Praise for *Unlocking Multilingual Lear[n]*

There is so much to love about Unlocking Multilingual Learners' Potential. *The authors have created a truly readable text packed with practical suggestions for all educators who teach multilingual learners (MLs)! English language development (ELD) educators will find the focus on advocacy and leadership provides them with new ideas to take their practice to the next level. Content educators will appreciate the many easy-to-incorporate strategies for developing oral language and reading within their own academic content classes. And finally, the emphasis on teacher collaboration is vital to get everyone on board with an agenda that stresses equity and excellence for our culturally and linguistically diverse learners. This text will undoubtedly be a hit with school PLCs and teacher education programs.*

Tim Boals, WIDA Executive Director
University of Wisconsin–Madison

With so many resources available today and so little time to review them all, it becomes harder and harder for educators to know what to read and when to read it. What the authors offer to educators of multilingual learners with this book is the unique opportunity to find in one resource a synthesis of the current research, examples of its impact in the classroom through authentic classroom vignettes, and a wealth of tools to get started in their own classrooms. The authors have successfully combined their own expertise with that of colleagues and educators to bring to the field a valuable tool for professional growth and collaboration. Thank you!

Mariana Castro, Deputy Director
Wisconsin Center for Education Research

Collecting, analyzing, and using various data points are key to supporting positive outcomes that center on the unique needs of multilingual students. Staehr Fenner, Snyder, and Gregoire-Smith provide data-ready resources that can be easily embedded across content areas and into instructional practices. The strategies highlighted in this edition help teachers afford more opportunities for students, especially newcomers and Students with Limited/Interrupted Formal Education (SLIFE), to practice, collect, reflect, and analyze their own learning experiences.

Ayanna Cooper, Author/Educator
ACooper Consulting

Continuing their advocacy for multilingual learners to obtain an equitable education, the authors offer a remarkable framework to guide teachers to better understand the complex nature of teaching diverse students. This book not only examines why a supportive school environment matters but also offers detailed, research-informed instructional strategies applicable to every class. It is a must-read for all teachers of multilingual learners!

Maria G. Dove, EdD, Professor
Molloy College, New York, Graduate Education TESOL Programs

Unlocking Multilingual Learners' Potential: Strategies for Making Content Accessible offers a treasure trove of practical resources and ideas for all teachers—and not just those with MLs in their classrooms.

Larry Ferlazzo, Teacher and Author
The Student Motivation Handbook: 50 Ways to Boost an Intrinsic Desire to Learn

The authors masterfully unravel the intricacies of teaching and supporting multilingual learners. Seen through a series of core beliefs within an equitable educational framework, each chapter reveals an important theme in enacting effective instructional strategies that advance ML learning. Their focus on teacher collaboration in furthering students' language development and academic achievement provides insight into implementing their carefully delineated steps. With its many application activities, this book offers both content and language teachers a myriad of ideas for working with MLs integral to their classroom practices.

Margo Gottlieb, Co-founder and Lead Developer for WIDA
Wisconsin Center for Education Research, University of Wisconsin–Madison

The authors have created a practitioner-friendly guide for educators of MLs to help create welcoming school and classroom environments, build cultural responsiveness, and increase educators' toolboxes for serving MLs. The authors speak with experienced teacher voices and have a gift for making the complex simple through explicit explanation, classroom examples, and use of tools for instruction and assessment. This is a must-read for preservice educators of MLs who are seeking authentic professional learning to meet the needs of their MLs.

Janet E. Hiatt, EL/Title III Consultant
Heartland Area Education Agency, Iowa

Unlocking Multilingual Learners' Potential: Strategies for Making Content Accessible *not only offers a fresh perspective on approaching the education of multilingual learners but also provides readers with practical and comprehensive guidance on how to ensure success for MLs. I am honored to endorse this book from leading experts who continue to demonstrate uncompromising dedication to and advocacy for MLs, while also offering ready-to-implement strategies and examples of successful practices.*

Andrea Honigsfeld, Professor
Molloy College, New York

Teachers and administrators often read books that later end up on the shelf covered in dust. Unlocking Multilingual Learners' Potential: Strategies for Making Content Accessible *is not one of them. It is a practical pedagogical guide that helps* all *teachers realize their role as a teacher of multilingual learners. Teachers will especially love how it builds their background knowledge as well as provides actual strategies that work for MLs.*

Samuel Klein, Supervisor, ESOL/HILT
Department of Instruction, Arlington Public Schools

Unlocking Multilingual Learners' Potential *is a powerful and valuable guide for deepening all educators' understandings, practices, and beliefs that contribute to the success of multilingual language learners. The authors provide a framework for educating MLs explained with practical tools, helpful examples, scenarios, and activities that promote the implementation of best practices with this population of students. A must-have for schools looking to establish a shared schoolwide responsibility for educating MLs.*

Jacqueline LeRoy, former Director of ENL,
World Languages and Bilingual Education
Syracuse City School District

For anyone needing a blueprint for how to successfully work with and instruct multilingual language learners, Unlocking Multilingual Learners' Potential *is a one-stop shop. This book is a beacon of light for schools and practitioners who are new to MLs and want to implement exemplary practices.*

Giselle Lundy-Ponce, ML Policy Expert
American Federation of Teachers

There is no book I recommend to teachers more often. This comprehensive, practical guide is everything a teacher needs to understand and apply strategies that will truly improve outcomes for students learning English. In this new edition, Staehr Fenner, Snyder, and Gregoire-Smith are responsive to the most salient issues today in the field of ESOL, as schools across the U.S. strive to provide high-quality education to growing numbers of Students with Limited/Interrupted Formal Education (SLIFE) and to ensure effective, research-based literacy instructional practices for all multilingual learners. Unlocking Multilingual Learners' Potential remains an indispensable part of any district's professional learning plan.

April Perkins, Director of Multilingual Programs
South Portland School Department

As part of the Title III English Learner Support Grant through the Ohio Department of Education, Painesville City Local Schools worked through the Unlocking text with their EL Department. Professional learning sessions were led by SupportEd and covered vocabulary development, scaffolding, academic and oral language development, building background knowledge, and formative assessments. The content in the Unlocking text provided easy-to-understand examples, scenarios, and suggestions. In addition, the text encouraged staff discussion and collaboration on implementation ideas. The material not only aligned to the goals of the grant, but the SupportEd team also went above and beyond to align their materials and instruction with other district initiatives for general instructional frameworks. Of all of the professional development series I have been a part of in my twenty years in education, SupportEd was by far the most well-organized, informative series. Their team was overly accommodating of the day-to-day struggle of districts and flexible in their planning and delivery to ensure the district was provided with the support and learning opportunities they needed as well as requested. I would highly recommend their team and their materials to any district or school looking to improve their EL instructional knowledge and skill sets.

Shannon Ranta, Coordinator of Curriculum and Data Specialist
ESC of the Western Reserve

Every K–12 teacher needs to be effective with multilingual learners (MLs). This practical, asset-oriented book helps teachers put theory into action to unlock MLs' potential!

Tonya Ward Singer, Author & Founder,
Courageous Literacy LLC

This second edition of Unlocking Multilingual Learners' Potential: Strategies for Making Content Accessible *should be in the hands of new and veteran educators. As its predecessor, in this second edition the authors draw from current research and practice and brilliantly present a user-friendly guide for supporting students' success. Look no further if you are seeking a professional book to support our ever-changing multilingual learners to work, collaborate, and flourish together.*

Debbie Zacarian, Author & Founder,
Debbie Zacarian, EdD and Associates, LLC

Unlocking Multilingual Learners' Potential

Second Edition

This book is dedicated to all teachers of multilingual learners.

May you find the joy and passion that working with these students brings.

We also dedicate this book to our families,

David, Zoe, Maya, and Carson Fenner,

Gus, Sylvia, and Iris Fahey, and

Jason, Wiley, Liana, and Easton Smith,

for the boundless love and support they offer.

Unlocking Multilingual Learners' Potential

Strategies for Making Content Accessible

Second Edition

Diane Staehr Fenner

Sydney Snyder

Meghan Gregoire-Smith

Foreword by Emily Francis

CORWIN

FOR INFORMATION:

Corwin

A SAGE Company

2455 Teller Road

Thousand Oaks, California 91320

(800) 233-9936

www.corwin.com

SAGE Publications Ltd.

1 Oliver's Yard

55 City Road

London EC1Y 1SP

United Kingdom

SAGE Publications India Pvt. Ltd.

Unit No 323–333, Third Floor, F-Block

International Trade Tower Nehru Place

New Delhi 110 019

India

SAGE Publications Asia-Pacific Pte. Ltd.

18 Cross Street #10-10/11/12

China Square Central

Singapore 048423

Vice President and
  Editorial Director: Monica Eckman

Publisher: Megan Bedell

Content Development
  Manager: Lucas Schleicher

Content Development Editor: Mia Rodriguez

Senior Editorial Assistant: Natalie Delpino

Production Editor: Tori Mirsadjadi

Copy Editor: Michelle Ponce

Typesetter: C&M Digitals (P) Ltd.

Cover Designer: Scott Van Atta

Marketing Manager: Melissa Duclos

Library of Congress Cataloging-in-Publication Data

Names: Fenner, Diane Staehr, author. | Snyder, Sydney, author. | Gregoire-Smith, Meghan, author. | Francis, Emily (ESL teacher), writer of foreword.

Title: Unlocking multilingual learners' potential : strategies for making content accessible / Diane Staehr Fenner, Sydney Snyder, Meghan Gregoire-Smith ; foreword by Emily Francis.

Other titles: Unlocking English learners' potential

Description: Second edition. | Thousand Oaks, California : Corwin, [2024] | Includes bibliographical references and index.

Identifiers: LCCN 2023041431 | ISBN 9781071902660 (paperback : acid-free paper) | ISBN 9781071902677 (epub) | ISBN 9781071902684 (epub) | ISBN 9781071902691 (pdf)

Subjects: LCSH: English language—Study and teaching—Foreign speakers. | Language arts—Correlation with content subjects. | English teachers—Training of. | Classroom environment. | Education—Curricula. | Second language acquisition.

Classification: LCC PE1128.A2 F38 2024 | DDC 428.0071—dc23/eng/20231120

LC record available at https://lccn.loc.gov/2023041431

This book is printed on acid-free paper.

24 25 26 27 28 10 9 8 7 6 5 4 3 2 1

Contents

Website Table of Contents   xv

Foreword by Emily Francis   xix

Acknowledgments   xxv

About the Authors   xxvii

Introduction   1

    Why We Wrote a Second Edition   1

    What's New in This Edition   2

    How This Book Is Structured   2

Chapter 1. Why You Need This Book to Support MLs   7

    Who Are MLs?   8

    What Is the Sense of Urgency Around MLs' Equitable and
       Excellent Education?   10

    What Is the Framework for Equitable and Excellent ML Education?   13

    What Are the Core Beliefs That We Use to Frame Our Work
       With MLs and This Book?   14

    How Do I Get Started Using All Five Core Beliefs?   29

    Conclusion   32

**Chapter 2. Using a Culturally Responsive Framework
to Leverage the Strengths and Meet the Needs of MLs**   33

    What Is Culture?   35

    Why Does Culture Matter for MLs' Teaching and Learning?   39

    What Is Culturally Responsive Teaching?   41

    What Are the Guiding Principles of Culturally Responsive Teaching?   42

    What Is the Role of Collaboration in Developing a Culturally
       Responsive Classroom?   61

What Is the Role of Equity, Advocacy, and Leadership in
    Developing a Culturally Responsive Classroom?   62

Next Steps   63

Conclusion   63

Chapter 3. Scaffolding Instruction for MLs   65

What Is a Scaffold?   66

What Are Different Types of Scaffolds?   69

What Types of Instructional Materials Can I Use to Scaffold Instruction?   71

What Instructional Practices Can I Use to Scaffold Instruction?   77

What Instructional Groupings Can I Use to Scaffold Instruction?   80

What Steps Should I Take to Scaffold a Unit?   82

What Is the Role of Collaboration in Scaffolding Instruction for MLs?   90

What Is the Role of Equity, Advocacy, and Leadership in
    Developing Scaffolded Materials?   91

Next Steps   91

Conclusion   94

Chapter 4. Peer Learning: Fostering MLs' Oral Language Development and Content Understanding   95

Why Is it Important to Focus on Peer Learning for MLs?   98

How Do I Develop Effective Peer Learning Activities for MLs?   99

What Practices Can MLs Engage in to Support Their Participation
    and Engagement in Peer Learning Activities?   104

What Are Some Effective Peer Learning Activities for MLs?   117

How Can I Collaborate Around Peer Learning for MLs?   122

What Is the Role of Equity, Advocacy, and Leadership in Supporting
    Peer Learning for MLs?   123

Next Steps   123

Conclusion   126

Chapter 5. Teaching Academic Language to MLs at the Word/Phrase Level   129

What Is Academic Language?   132

What Is the Purpose of Academic Language, and How Is it Structured?   133

Why Is Academic Language Important?   136

What Is the Word/Phrase Level? 137

Why Teach Academic Vocabulary to MLs? 139

How Should I Select Vocabulary for Intentional Instruction? 140

How Can I Assess Students' Initial Understanding of
These New Words? 144

What Strategies Should I Use for Teaching Academic Vocabulary? 146

What Activities Can I Use to Help MLs Practice New Vocabulary? 150

How Can I Support MLs in Becoming Independent Learners of
New Vocabulary? 154

How Do I Put All of the ML Vocabulary Strategies Together? 157

What Is the Role of Collaboration in Teaching Academic
Vocabulary to MLs? 159

What Is the Role of Equity, Advocacy, and Leadership in Teaching Academic
Vocabulary to MLs? 160

Next Steps 160

Conclusion 163

Chapter 6. Teaching Academic Language to MLs at the Sentence and Discourse Level 165

Why Don't MLs Just Need Assistance With Vocabulary? 167

What Is the Sentence Level? 167

What Is the Discourse Level? 170

How Do I Increase My Awareness of the Academic Language MLs
Need to Access Challenging Content? 174

How Can I Figure Out What Academic Language Might Be
Challenging for MLs? 175

How Do I Teach Academic Language to MLs at
the Sentence Level? 180

How Do I Teach Academic Language to MLs at
the Discourse Level? 185

What Is the Role of Collaboration When Planning Lessons
That Integrate Academic-Language Instruction and
Content Instruction? 192

What Is the Role of Equity, Advocacy, and Leadership to Promote
Academic-Language Development? 193

Next Steps 194

Conclusion 195

Text Sequencing Answer Key 196

Chapter 7. Activating and Teaching MLs Background Knowledge 197

Reflection: How Do I Feel About Teaching Background Knowledge to MLs? 198

How Can I Raise My Awareness About the Importance of MLs' Background Knowledge? 199

What Does the Research Say About Background Knowledge? 201

What Is a Framework I Can Use for Building MLs' Background Knowledge? 202

Step 1: How Do I Find Out MLs' Prior Knowledge on a Particular Topic or Text? 203

Step 2: How Do I Decide How Much Background Knowledge to Provide to MLs? 204

Step 3: How Do I Activate MLs' Background Knowledge That They Already Possess? 206

Step 4: What Are Some Strategies for Concisely Teaching MLs Background Knowledge? 208

What Are Some Examples of Teaching Background Knowledge? 210

How Can I Apply the Four-Step Framework When Teaching Background Knowledge to MLs? 213

How Do I Build or Activate MLs' Background Knowledge in Mathematics? 218

What Is the Role of Collaboration in Teaching Background Knowledge? 222

What Is the Role of Equity, Advocacy, and Leadership in Teaching Background Knowledge? 223

Next Steps 224

Conclusion 226

Application Activity Responses 227

Chapter 8. Engaging MLs in Reading and Writing in the Content Areas 229

Our Lens 230

What Does Research Say About Engaging MLs in Reading and Writing Across Content Areas? 230

How Can I Use Peer Learning Routines and Scaffolded Instruction to Support MLs in Reading and Writing Across Content Areas? 235

What Is the Role of Collaboration in Supporting MLs in Reading and Writing? 255

What Is the Role of Equity, Advocacy, and Leadership in Engaging MLs in Reading and Writing in All Subjects? 256

Next Steps 260

Conclusion 262

What Is Formative Assessment?   264

What Does the Research Say on Assessment for MLs in General?   267

What Is the Role of Formative Assessment With MLs?   269

How Do I Structure the Formative-Assessment Process for MLs?   270

How Can I Collect and Interpret Formative-Assessment Evidence
     to Inform Instruction of MLs?   272

What Is Assessment Validity for MLs, and How Can I Ensure My
     Formative Assessments Are Valid?   275

How Can I Ensure That Formative Assessments Are Valid for MLs
     of Varying Proficiency Levels?   278

How Do I Scaffold Formative Assessments for MLs?   279

How Does the Formative-Assessment Process for MLs Unfold in a Classroom?   282

What Is the Role of Collaboration in Creating and Using Formative
     Assessments for MLs?   290

What Is the Role of Equity, Advocacy, and Leadership in Creating
     and Using Formative Assessments for MLs?   290

Next Steps   292

Conclusion   295

Final Thoughts   296

References   **297**

Index   **307**

Visit the companion website at
https://resources.corwin.com/FennerUnlocking2E
for downloadable resources.

Note From the Publisher: The authors have provided video and web content throughout the book that is available to you through QR (quick response) codes. To read a QR code, you must have a smartphone or tablet with a camera. We recommend that you download a QR code reader app that is made specifically for your phone or tablet brand.

Website Table of Contents

List of Online Resources

Access the following downloadable resources at **https://resources.corwin .com/FennerUnlocking2E**

Reflection Questions for Chapters 1 through 9

Chapter 1. Why You Need This Book to Support MLs

Figure 1.4   Recognizing MLs' Strengths

Figure 1.9   ML Advocacy Equity Audit

Chapter 2. Using a Culturally Responsive Framework to Leverage the Strengths and Meet the Needs of MLs

Application Activity 2.2   My Multicultural Self

Figure 2.3   What I Know About My ML

Video: Building Relationships With Multilingual Families Through Family Engagement Events

Chapter 3. Scaffolding Instruction for MLs

Figure 3.1   Categories of Scaffolds

Figure 3.9   Scaffolded Unit Planning Checklist

Chapter 4. Peer Learning: Fostering MLs' Oral Language Development and Content Understanding

Figure 4.10   Peer Learning Activity Checklist

Figure 4.14   Peer Learning Activity Planning Template

Chapter 5. Teaching Academic Language to MLs at the Word/Phrase Level

Figure 5.15   Vocabulary Instruction Checklist

Figure 5.16   Academic-Vocabulary Planning Template

Chapter 6. Teaching Academic Language to MLs at the Sentence and Discourse Level

Figure 6.6   Checklist for Increasing Academic-Language Awareness

Chapter 7. Activating and Teaching MLs Background Knowledge

Figure 7.4   Flowchart for Determining Background Knowledge to Teach MLs

Figure 7.16   Activating and Building MLs' Background Knowledge Planning Tool

Video: Activating and Building Background Knowledge

Chapter 8. Engaging MLs in Reading and Writing in the Content Areas

Figure 8.5   Three Read Protocol: Steps, Key Questions, and Possible Scaffolds for MLs

Figure 8.8   Dining Partners

Chapter 9. Formative Assessment for MLs

Figure 9.16   ML Formative Assessment Checklist

Figure 9.17   ML Formative Assessment Planning Tool

Video: Students Engaging in Self-Assessment

Online-only Appendices

Appendix A: Unlocking MLs' Potential Unit Planning Template

Appendix B: Unlocking MLs' Potential Unit Planning Template Completed Example

Appendix C: Classroom Checklist to Foster a Language Learning Environment for MLs

Appendix D: Culturally Responsive School Checklist and
          Goal Setting

Appendix E: Scaffolding for MLs' Self-Assessment

Appendix F: Checklist for Supporting MLs' Academic-Language
          Development in Speaking and Writing

Foreword

By Emily Francis

If the *Unlocking Multilingual Learners' Potential: Strategies for Making Content Accessible* book is not on your teacher's bookshelf, you are missing out. This book is a gem and a must-have resource for all general education and English language development (ELD) teachers.

Whenever I come across a professional development book for educators that specifically focuses on multilingual learners (MLs), particularly on unlocking their full potential, my heart fills with joy. Additionally, it makes me reflect upon the missed opportunities I had while attending school in the United States as an ML. It is difficult for me to imagine myself as a 15-year-old ML sitting in a classroom trying to make sense of what my teachers were teaching. Looking around high school halls for something or someone to validate my humanity, strengths, and culture. For me, this only happened in bathroom mirrors.

Instead of developing the identity I had already constructed for 15 years, I found myself at a place where I was forced to build a new personal and academic identity—an experience that made a negative imprint in my future years. You see, when I began my ML experience here in the United States, I had lived 15 years of my life surrounded by Guatemalan cultural experiences that shaped who I am. At a very early age, I learned to survive very difficult experiences that perhaps others have only read about or watched in movies. I had taken on a motherhood role while my mother worked countless hours and even left our home country to come to the United States to make a way for us. I had learned how to run our family business, which consisted of selling oranges at the local market or selling door-to-door in our local neighborhoods; all this just to afford shelter over our heads and have beans, rice, and tortillas on our table. I had traveled as an unaccompanied and undocumented immigrant across countries to come to a place that offered the opportunity of education and new life.

My hope in 1994 as I entered high school as a Student with Limited/Interrupted Formal Education (SLIFE) was not to start over as a blank slate or to rebuild my identity; on the contrary, I hoped to continue developing my identity upon the assets I had within me.

But it did not take me long to process the message the school environment was sending about my cultural identity and my home language. Because I found my identity threatened, I felt the need to protect it by hiding it away. I began the process of assimilation where all that mattered was learning English and meeting the academic expectation all teachers had of me . . . regardless of my language proficiency and at the cost of racial trauma. While questioning my humanity and whether my experiences were even worth caring about, I met my ELD and academic goal by obtaining 42 high school credits by 1997.[1] Unfortunately, I did not graduate. A New York State Regents exam put a hold on my academic success as a high school student.

So, as a high school dropout and while absorbing our society's message about my existence, I operated dysfunctionally within our society for several years. However, in 2004 I began putting my broken pieces back together while putting myself through school at a community college and reconstructing my academic identity. I was determined to not only become the educator I desperately needed while I was in school but also to impact students' educational experiences positively. My experience as an ML inspired me to become an ELD teacher knowing that this role affords me a deep understanding of the challenges my students must overcome to find success.

In 2012, during my first year as an ELD teacher, I received a call from the front office about José, a newcomer from Mexico enrolling in a U.S. school for the first time. My heart leaped with joy and on the way to the office I began brainstorming from all my personal experiences and from all the learning I had acquired while becoming an educator. I was thinking about all the ways, not just me, but as our school community, we could build a place where our new student could thrive not only academically but also linguistically and emotionally.

That school year, José began his academic experience with us. However, we intentionally focused on his assets, passion, cultural experiences, and home literacy development. He was encouraged to use his home language to access content, present research projects in his language, and freely interact with peers in a comfortable environment. General education teachers worked closely with me to ensure we were employing up-to-date strategies to support his academic and linguistic needs. He participated in our school's Spanish Spelling Bee competition where the entire school witnessed his potential and literacy skills. This identity-affirming environment had a very positive impact on José's life. We had created a place with a strong sense of belonging that activated his voice and developed his academic identity. During his last year at our elementary school, José exited the ELD program and obtained passing scores on his math, English language arts

---

[1] Emily had the required number of credits to graduate, but she did not receive the score that she needed on the New York State United States History and Government Regents examination to allow her to graduate.

(ELA), and science end-of-grade testing. This school year, José is crossing the stage and graduating high school.

During my fifth year as an ELD teacher, Drs. Staehr Fenner and Snyder's book *Unlocking English Learners' Potential: Strategies for Making Content Accessible* was released. I purchased the book and joined a Twitter book study/chat. Little did I know the impact this book was about to have on my life and career. At a personal level, I felt like this book was healing the wounds I received during my educational experience by acknowledging that the poor instruction and the low expectations I experienced while attending high school in the United States translated to inequity and injustice that impacted me greatly in a negative way. I honestly felt like Chapters 1 and 2 were like cool water to my soul. Here is a book with a framework for equitable ML education with core beliefs focused on students' assets, culture, home languages, and identities.

Professionally, I felt reaffirmation of so many practices I had put in place for five years as an ELD teacher. I found myself marking on the book all the areas that would share something I had already put into practice. I smiled every time I highlighted an affirmation in the book.

I was also enlightened on so many topics that strengthened my instruction with guidelines that became part of my everyday instruction. From that day forward, this book became part of my lesson planning as I crafted lessons that were equitable and excellent for my students. Moreso, this book made me a more culturally competent educator. Just because I had some shared experiences with my students, that was not enough to have the cultural competence I needed to serve my MLs with equity and justice. This book allowed me to reflect carefully and intentionally on my cultural values and beliefs that today shape my expectations for my students, then make it intentional to learn more about my students by recognizing their values and beliefs that may be different than mine. These are key components to becoming a culturally competent educator with a mindset of respecting and building on my students' assets, backgrounds, and experiences.

In 2018, an opportunity came for me to begin working with newcomer students at Concord High School in Concord, North Carolina. The plan was to implement a full inclusion model where our students were spending more time in core instructional courses and receiving support from me, their ELD teacher, throughout the day. I did not doubt that the framework and strategies I acquired from the *Unlocking English Learners' Potential: Strategies for Making Content Accessible* book were exactly what I needed to implement this program with passion, integrity, and equity.

Today, five years later, we continue to implement this framework and employ many of the strategies for academic success found within these chapters.

So, it is 2023, and I get a first look at the second edition of this amazing book. It is a joy, an honor, and a humbling opportunity to see the new additions and revisions.

I am thrilled to see that Dr. Staehr Fenner, Dr. Snyder, and new coauthor Ms. Gregoire-Smith are still hard at work in our field and saw the urgent need to revisit this essential resource for educators and added much-needed components such as a focus on SLIFE students, shifting the language from EL to ML, and removing strategies no longer effective in our practice. The addition of peer learning to foster MLs' oral language and content understanding is one of my favorites. I do believe that the pandemic stole from our students the skills to engage in conversation whether in social or academic settings. The strategies provided are not only helpful for MLs but are great for all students to develop oral language with success. I consider Chapters 3–9 to be heavy in content but loaded with doable strategies that wrap up with a focus on the role of collaboration in teaching MLs and the role of equity, advocacy, and leadership in teaching, which I see both as fundamental to support our MLs. This is critical now that many districts are implementing more and more inclusive instructional models where the ELD teacher provides support to both the mainstream classroom teacher and the MLs within the classroom. This book has a clear focus on MLs' success relying on all adults surrounding the students, not only the ELD teacher.

Throughout the chapters, you will read scenarios that will provide an accurate picture of the strategy in practice.

As a full-time ELD teacher and fearless advocate for the instructional support our MLs deserve, let me share with you how I implement this book:

- I follow the five core beliefs, which are research-based with practical tools to apply them.

- I apply Culturally Responsive Pedagogy after recognizing the culture and experiences that shape our students' learning.

- I elevate vs. value students' home language and experience by amplifying translanguaging practices and displaying students' work.

- I provide content teachers a clear understanding of instructional scaffolds for MLs.

- I encourage participation through strategies that promote engagement for all students including our MLs and SLIFE students.

- I share a clear understanding of how social and academic language is constructed and developed.

- I integrate practice with academic vocabulary and vocabulary practices.

- I incorporate reading and writing activities that are equitable ⇒ challenging and on grade level, including engineering text for MLs and SLIFE students.

- I implement identity text projects where students demonstrate their cultural background through a multimodal text created by students.

- I implement equitable assessments and differentiated assessment and grading.

Do not be intimidated by this long list of practices my school is implementing based on *Unlocking Multilingual Learners' Potential: Strategies for Making Content Accessible*. This implementation does not happen from one day to another—it is a process. The key is starting somewhere and working your way through all the amazing practices shared in the book. My first tip is to do an equity audit and an inventory. An equity audit that advocates for MLs' rights and the education they deserve. Conduct an inventory of your cultural views and experiences. Create a climate of shared responsibility where all adults on campus feel the urgency to begin building a safe place for all MLs and SLIFE. This is hard work and requires vulnerability. However, it is at this crossroads that students will meet you and see that there are teachers who care and believe they matter. Students will feel comfortable enough to share about themselves and this will give you the windows of knowledge about their life experiences you need to make Chapters 3 to 9 (content and language strategies) doable for their success.

From teacher to teacher, know that you are not alone. We are all trying to do what is best for our students. Just the fact that you picked up this book and are reading these words says that you care for your MLs and want what is best for them. We are in this together. Let's connect and together UNLOCK our students' FULL potential.

Acknowledgments

A central theme of *Unlocking Multilingual Learners' Potential* is collaboration. We could not have written this book without our collaboration with students, educators, colleagues, and friends. We feel incredibly fortunate to be part of such an amazing network of individuals working in support of multilingual learners (MLs) and their families. The process of writing goes far beyond the work of the three of us, and as a result, there are quite a few people we'd like to acknowledge and thank.

We would first like to deeply thank our SupportEd colleagues, without whom this book would not have been possible. Michele Iris provided the fabulous graphics that brought our content to life. We are so appreciative of her creativity and openness to brainstorming new ideas to visually demonstrate our concepts. Jasmine Singh offered her critical eye to carefully review each chapter and identify inconsistencies, and she also supported the development of graphics. Mindi Teich and Shannon Smith brought their ELD expertise to the book and provided us with thoughtful suggestions and insights to make the book stronger. A big thank-you to Diane Choi for her help on the model unit plan and for all the work she did on other projects that allowed us time to write. And finally, thank you to Galen Murray and Tamara Echols for all their behind-the-scenes encouragement. We also want to give a big shout-out to our fabulous SupportEd consultants, who consistently share new strategy ideas and research with us and help us grow as teacher educators. Thank you to Nancy Batchelder, Kent Buckley-Ess, Jessica Fundalinski, and Dr. Eleni Pappamihiel. We'd also like to share our sincere appreciation for ELD educator and author Emily Francis for writing the inspirational foreword that set the tone for the entire book.

In addition, we would like to express our gratitude to all the educators who contributed to this book by sharing a strategy, letting us work with their students, and having discussions about practice. We especially appreciated the contributions of Anah Alie, Amanda Angstadt, Susan Bitler, Amanda Brudecki, Myunghee Chung, Erica Daniels, Becky Hoover, Tan Huynh, Jill Kester, Maureen McCormick, Jennifer Rawlings, Jennifer Saunders, Rebecca Thomas, Katie Toppel, and Chrystal Whipkey. We are so grateful to be able to include authentic examples of resources and activities in each chapter. We also want to thank Reading School District (PA) and Montgomery County Public Schools (MCPS) for the opportunity to collaborate with educators in their districts. That work as well as our work in other districts informed every chapter in this book.

The other critical part of our team effort was made up of multiple Corwin colleagues who each contributed specific expertise. We are especially appreciative of Corwin Program Director and Publisher for Equity and Professional Learning, Dan Alpert, who was an immediate supporter of both the first edition of this book and our desire to write a second edition. Dan has been our champion and source of inspiration for more than a decade through many projects, and we treasure his insight, his dedication to MLs, and his continued calming encouragement. In addition, we would like to give a special shout-out to Lucas Schleicher, content development manager, who responded to more of our questions than we can count and provided endless amounts of support in this process. Also, we say thank you to Megan Bedell, acquisitions editor, Mia Rodriguez, content development editor, and Tori Mirsadjadi, production editor for their continued assistance during the publication process, as well as Michelle Ponce for carefully copy editing the book. We would also like to share our gratitude for Melissa Duclos, senior marketing manager, for all she did to spread the word about our work.

Last but not least, we'd like to thank our families for their encouragement while we were writing and revising the second edition of the book. Diane thanks her husband, David, and children, Zoe, Maya, and Carson. Sydney thanks her husband, Gus, and children, Sylvia and Iris. Meghan thanks her husband, Jason, her children, Wiley, Liana, and Easton, and her parents, Jane and Michael. We are especially encouraged to see our own children learning about the book-publishing process through witnessing it firsthand, and we are hopeful our kids appreciate that their moms wear multiple hats.

About the Authors

Diane Staehr Fenner, PhD, is the president of SupportEd (SupportEd .com), a woman-owned small business located in the Washington, DC, metro area that she founded in 2011. SupportEd is dedicated to empowering multilingual learners and their educators. Dr. Staehr Fenner leads her team to provide ML professional development, coaching, technical assistance, and curriculum and assessment support to school districts, states, organizations, and the U.S. Department of Education. Prior to forming SupportEd, Dr. Staehr Fenner was an English language development (ELD) teacher, dual language assessment teacher, and ELD assessment specialist in Fairfax County Public Schools, VA. She speaks German and Spanish and has taught in Berlin, Germany, and Veracruz, Mexico. Dr. Staehr Fenner grew up on a dairy farm in central New York and is a proud first-generation college graduate. She has written eight books on ML education (and counting), including coauthoring *Culturally Responsive Teaching for Multilingual Learners: Tools for Equity* and authoring *Advocating for English Learners: A Guide for Educators*. She is a frequent keynote speaker on ML education at conferences across North America. She earned her PhD in Multilingual/Multicultural Education at George Mason University and her MAT in TESOL at the School for International Training. You can connect with her by email at Diane@SupportEd.com or on Twitter at @DStaehrFenner.

Sydney Snyder, PhD, is a principal associate at SupportEd. In this role, Dr. Snyder coaches ML educators and develops and facilitates interactive professional development for teachers of MLs. She also works with the SupportEd team to offer technical assistance to school districts and educational organizations. Dr. Snyder has extensive instructional experience and has worked in the field of English language development for over 25 years. She started her teaching career as a Peace Corps volunteer in Guinea, West Africa. This experience ignited her passion for language teaching, culturally responsive instruction, and ML advocacy. Dr. Snyder is coauthor of *Culturally Responsive Teaching for Multilingual Learners: Tools for Equity* and contributing author to *Breaking Down the Monolingual Wall.* She served as an English Teaching Fellow at Gadja Mada University in Yogyakarta, Indonesia. She earned her PhD in Multilingual/ Multicultural Education at George Mason University and her MAT in TESOL at the School for International Training. You can connect with her by email at Sydney@SupportEd.com or on Twitter at @SydneySupportEd.

Meghan Gregoire-Smith, MA, is a multilingual learner (ML) coach at SupportEd. In this role, Ms. Gregoire-Smith coaches ML educators and develops and facilitates interactive professional development for teachers of MLs. Ms. Gregoire-Smith began her career teaching English as a foreign language (EFL) to young adults in Guayaquil, Ecuador. Her time in Ecuador sparked her love of language teaching. She then spent over a decade supporting MLs in Anne Arundel County Public Schools, Maryland, first as an elementary English language development teacher and then as an ELD Teacher Specialist. As an ELD Teacher Specialist, Ms. Gregoire-Smith wrote the K–12 ELD curricula, planned and delivered professional development around best practices for working with MLs, and provided coaching for ELD teachers new to the profession. Ms. Gregoire-Smith's experiences as an ELD teacher and teacher specialist led to a passion for supporting educators of MLs through high-quality professional development and coaching. She earned her Master's in TESOL from the University of Maryland, Baltimore County. You can connect with her by email at Meghan@ SupportEd.com or on Twitter at @MeghanGSmith.

Introduction

Why We Wrote a Second Edition

Since *Unlocking English Learners' Potential: Strategies for Making Content Accessible* was published in 2017, we have continued to work extensively with educators of multilingual learners (MLs) to implement the strategies shared in the book. We have also framed ongoing coaching projects in several school districts around the content of *Unlocking* and have seen trends in terms of teachers' strengths and needs in implementing these strategies to support MLs. As a result, we decided we needed to add to the activities and tools from the first edition that align with each chapter based on our collaborative work with K–12 educators. In addition, since the first edition of *Unlocking* was published, there has been new research on effective strategies to support MLs' acquisition of language and engagement with grade-level content, and we wished to give the research we draw from a refresh. This second edition of *Unlocking* has allowed us the opportunity to update the research that we include so as to provide the most relevant theory that undergirds the instructional practices that we share.

We have also seen the impact that interrupted schooling and virtual learning had on MLs' language development opportunities and learning and recognize the urgent need to revisit what we know about the best way to build on MLs' assets and further their growth. For example, through our work, we have noticed a need to be more explicit about strategies to support MLs in reading and writing across content areas, including the elevated importance of peer interactions to foster growth in literacy and content understanding. Additionally, we are frequently asked about unique strategies to support the specific learning needs of ML newcomer students (students who have been in the country for less than a year) and students with limited or interrupted formal education (SLIFE). The second edition of our book gives us the opportunity to highlight our collaboration with educators and districts and to incorporate new strategies for supporting MLs' language and literacy development, including much-needed strategies for newcomers and SLIFE.

What's New in This Edition

In addition to updating the classroom examples, instructional strategies, and research in each chapter, we have also made several other changes in the second edition. Some highlights of the new or modified content follow.

- In order to take a more assets-based approach in the second edition, we use the terms *multilingual learner* and *emergent multilingual learner* instead of *English learner*. Please see Chapter 1 for our rationale for this shift and the definition of these terms. In addition, we are using the term English language development (ELD) teacher instead of ESOL teacher to refer to teachers who specialize in MLs' language development.

- We have revised our five core beliefs (formerly called guiding principles) to include a belief framed around the importance of peer learning opportunities for MLs. While we have always understood peer learning to be a valuable support for MLs, the urgency for incorporating these practices into daily instruction has become even more pronounced. For more on our rationale for this shift, see Chapter 1.

- To respond to the many questions that we have received about strategies for supporting ML newcomer students and SLIFE, we have added a section in Chapters 2–9 to focus on practices specific to leveraging the strengths and meeting the needs of these populations of MLs. In these chapters, we provide specific considerations in the instruction of ML newcomer students and SLIFE related to that chapter's topic. Then we provide a scenario to illustrate how these unique considerations might be applied in a school or classroom.

- We revised Chapter 8 to focus more broadly on supporting MLs in reading and writing in the content areas rather than focusing only on text-dependent questions. Chapter 8 now includes a variety of recommendations for incorporating scaffolded instruction and peer learning opportunities into reading and writing activities for MLs.

UNLOCKING RESOURCES

To read a QR code, you must have a smartphone or tablet with a camera. We recommend that you download a QR code reader app that is made specifically for your phone or tablet brand.

resources.corwin .com/FennerUnlocking2E

- We developed a unit planning template that is aligned to the research-based instructional practices presented in the book. Chapters 3–9 include the relevant section of the unit planning template so that, if you would like, you can develop a complete unit plan as you progress through the book. The complete unit planning template and a model unit plan are provided in the appendices on the online companion website. To access the companion website, please visit resources.corwin.com/FennerUnlocking2E.

How This Book Is Structured

As we wrote the second edition of book, we imagined all of the different types of current and future educators who might use it and took steps to adapt the content, as well as the structure, of the book to reach a wide audience. We have heard from countless educators in varied roles, including preservice teachers, teacher educators, content teachers, ELD teachers, support staff, and administrators about how practical and relevant the first edition of the book has been for them, and we wanted to ensure it continues to be relevant for everyone who reads it. First, we were sure to frame the book around solid research that grounds the ML strategies you will encounter and apply. Next, we structured the book in a way that provides the background that teachers with less training in working with MLs will need in order to understand the research, the rationale, and the use of particular strategies. At the same time, we also included ample modeling and examples, application activities, and reflection questions that can support even an experienced teacher of MLs in deepening their understanding and use of the selected research-based strategies, weaving in scenarios that span grade levels and content areas. We are confident that anyone from kindergarten dual-language teachers to high school mathematics teachers can find useful strategies that they can apply in their context. Further, we have included ample opportunities in the book for reflection so that educators can focus on their intentionality in selecting certain strategies, voicing their rationale for why and how they would use such strategies to support MLs. The online companion website that accompanies this book includes a compilation of all the reflection questions in the book with space to write your responses. You can print out this document and jot down your responses as you read. To access the companion website, please visit resources.corwin.com/FennerUnlocking2E

UNLOCKING RESOURCES

resources.corwin .com/FennerUnlocking2E

In addition to ensuring the book is relevant for all educators, we have structured the book so that you can use it independently, as part of a course, or within a professional learning community (PLC), where ideally, ELD teachers and content teachers can discuss and interact with the material together. The book is organized so that the first two chapters introduce our organizational framework and provide overarching instructional practices for MLs that are meant to be implemented in combination with other strategies shared in Chapters 3–9 of the book. Chapters 3–9 then each introduce a very specific instructional practice in a multilayered fashion that you can incorporate into your instruction. Each chapter includes scenarios that allow you to reflect on how the practice might be applied to a particular classroom setting and tools to help you implement the practice in your own setting. If you are reading this book as part of a PLC or in a coteaching partnership, you could select any of Chapters 3–9 to read, discuss, and implement in your classroom. In addition, for ready-to-use, practical tools to support these instructional practices, please visit SupportEd.com/unlocking-toolbox.

SupportEd TOOLBOX

For ready-to-use, practical tools to support culturally responsive teaching, please visit SupportEd.com/ unlocking-toolbox.

Even though integrating research-based strategies is crucial to MLs' success, educators must also constantly monitor and strengthen their professional skills with other educators to most effectively serve MLs. Our approach to working with MLs is unique, and so is this book. Because we believe the principles of collaboration, equity, advocacy, and leadership are fundamental to supporting MLs, we have woven these ideas into each chapter. As a result, we have included two sections at the end of each chapter that identify the role collaboration can have in relation to each specific instructional practice and also how equity, advocacy, and leadership can play out in the facilitation of each practice. This book offers you a space in which you can hit the pause button, reflect on your own practice and your relationship with your colleagues, and recharge your batteries to better support MLs. We encourage you, as you implement the different practices recommended in this book, to examine how you can build on your collaboration with your colleagues in the service of equitable and excellent education for MLs. We also hope you will reflect on how you can bolster your advocacy and leadership skills to share the new considerations, approaches, and strategies that you are implementing with other educators as a result of your learning in this book. This book will provide you with the opportunities to begin conversations not only around instructional practices that all teachers can use to support their MLs but also around ways in which teachers can continue to enhance their own professional development and grow as leaders and advocates for MLs. Now that we have provided you this overview, a summary of each chapter follows.

Chapter 1: Why You Need This Book to Support MLs

Chapter 1 identifies the urgent need to provide MLs with the type of instructional support that they require to succeed academically and recognizes that they are equal members of any classroom. The chapter provides an overview of the current educational context, demographics, research, and climate within which MLs are being educated. We also introduce the five core beliefs that define our work with MLs and their educators. These beliefs provide an easily accessible theoretical framework that forms the foundation for the remaining chapters in the book.

Chapter 2: Using a Culturally Responsive Framework to Leverage the Strengths and Meet the Needs of MLs

Chapter 2 provides an understanding of the crucial role culture plays in the education of MLs. The chapter includes working definitions of culture and culturally responsive teaching, a description of the characteristics of culture, and strategies to support culturally responsive teaching. It also provides opportunities for you to reflect on your own culture and how it shapes your instruction, classroom expectations, and interactions with MLs.

Chapter 3: Scaffolding Instruction for MLs

Chapter 3 shares an overview of what scaffolds are and why they are essential to incorporate into instruction and assessment for MLs. The chapter's deeper focus is on research-based strategies for selecting and developing scaffolds based on such factors as the academic task at hand and MLs' English proficiency levels, as well as other student background factors. The chapter includes examples of a variety of different types of scaffolds, checklists, and practical tools for you to plan and implement scaffolded lessons and units for MLs in your context.

Chapter 4: Peer Learning: Fostering MLs' Oral Language Development and Content Understanding

Chapter 4 begins with a discussion of the importance of integrating peer learning opportunities into content-based instruction of MLs framed around relevant research. It introduces and provides examples of four student practices that will foster MLs' engagement in peer learning activities in order to support their oral language development and their understanding of challenging content. The chapter also includes tools that you can use when planning and incorporating oral language activities into your instruction and offers recommendations for different types of peer learning activities.

Chapter 5: Teaching Academic Language to MLs at the Word/Phrase Level

Chapter 5 is the first of two chapters dedicated to explicitly teaching academic language to MLs. This chapter defines what academic language is and shares why it is critical for MLs to acquire academic language in order to engage with challenging content and be fully integrated into content classrooms. Then, it takes a deeper dive into why the focused teaching of academic vocabulary is critical to MLs' academic achievement. Recognizing that teachers must select vocabulary for MLs carefully and judiciously, the chapter includes research-based guidelines on selecting the vocabulary to teach that will have the most benefit for MLs as well as strategies for teaching and reinforcing those new words. The chapter also offers a tool for planning lessons based on content-specific vocabulary.

Chapter 6: Teaching Academic Language to MLs at the Sentence and Discourse Level

Building on Chapter 5, Chapter 6 examines teaching academic language at the sentence and discourse levels. It includes practical examples of how to analyze a text's academic language and how to teach a sample of the linguistic forms and functions necessary for MLs to interact with challenging grade-level texts and topics. The chapter gives you guidance on how to leverage different types of teachers' strengths in order to effectively collaborate to integrate instruction of academic language at the sentence and discourse levels, weaving together academic language and content instruction.

Chapter 7: Activating and Teaching MLs Background Knowledge

Chapter 7 presents research on the role of background knowledge in MLs' engagement with academic content. This chapter addresses the need to develop a new approach to activating and teaching background knowledge to MLs, including a specific focus on supporting background knowledge in mathematics. It presents a four-step framework for deciding which types of background knowledge to teach MLs as well as ways to activate and teach background knowledge concisely. The chapter models several activities that you can use in your own planning and instruction to help you put our ML background knowledge framework into practice.

Chapter 8: Engaging MLs in Reading and Writing in the Content Areas

Chapter 8 first synthesizes a new body of relevant research on engaging MLs in literacy practices. Then, it presents an integrated series of activities to scaffold MLs' engagement with reading and writing in the content areas. The chapter emphasizes the connection between reading and writing practices and offers strategies for incorporating classroom activities that provide opportunities for both. Building on Chapter 4, Chapter 8 offers a variety of ways to incorporate peer learning as a tool for supporting MLs in unlocking the meaning of complex texts and strengthening academic writing.

Chapter 9: Formative Assessment for MLs

Chapter 9 highlights the necessity of creating formative assessments that measure MLs' acquisition of academic language and content. The chapter includes a definition of formative assessment and provides a summary of relevant research on the practice of formative assessment for MLs. It also includes guidance on creating valid classroom assessments for MLs based on MLs' English proficiency levels and offers you the opportunity to apply what you've learned to your own formative assessment of MLs.

WHY YOU NEED THIS BOOK TO SUPPORT MLs

1

Times have changed. In the past, English language development (ELD) teachers tended to physically remove multilingual learners (MLs) from the content or grade-level teachers' classrooms, providing them ELD instruction in a separate location (sometimes a closet, a hallway, or a basement room). Now, many schools, districts, and states have shifted to integrated instructional models in which MLs spend the majority—if not all of—their time with their grade-level peers. In this integrated model, ELD teachers and content teachers collaborate and/or coteach to share the responsibility (and the joy) of teaching both content and academic language to MLs (Staehr Fenner, 2014a).

Research clearly demonstrates the benefits of integrating the instruction of grade-level content and academic language for MLs (August, 2018). At the same time, we also want to acknowledge how much teachers have on their plates these days—content teaching, literacy and language development, and social-emotional support (just to name a few educational priorities). In order to be able to effectively incorporate ML instructional strategies to support content learning and integrate ELD opportunities, content teachers need models, practice, and guidance. Similarly, in order for ELD teachers to be able to share their expertise on language development and scaffolded instruction, they need assistance in how to effectively collaborate with content teachers in support of MLs. It is also critical that they be part of a school culture that values their expertise and that they have the time for effective collaboration to take place (Honigsfeld & Dove, 2022). Based on our work with MLs, our collaboration with ML educators in a wide variety of roles, and our review of research in the field, we have developed a framework for equitable ML education that we present in this chapter.

In this chapter, we will first provide an overview of who MLs are. Next, we will outline the sense of urgency in providing MLs the instruction that they need to be successful in today's challenging classrooms and also be respected and valued on a social-emotional level. The bulk of the chapter will focus on the five core beliefs that frame the content of this book, as well as all of our work with MLs. For each core belief, we provide a brief research-based rationale for the belief, as well as practical tools for you to use to apply the core belief to your own practice. The chapter ends with the opportunity for you to develop your own core beliefs, create a grade-level team, department, school, or district vision for the equitable education of MLs, and craft your own "elevator speech" to define your role in unlocking MLs' potential.

Who Are MLs?

As we mentioned in the "What's New in This Edition?" introduction to this book, one shift that we have made in the second edition is using the term multilingual learner to replace English learner. This shift in terminology represents a more assets-based view of students as the term *English learner* "prioritize[s] English as the student's language, while ignoring the additional language(s) a student may already speak or may be developing" (Columbo et al., 2018). In contrast, the term *ML* brings to the forefront the understanding that regardless of their level of English proficiency, each student (or learner) enters the classroom with valuable cultural and linguistic assets. Several state agencies and national organizations (e.g., National Association of English Learner Program Administrators [NAELPA], TESOL International Association, and WIDA) have adopted the term *ML*.

In discussing terminology, it's important to note that the term *ML* incorporates a broader group of students than the term *EL*. **MLs are any students whose parents or guardians report speaking one or more language(s) other than or in addition to English in the home. MLs may or may not qualify for ELD services due to their level of English proficiency** (Snyder et al., 2023; Snyder & Staehr Fenner, 2021). In order to distinguish between MLs as a whole and MLs who qualify for ELD services, particularly in the discussion of data on a nationwide level, we use the term *emergent ML*. **Emergent MLs are MLs who qualify for ELD services. The federal government identifies these students using the term *English learners*.** Let's take a look at what this distinction means in terms of numbers of students. In the 2019-2020 school year, over five million, or more than 10 percent, of the school-aged population was eligible to receive specialized ELD services (National Center for Education Statistics, 2021). In that same year, more than twelve million or nearly 23 percent of children ages 5-17 in the United States were identified as MLs, as reported in the U.S. census data. In Figure 1.1 you can see that more than double the number of students who qualified for ELD services are considered to be MLs.

As is often the case when discussing terminology, this shift to the use of ML is not without its challenges (Snyder et al., 2023). Dr. Julie Sugarman, senior policy analyst for PreK–12 education at the Migration Policy Institute's National Center on Immigrant Integration Policy, explains, "while it's helpful to have an overarching term for all students with exposure to or fluency in multiple languages, it's also really important to remember that students who are identified as English learners with the federal definition have protections and learning needs that states, districts, and schools are legally obligated to manage." (personal communication, February 13, 2023, as cited in Snyder et al., 2023).

FIGURE 1.1   POPULATION OF EMERGENT MLs AND ML SCHOOL-AGED CHILDREN IN THE UNITED STATES

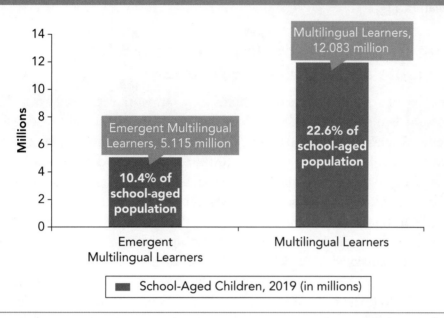

School-Aged Children, 2019 (in millions)

Sources: National Center for Education Statistics (2021); U.S. Census Bureau (2019a); U.S. Census Bureau (2019b).

We also agree that while it is critical to use language that fosters an assets-based view of students, it is also essential to make sure that the specific strengths and needs of individual MLs are identified and responded to. In this book, we explore many strategies (e.g., peer learning, academic-language instruction) that are beneficial to MLs regardless of their level of language proficiency in English. However, we also take steps to highlight strategies that are specific to emergent MLs at varying stages of English language development (ELD). We make these distinctions by using the term *emergent ML*, by including English language proficiency (ELP) levels in our scenarios, by incorporating an ML Newcomer Student and SLIFE section at the end of each chapter, and by highlighting ELP levels in our scaffolding framework. With the reflection questions that follow, consider the terminology that is used in your district.

REFLECTION QUESTIONS

1. What terminology does your district use to describe students whose parents or guardians report speaking one or more language(s) other than or in addition to English in the home?

2. What terminology does your district use to describe students who qualify for ELD services based on their level of English proficiency?

3. What procedures does your district have in place to identify the unique strengths and needs of individual MLs?

  Available for download at **resources.corwin.com/FennerUnlocking2E**

The need for assets-based terminology when referring to MLs is just one piece of a broader and urgent appeal to support MLs' equitable and excellent education.

What Is the Sense of Urgency Around MLs' Equitable and Excellent Education?

Our sense of urgency for this book stems from our work with teachers and MLs across the United States and Canada and our synthesis of current research and practice. Issues of inequitable educational opportunities that have long been present in our schools were brought to the forefront in recent years for MLs, students of color, students receiving special educational services, and students coming from low socioeconomic backgrounds, among others. These students were disproportionally impacted by school closures, shifts to virtual learning, rising living costs, and other factors impacting students' physical and mental well-being (Sahakyan & Cook, 2021; U.S. Department of Education, Office for Civil Rights, 2021; Villegas & Garcia, 2022). Two areas of continued inequity for MLs include their educational outcomes and opportunities and their access to qualified teachers and administrators who share their cultural and linguistic backgrounds or have training in meeting the needs of MLs. We will explore these two areas next.

Educational Opportunities and Outcomes for MLs

MLs tend to experience significant gaps in educational opportunities and outcomes. While it is difficult to find disaggregated data for MLs as a whole, data specific to emergent MLs (MLs qualifying for ELD services) highlights several areas of inequity. Emergent MLs as a subgroup achieve below national averages for student proficiency rates on state math, language arts, and science exams (Office of English Language Acquisition [OELA], 2021d). However, it is essential to keep in mind that emergent MLs are a dynamic group with students being reclassified as they gain English proficiency (U.S. Department of Education, n.d.). In fact, there is growing evidence in some states to show that students who formerly qualified for ELD services and have been reclassified are outperforming native English speakers who never qualified for ELD services (Jorgensen, 2019; U.S. Department of Education, 2023; Villegas & Ibarra, 2022).

Additionally, emergent MLs tend to be underrepresented in honors and gifted programs as well as Advanced Placement (AP) and International Baccalaureate (IB) classes (OELA, 2021b, 2021c). During the 2017-2018 school year, only 1.5 percent of emergent MLs were enrolled in gifted and talented programs compared to 7.2 percent of students who were not emergent MLs (OELA, 2021c). Similarly, during the 2017-2018 school year, fewer than one in ten emergent MLs were enrolled in AP courses when these courses were offered by their school compared to more than one in five students overall (OELA, 2021b). Emergent

MLs are also underrepresented in dual enrollment courses, which are courses in which students simultaneously earn credit for both a high school diploma and a college degree. In 2017-2018, fewer than 4 percent of emergent MLs were enrolled in dual enrollment courses compared to 11 percent of the total school population (OELA, 2022).

These types of inequities also extend to ML student retention rates. In Grades K–12, emergent MLs represented 10 percent of students enrolled in public schools nationwide but 14.3 percent of students retained during the 2017–2018 school year (OELA, 2021a). While we have provided a national overview of some areas of inequities for MLs, we encourage you to review similar data for your school or district in order to identify where advocacy for MLs might be needed.

Teacher Demographics and Professional Development

A second area of inequity for MLs is that many MLs do not have teachers who represent their racial, cultural, and linguistic backgrounds (Ingersoll et al., 2018). The number of teachers of color is increasing nationally in the United States. However, there still remains a noteworthy gap between the percentages of students of color and the percentages of teachers of color in U.S. public schools (Ingersoll et al., 2018; Schaeffer, 2021). During the 2018-2019 school year, 47 percent of U.S. public school students identified as non-Hispanic white, 27 percent as Hispanic, 15 percent as Black, and 5 percent as Asian. Approximately 1 percent or fewer identified as Pacific Islander, American Indian, or Alaska Native; and around 4 percent were of two or more races (Schaeffer, 2021). In contrast, the National Center for Educational Statistics (NCES) data show that 79 percent of public school teachers identified as non-Hispanic white during the 2017–2018 school year (Schaeffer, 2021). Additionally, 7 percent identified as Black, 9 percent as Hispanic, 2 percent as Asian American, and fewer than 2 percent of teachers identified either as American Indian or Alaska Native, Pacific Islander, or of two or more races. There are similar patterns for racial and ethnic diversity in principals. In 2017–2018, approximately 78 percent of principals were non-Hispanic white, compared with 11 percent who were Black, 9 percent who were Hispanic, and 1 percent who were Asian American (Schaeffer, 2021). Figure 1.2 illustrates this gap.

Although a common racial, ethnic, cultural, or linguistic background is not a prerequisite for effective instruction of MLs, the fact that a significant percentage of educators are white, middle class monolinguals does emphasize the need for educator professional development centered on effective teaching and social-emotional support for MLs. In order to bolster educational opportunities and respond to educational inequities for MLs, teachers must value MLs' cultural and linguistic assets and be prepared to use and sustain students' assets during instruction (Banks & Banks, 2019; Gay, 2010; Ladson-Billings,

FIGURE 1.2   RACIAL AND ETHNIC MAKE-UP OF PUBLIC SCHOOL STUDENTS, TEACHERS, AND PRINCIPALS[1]

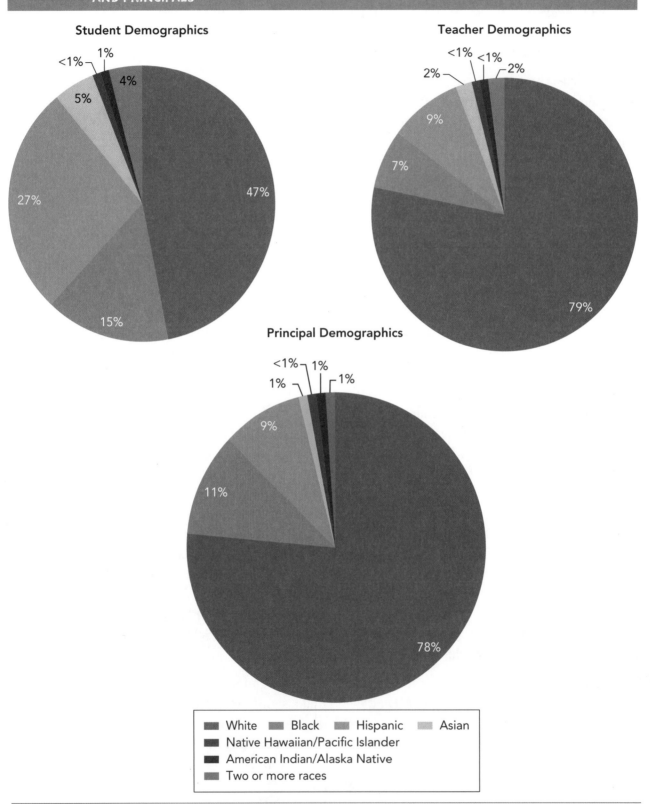

Sources: Schaffer, K. (2021), National Center for Education Statistics (2022).

_____

[1]These percentages are approximates based on available data.

2004; Paris & Alim, 2017). ML equity and excellence extends to our moral obligation as educators to ensure that our MLs, who often navigate complex, conflicting cultural balances between home and school, are supported on a social-emotional, holistic level (Staehr Fenner & Teich, in press). MLs must know that their teachers are providing a safe space in which they can learn and also trust their teachers enough to reach out to them if a personal factor is presenting a barrier to their learning. At a time in which concerns about student mental health and well-being have reached a crisis point, we must be especially vigilant and collaborate to provide a support network for our MLs, who may be recovering from trauma, and encourage them to learn and thrive on many levels. The types of student-teacher relationships that will foster this safe space begin in the classroom and set the stage for MLs to feel valued, a part of the community, and ready to learn (Staehr Fenner & Teich, in press).

Despite the fact that numbers of MLs continues to rise, the number of certified ELD educators has decreased (Najarro, 2023). During SY 2017–2018, 32 states, the District of Columbia, and Puerto Rico did not meet their projected needs for bilingual or ELD teachers (OELA, 2021a). Furthermore, in an analysis that we conducted in 2020, we found that only four states have teacher recertification requirements for general-education teachers that included professional development on instructional practices for MLs (Duggan et al., 2020). Thus, there is an urgent need for professional development to support educators as they become prepared for and invested in working with culturally and linguistically diverse students and families in service to a more equitable and excellent education for MLs.

What Is the Framework for Equitable and Excellent ML Education?

Through our work with all educators who serve MLs—including content teachers, ELD teachers, specials teachers, school counselors, administrators, and others—we recognize the importance of a framework that identifies and addresses the need for all teachers to adjust their instruction to recognize MLs' strengths, as well as to support their needs. This framework for equitable and excellent ML education encompasses many areas related to instruction that are necessary for MLs to meaningfully engage in challenging content classes and develop their language skills. In addition, our framework is unique in that it also recognizes the need for all teachers of MLs to collaborate and operate within a context of equity, advocacy, and leadership to continually develop as professionals in order to best support MLs. The framework is driven by our five core beliefs. Figure 1.3 provides a visual representation of the framework.

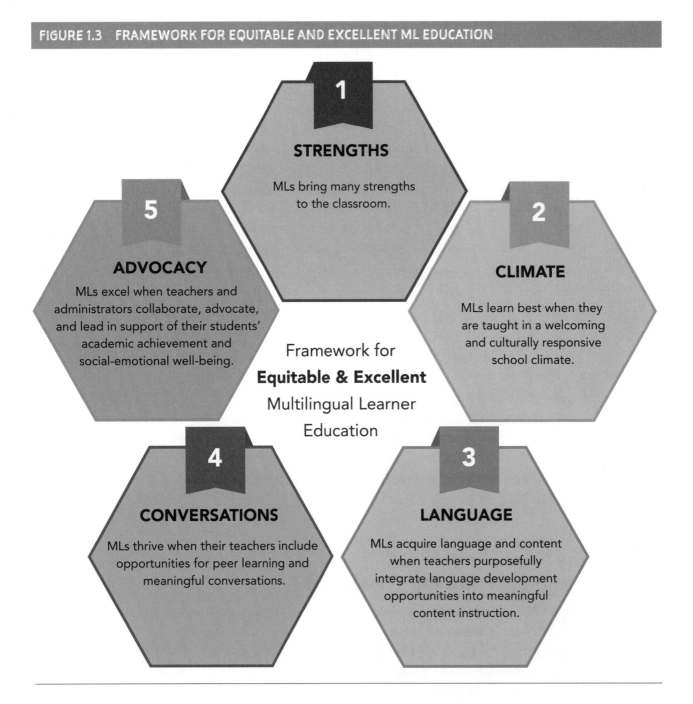

What Are the Core Beliefs That We Use to Frame Our Work With MLs and This Book?

In our work supporting MLs and their teachers, we often analyze complex educational issues and try to make sense of them as they apply to MLs, phrasing our findings and recommendations in a way that resonates with educators in different roles. Along those lines, we have developed a set of five core beliefs that synthesize our beliefs, grounded in research and practice, about the education of MLs. You will see these core beliefs exemplified in our recommendations and strategies throughout the chapters of this book. In this chapter, for each core belief, we provide an explanation of what that belief means to us, we briefly share the research on which it is based, and we also leave you with reflection questions and practical tools that you can use to support your understanding of each core belief as it applies to your context. Our core beliefs are as follows:

1. MLs bring many strengths to the classroom.

2. MLs learn best when they are taught in a welcoming and culturally responsive school climate.

3. MLs acquire language and content when teachers purposefully integrate language development opportunities into meaningful content instruction.

4. MLs thrive when their teachers include opportunities for peer learning and meaningful conversations.

5. MLs excel when teachers and administrators collaborate, advocate, and lead in support of their students' academic achievement and social-emotional well-being.

Core Belief 1: MLs bring many strengths to the classroom.

MLs enter the classroom with diverse cultural and linguistic experiences that we feel are often unintentionally overlooked or underappreciated by their schools and teachers. In order to effectively educate MLs, it is important to first recognize the knowledge and skills that they already have and what they bring to the educational landscape. Moll et al. (1992) coined the term **funds of knowledge** to refer to these **accumulated bodies of knowledge and skills that MLs bring to the classroom**. MLs' home languages, knowledge, and cultural assets should be incorporated into instruction, so as to honor students' backgrounds and experiences, sustain their cultural and linguistic practices, and support their academic learning (August, 2018; National Academies of Sciences, Engineering, & Medicine [NASEM], 2017; Paris & Alim, 2017). For example, refugee students may enter the U.S. education system with gaps in their education due to interrupted schooling, emerging literacy skills in their home language, and beginner-level English language proficiency (ELP). However, those same students might bring with them a passionate desire to learn, a strong oral tradition of sharing knowledge, persistence in overcoming obstacles, and creative problem-solving skills. A teacher educating these students should look for ways to build on these strengths as a tool for instruction, such as having oral language activities linked to writing tasks.

As we build relationships with students, we learn about their strengths and are better positioned to use students' lived experiences as foundations for learning (Snyder & Staehr Fenner, 2021; Staehr Fenner & Teich, in press). Providing MLs opportunities to share their backgrounds, experiences, and ideas benefits other students as well. Listening to and responding to diverse perspectives helps prepare all students to live in a multicultural society and interact with individuals from different backgrounds (Gorski, 2010; Snyder & Staehr Fenner, 2021). In addition, with all states recognizing the value of bilingualism and biliteracy through the Seal of Biliteracy,[2] MLs can serve as needed language models for non-MLs studying world languages and in dual-language settings. They can also share cultural and linguistic insights in less formal ways during content instruction. For example, in a discussion on U.S. elections, MLs who were born in countries outside the United States might share what the election process looks like in their home countries if they feel comfortable doing so. Such straightforward ways to include MLs and highlight their perspectives can go a long way in creating an environment conducive to building their trust and facilitating deeper learning. We explore this idea in greater depth in Chapter 2 when we discuss using an assets-based approach in our work with MLs and leveraging MLs' cultural and linguistic assets. Application Activity 1.1 is an opportunity for you to reflect on the ways in which you recognize MLs' strengths in your role.

APPLICATION ACTIVITY 1.1: RECOGNIZING MLS' STRENGTHS

Consider the following reflection questions to help you better understand your perspective when working with MLs. For each question, answer *yes*, *sometimes*, or *no*. For any question that you answer with a *sometimes* or a *no*, write down a question or idea that you have about how to shift toward an assets-based perspective in this area. Then, answer the reflection questions.

FIGURE 1.4 RECOGNIZING MLs' STRENGTHS

REFLECTION QUESTION	YES	SOMETIMES	NO	QUESTION OR IDEA FOR A SHIFT TO A STRENGTHS-BASED APPROACH
1. Do I view students' cultural and linguistic backgrounds as a valuable source of knowledge and skills that I can build on in my lessons?				
2. Do I view diverse perspectives as a beneficial resource for all students and look for ways to incorporate these diverse perspectives into my teaching?				
3. Do I recognize and appreciate that ML families may contribute to their children's educations in varied and sometimes unseen ways?				

[2]State Laws Regarding the Seal of Biliteracy: https://sealofbiliteracy.org.

REFLECTION QUESTION	YES	SOMETIMES	NO	QUESTION OR IDEA FOR A SHIFT TO A STRENGTHS-BASED APPROACH
4. Do I hold my MLs to the same high standards as other students?				
5. Do I recognize that MLs who are struggling in my class may be doing so because they need additional forms of support to acquire language and content knowledge that they are not currently receiving, or they may need additional social-emotional support?				

APPLICATION ACTIVITY 1.1: REFLECTION QUESTIONS

1. What is an area of strength for you in terms of recognizing MLs' strengths?

_____

_____

2. What is an area where you would like to improve in terms of recognizing MLs' strengths?

_____

_____

Core Belief 2: MLs learn best when they are taught in a welcoming and culturally responsive school climate.

A school culture that supports equitable and excellent educational opportunities for MLs includes schoolwide beliefs about the potential of MLs, interest in and appreciation for MLs' culture, and the desire to foster positive relationships with the MLs and their families. Dr. Cooper (2021), in her book *And Justice for ELs*, highlights the pressing need for a whole-school approach to meeting the needs of MLs. She writes, "Misconceptions about linguistic diversity, racial identity, cultural diversity, citizenship, and how one might feel included (or excluded) with a learning community can pose persistent challenges that affect [MLs'] language instruction and overall sense of belonging" (p. 6). As the leaders of the school, principals and assistant principals influence this culture in terms of their commitment to the academic success of MLs, how they speak to and about MLs and their families, the types of professional development they offer staff, and how they evaluate teachers' work with MLs (Alford & Niño, 2011; Staehr Fenner et al., 2015). Unfortunately, many school administrators have received insufficient training in culturally responsive teaching practices to foster a school climate that fully embraces MLs as part of the school community and effectively supports their language and content learning (Callahan et al., 2019; Khalifa, 2018; Staehr Fenner, 2014a).

In building a school culture that supports high achievement for all MLs, shared beliefs at the school level should include recognition of the benefits of multilingualism, an appreciation of MLs' culture, and the need to overcome stereotypes and a deficit paradigm. School leaders must be prepared to reflect on their own biases and gaps in knowledge about supporting ML populations (Bryan et al., 2019; Cooper, 2021). Callahan et al. (2019) argue that school leaders must recognize students' linguistic civil rights (equitable access to instruction) and also have a "research-based understanding of bilingual and [ELD] instructional programs that frame language as a resource and right, rather than a problem" (p. 291). They further argue that, in order to be responsive to the needs of MLs in their context, it is essential to have a shared dialogue with teachers, families, and staff. To engage in these types of dialogues with families, it is critical to build strong partnerships with ML families and foster a welcoming climate. We explore strategies for building these types of partnerships in greater detail in Chapter 2. Application Activity 1.2 is a collaborative activity that you can take part in with your school leadership team or as a department to reflect on your school environment.

APPLICATION ACTIVITY 1.2: SCHOOL ENVIRONMENT CHECKLIST

Review the questions on your school environment in relation to MLs and ML families. Identify possible areas that you might want to strengthen.

FIGURE 1.5   SCHOOL ENVIRONMENT CHECKLIST

AT OUR SCHOOL, DO WE . . .	YES	NO
Take time as staff members to reflect on our own biases and gaps in knowledge around supporting MLs?		
Have a school mission that is inclusive of MLs and values multilingualism and multiculturalism?		
Use a research-based program model and strategies for developing MLs' content knowledge and language skills?		

AT OUR SCHOOL, DO WE . . .	YES	NO
Create a welcoming environment for ML families (e.g., have signs in ML families' home languages, display maps and flags of MLs' home countries, offer school tours to new families in their home language)?		
Prioritize relationship building with ML families (e.g., host ML family events, give staff opportunities to learn common phrases in families' home languages and key information about families' cultures)?		
Communicate effectively with families in their preferred language (e.g., information shared in families' home languages, bilingual staff or bilingual volunteers available to meet with families)?		
Provide services that remove barriers that prevent ML families from attending school events (e.g., childcare, interpreters, and transportation)?		

Source: Adapted from Breiseth, L., Robertson, K., & Lafond, S. (2011).

Action Steps: To make a more welcoming environment for MLs and families of MLs, we will . . .

1.

2.

3.

Core Belief 3: MLs acquire language and content when teachers purposefully integrate language development opportunities into meaningful content instruction.

In order to assist MLs in meeting challenging content standards, they will need language instruction that closely corresponds to the content they are learning. WIDA, a national organization that provides language development resources and assessments for MLs, created an ELD Standards Framework (WIDA, 2020a). This framework, first developed in 2012 and then most recently revised in 2020, highlights the way in which content and language are integrated for MLs. WIDA (2020a) explains that MLs "develop content and language concurrently, with academic content as a context for language learning and language as a means for learning academic content" (p. 19). In other words, direct instruction in academic language and language skills that provide a bridge to content standards will bolster MLs' achievement in specific content areas. And language will be acquired most effectively when it is taught through meaningful content that includes opportunities for students to practice using the four domains of language (i.e., listening, speaking, reading, and writing).

The WIDA ELD Standards Framework (WIDA, 2020a) has identified four key language uses (i.e., narrate, inform, explain, and argue) that can be helpful in thinking about how to determine language objectives and support the integration of content and language. **Language objectives are learning objectives that specifically focus on students' language use and language development.** Let's consider how teachers might use this information in practice.

In Figure 1.6, you can see the WIDA ELD Standard and one of the language expectations for explaining in science in Grades 2–3. **A language expectation is the language that students need to be able to understand and produce in a specific content area and grade level.** The language expectation included in Figure 1.6 is one example of how students can be expected to use language when providing a scientific explanation. We have added a possible **student-friendly language objective (a language objective that is understandable to students)** based on that language expectation. When you begin sharing student-friendly language objectives with MLs, you give them opportunities to think more about their language use and language development and become more independent learners. We have also included a possible mini lesson to support the language objective. **A mini lesson is a short lesson in which you practice one aspect of language.** Developing student-friendly language objectives and ideas for language mini lessons is a great place for the ELD teacher to take the lead in a cotaught classroom.

FIGURE 1.6   USING LANGUAGE STANDARDS TO WRITE STUDENT-FRIENDLY LANGUAGE OBJECTIVES

WIDA ELD STANDARD 4 GRADES 2–3 LANGUAGE FOR SCIENCE (KEY LANGUAGE USE: EXPLAIN)	
Language Expectation: MLs will construct scientific observations that develop a logical sequence between data or evidence and a claim.	
Possible student-friendly language objective: I will explain orally how my claim is supported by evidence.	**Possible mini lesson:** Academic language for supporting claims with evidence (e.g., Our data shows . . . , I observed that . . .)

Source: Adapted from WIDA English Language Development Standards, 2020 Edition, https://wida.wisc.edu/teach/standards/eld/2020 (2020a), p. 94.

REFLECTION QUESTIONS

1. What do you notice about how the language expectation can be used to develop a student-friendly language objective?

2. What do you notice about how the language objective can be used to determine possible language mini lessons?

3. What questions do you have about language objectives or integrating language and content instruction?

 Available for download at **resources.corwin.com/FennerUnlocking2E**

As more districts move toward collaborative, inclusive models of ELD instruction in which MLs receive language support as part of their content classes, MLs will benefit when their teachers learn how to teach language and content in an integrated way. The strategies presented in this book are intended to facilitate the teaching of language and content in tandem by ELD as well as content teachers. We recognize it can be a challenge to step outside your area of expertise, especially when you may not have received adequate resources or training on teaching MLs. However, we hope that as you work through the chapters and try out the strategies used in this book (ideally, together with a colleague or two), you will gain increasing confidence in how to better support your MLs as they acquire language and content. Figure 1.7 outlines some—but not all—ways a content and an ELD teacher can plan and prepare for, teach, and assess lessons that incorporate academic-language instruction along with content instruction. We will explore more strategies for collaborating in support of MLs' academic language development in Chapters 5 and 6.

FIGURE 1.7   POSSIBLE ROLES OF TEACHERS IN TEACHING LANGUAGE AND CONTENT

COMPONENTS OF INSTRUCTION	CONTENT TEACHER	ELD TEACHER	BOTH
Planning and preparing for the lesson	• Select content • Identify content objectives • Identify content-specific vocabulary and language needed for students to meet content objectives	• Analyze language demands of lesson and texts • Identify language objectives • Develop supporting materials for MLs	• Reach consensus on language objectives • Determine key vocabulary • Decide on strategies for teaching and practicing academic language at sentence and discourse levels

(Continued)

(Continued)

COMPONENTS OF INSTRUCTION	CONTENT TEACHER	ELD TEACHER	BOTH
Teaching the lesson	• Incorporate additional opportunities to practice academic language into lesson • Coteach large group of students, embedding scaffolds for MLs	• Work with small groups of MLs as needed to support language development • Coteach whole class, embedding scaffolds for MLs	• Teach academic vocabulary and language • Teach language-focused mini lessons (e.g., compound sentence structure or connecting ideas at discourse level)
Assessing student learning	• Develop assessment of content objectives • Determine scoring mechanism (e.g., rubric or checklist)	• Add assessment of language to assessment of content for MLs • Scaffold assessment as needed for MLs (e.g., word banks, bilingual glossaries, or visuals)	• Determine how MLs will be assessed • Reflect on MLs' assessment results, and determine how to adjust instruction of content and language • Work with MLs needing additional support

Core Belief 4: MLs thrive when their teachers include opportunities for peer learning and meaningful conversations.

In our work with some educators of MLs, one of our greatest takeaways is the missed opportunities for peer interactions. Imagine the difference between a teacher leading a whole class discussion in which the teacher asks a series of questions and a couple of students—usually the same ones who raise their hands all the time—are called on to respond versus a teacher posing a well-developed prompt and students discussing it in pairs. Consider the dramatic difference in terms of student engagement and students' opportunities for language use.

While every question we ask the class isn't a peer learning opportunity, the strategic inclusion of peer learning opportunities throughout a lesson can have significant impact on MLs' language development, understanding of content, and feeling of belonging (August, 2018; NASEM, 2017; Zwiers, 2019). Well-structured peer learning opportunities support language development because there is an opportunity for MLs to receive feedback on their language use, to develop greater understanding of the grammatical structures of English, and to be pushed to interact at higher proficiency levels (August, 2018). Additionally, peer learning supports students' understanding and engagement with course content and helps build stronger social-emotional skills and student agency (Staehr Fenner & Teich, in press; Zwiers, 2019). Zwiers (2019) explains that as students interact with each other they gain understanding about how others think and feel about different topics and how they express their feelings. These type of interactions help build empathy for others which is so critical in creating a safe space for student learning. Additionally, when students are given the space to co-create ideas and ways to express these ideas, their sense of agency grows (Zwiers, 2019).

In order to foster a safe space for effective peer learning, the teacher must consider the routines that they will teach to support effective peer-to-peer interactions, the steps that they will take to build a safe space for MLs to take risks with their language, and the room setup. Without these structures in place, peer learning activities may fall flat. In addition, once a safe space has been created and students are familiar with peer learning routines, these types of activities can be incorporated into learning with minimal preparation. In Application Activity 1.3, consider the classroom look-fors from our Classroom Checklist (Figure 1.8), and answer the reflection questions. The complete checklist can be found on the online companion website in Appendix C. To access the companion website, please visit resources.corwin.com/FennerUnlocking2E.

UNLOCKING RESOURCES

resources.corwin
.com/FennerUnlocking2E

APPLICATION ACTIVITY 1.3: SETTING THE SCENE FOR PEER LEARNING

FIGURE 1.8   CLASSROOM LOOK-FORS FOR PEER LEARNING

I have . . .

- Clustered student desks in groups of 3–5 or used small tables to promote collaboration and peer interaction.

- Posted select talk moves needed to support pair and group discussions (e.g., "I think . . .", "I agree with you because . . ."). I will add new expressions throughout the year as I teach them.

- Planned for routines to learn about my students and support students in learning about each other (e.g., Morning Meeting, dialogue journals, icebreaker/community building activities).

- Identified and planned for teaching and modeling routines that will support structured peer interaction (e.g., turn and talk, think-pair-share, small group work).

- Planned how I will use language to support a welcoming, inclusive environment in the classroom (e.g., a personal morning greeting for each student which may include multiple languages, expectation that all student names will be pronounced correctly by everyone in the class).

- Planned how I will use language in the classroom that empowers or positions MLs to participate (e.g., highlight MLs' strengths, support use of MLs' home language or visuals to plan or share a response, acknowledge and build on what MLs say).

APPLICATION ACTIVITY 1.3: REFLECTION QUESTIONS

1. Which of the look-fors stands out to you? Why?

_____

_____

2. What is a step that you might take to implement one of the look-fors in your classroom or support others in implementing the look-for?

_____

_____

online resources ⟶ Available for download at **resources.corwin.com/FennerUnlocking2E**

We will explore peer learning in greater depth in Chapters 4 and 8.

Core Belief 5: MLs excel when teachers and administrators collaborate, advocate, and lead in support of their students' academic achievement and social-emotional well-being.

The work of promoting equitable educational opportunities for MLs implores us to draw on the skills of collaboration, advocacy, and leadership, which are skills many do not immediately consider that will have an impact on MLs' outcomes. We must collaborate with colleagues, students, families, and communities in support of MLs. We must also speak on behalf of those MLs and their families who have not yet developed a strong voice of their own due to their acquisition of English or knowledge of the U.S. education system (Staehr Fenner, 2014a) and use leadership skills to support our advocacy efforts. To that end, in each chapter of the book, we include a section on collaboration and another on advocacy, equity, and leadership to highlight possible strategies or needs related to the chapter topic.

Collaboration With Colleagues

As we mentioned earlier, educator collaboration is a powerful tool in supporting MLs' acquisition of language and content, but it also has additional far-reaching benefits. Teacher collaboration helps bring home the idea that all teachers are responsible for MLs' language development, social-emotional well-being, feeling of belonging, and academic success (Honigsfeld & Dove, 2018). Additionally, well-structured collaboration builds teacher capacity and supports a shared understanding of culturally responsive and sustaining practices (Honigsfeld & Dove, 2018).

ELD teachers can share their knowledge of second language acquisition and language pedagogy and can model strategies that will support content teachers in becoming teachers of language in addition to teachers of content (Honigsfeld & Dove, 2018; Maxwell, 2013; Valdés et al., 2014). Similarly, content teachers can share with ELD teachers the skills and knowledge that all students, including MLs, will need to be successful in a particular content area. Both types of teachers can support each other in ensuring that MLs' individual personal characteristics (e.g., motivation and learning preferences), as well as their backgrounds (e.g., literacy in the home language and amount and/or quality of previous schooling), are part of the schooling equation.

In order to foster such high-quality collaboration, schools must have a structure in place so that teachers can work together in a systematic and ongoing way and share their expertise with one another. Administrators must build time into schedules for collaboration to occur, make it a priority for the entire staff, and ensure it is happening.

Advocacy

Advocating for MLs can sometimes feel like a daunting task. In order to begin advocating for MLs, it's often helpful to get a sense of what the larger, systemic or programmatic advocacy issues may be to decide which direction your advocacy should take. Figure 1.9 provides an equity audit, which can help you reflect on your context at the school level. Working through this equity audit can assist you in deciding which areas of advocacy for MLs present the highest needs. You simply can't take on each potential injustice simultaneously, and prioritizing your top advocacy issue or issues will help you determine your path forward.

FIGURE 1.9   ML ADVOCACY EQUITY AUDIT

POTENTIAL ML ADVOCACY ISSUE	QUESTIONS TO ASK: TO WHAT DEGREE . . .	RESPONSE	ACTION ITEMS
Role of ELD teacher	Are ELD teachers working as experts and collaborating with general-education teachers?	Not at all Somewhat Extensively	
Instructional materials and curriculum	Are instructional materials and curriculum appropriate for MLs?	Not at all Somewhat Extensively	
Professional development	Does professional development focus on preparing *all* teachers to teach academic language and content to MLs?	Not at all Somewhat Extensively	

(Continued)

(Continued)

POTENTIAL ML ADVOCACY ISSUE	QUESTIONS TO ASK: TO WHAT DEGREE . . .	RESPONSE	ACTION ITEMS
Assessment	Are teachers aware of the linguistic demands of content assessments for MLs? Are they using valid formative assessments with MLs?	Not at all Somewhat Extensively	
ML family outreach	Are ML families' assets understood and valued? Are ML families aware of the school's expectations of all students and supports available to them?	Not at all Somewhat Extensively	
Teacher coaching	Are teachers receiving the professional development and coaching that they need to assist their MLs in accessing challenging content?	Not at all Somewhat Extensively	

Source: The concept is adapted from Betty J. Alford and Mary Catherine Niño's *equity audit*, which appears in *Leading Academic Achievement for English Language Learners: A Guide for Principals* (Alford, B. J., & Niño, M. C., 2011).

 Available for download at **resources.corwin.com/FennerUnlocking2E**

After you have taken the steps to determine which areas of advocacy you might like to prioritize at the school or district level, it's time to consider how you will approach your advocacy and how you will work to empower MLs to be stronger advocates for themselves. Just as we scaffold instruction for MLs, we also can scaffold our advocacy efforts. **Scaffolded advocacy is a concept in which MLs and their families are provided with just the right level of advocacy while at the same time being supported in developing their own advocacy skills** (Staehr Fenner, 2014a). The goal of scaffolded advocacy is for MLs and their families to advocate for themselves. In Figure 1.10, we offer ML advocacy steps and implementation suggestions for each step to collaborate and advocate on behalf of MLs.

Leadership

While it's always beneficial to reflect on your advocacy priorities and steps, in order to effectively advocate for MLs' equitable and excellent learning, you will also need to draw from and, in some cases, develop the necessary leadership skills to do so. While many definitions exist, one definition of **leadership is "the process of influencing . . . the behavior of others in order to reach a shared goal"** (Northouse, 2007). To advocate for MLs and support their equitable and excellent education, we encourage you to first increase your awareness of your own leadership skills and build upon those skills to make changes occur. As this is an area that teachers are typically not trained in, administrators can help develop these skills in their teachers. In our work with MLs, we have seen many educators rise up as leaders who successfully advocate for MLs, serve as allies to MLs, and bring about much-needed changes. It's truly inspiring to witness teachers serve MLs on multiple levels to impact change.

FIGURE 1.10 STEPS FOR ML ADVOCACY AND IMPLEMENTATION SUGGESTIONS

1 Begin thoughtfully

Consider all of the areas in which you can advocate for MLs and collaborate to benefit them. Choose one or two areas to focus on in which you have the agency to enact changes, and plan out what your action steps will look like.

2 Build alliances first with those who seem open

Begin by carefully considering colleagues who seem open to working with MLs and supporting them. Approach those colleagues first to ascertain whether they would like to collaborate with you.

3 Demonstrate empathy first

When collaborating with colleagues, show your empathy for their challenges and frustrations related to working with concepts outside of their area of expertise. Acknowledge those areas they find to be most challenging.

4 Respect educators' expertise

Voice your understanding of their area of expertise so you can leverage it together. Operating within a strengths perspective when it comes to your colleagues (as well as your students) will go a long way.

5 Operate from a strengths-based perspective of MLs

Intentionally highlight MLs' contributions to classrooms, such as their home language, culture, and/or families' commitment to education. When you hear deficit language offer an alternative strengths-based perspective.

6 Showcase ML achievement

Underscore the ways in which MLs make progress, be it academic or social. Often, MLs' progress may not be as apparent or obvious as it is with non-MLs.

7 Offer support and time for collaboration

Suggest concrete ways in which you can offer guidance to other teachers and/or administrators so that they can better serve MLs. Examples of supports include an ELD teacher sharing a graphic organizer for MLs with a content teacher or a content teacher sharing a content lesson plan ahead of time with an ELD teacher.

In order to leverage these leadership skills to advocate for MLs, it takes a strong foundation of interpersonal skills, many of which we are not explicitly taught or are not even mentioned in our preparation as educators. These interpersonal skills are increasingly important in today's educational landscape, which relies on more collaboration and innovation in order to lead and support MLs' equitable education. Figure 1.11 provides a self-awareness checklist and discussion questions about a sampling of crucial leadership skills that you may need to draw from to advocate for MLs and strengthen your voice as a leader. Consider how you would rate your leadership skills in each of the six areas.

FIGURE 1.11   LEADERSHIP SKILLS SELF-AWARENESS CHECKLIST

LEADERSHIP SKILL OR ATTRIBUTE	DESCRIPTION	MY RATING: LOW (1) TO HIGH (5)				
Character	The moral self that reflects the principles and ideals of the collective to which the leader belongs, including trustworthiness and credibility	1	2	3	4	5
Political skills	Social astuteness, networking ability, sincerity, integrity, honesty, charisma, and not being seen as manipulative	1	2	3	4	5
Nonverbal communication	Sensitivity to colleagues; use of culturally appropriate gestures, such as nodding in agreement; body openness	1	2	3	4	5
Conflict resolution	Managing one's own and others' emotional experiences, establishing norms and rules, and refocusing on tasks at hand	1	2	3	4	5
Interpersonal skills	Relationship development, trust, intercultural sensitivity, providing feedback, motivating and persuading others, showing empathy and support	1	2	3	4	5
Interpersonal communication skills	Connecting with others by using skills in sending and receiving culturally relevant nonverbal and emotional messages, listening and speaking skills, and effectively engaging others in conversation	1	2	3	4	5

Source: Adapted from Riggio, R. & and Tan, S. (2014).

REFLECTION QUESTIONS

1. What area(s) am I strongest in?

2. What area(s) am I weakest in?

3. What is one example of how each leadership skill affects my work with MLs?

4. What implications are there for my leadership in advocating for and supporting MLs?

 Available for download at **resources.corwin.com/FennerUnlocking2E**

How Do I Get Started Using All Five Core Beliefs?

We find in our work that educators have very little time to reflect on where we are in order to plan for where we'd like to go. This application activity will give you the gift of space for reflection. First, you will compare our core beliefs with your own. If you don't already approach your work with MLs from a set of core beliefs, this application activity will allow you the time and place for reflection in order to develop these. Based on your core beliefs and your role, you can create a vision for your grade-level team, department, school, or district's equitable and excellent instruction of MLs. Then, you will use your vision to create a succinct elevator speech to define your role and accountability in the process. By doing so, you will use this chapter's contents to create an aligned framework to support your work with MLs that will guide you as you work through the subsequent chapters.

APPLICATION ACTIVITY 1.4

Step 1. Using Figure 1.12, review our five core beliefs, compare them with your own, and add any comments you have.

FIGURE 1.12   COMPARISON OF CORE BELIEFS

OUR CORE BELIEFS	MY/OUR CORE BELIEFS	COMMENTS
1. MLs bring many strengths to the classroom.		
2. MLs learn best when they are taught in a welcoming and culturally responsive school climate.		
3. MLs acquire language and content when teachers purposefully integrate language development opportunities into meaningful content instruction.		
4. MLs thrive when their teachers include opportunities for peer learning and meaningful conversations.		
5. MLs excel when their teachers and administrators collaborate, advocate, and lead in support of their students' academic achievement and social-emotional well-being.		

Step 2. Drawing from your own core beliefs, create a vision for educating MLs in your school. Your grade-level team, department, school, or district needs to have a shared vision so that all stakeholders are working toward common goals and using common language. We suggest convening a group of educators committed to MLs'

(Continued)

(Continued)

equitable and excellent education to develop a shared vision statement for your grade-level team, department, school, or district. You may need to meet several times to revise and refine the vision statement, but your work will certainly pay off. Figure 1.13 provides some examples.

FIGURE 1.13   EXAMPLE VISION STATEMENTS

SCHOOL OR DISTRICT	VISION STATEMENT
Anne Arundel County Public Schools (MD)	"Our English learners will become empowered multilingual global citizens who are academically, linguistically, and culturally equipped for success in school and beyond."
Bellevue School District Multilingual Department (Bellevue, WA)	"To affirm and inspire each and every student to learn and thrive as creators of their future world while celebrating their cultural, racial, and linguistic identities."
Summit Hill School District 161 (Frankfort, IL)	"Our vision is to ensure that our English Language Learners have meaningful access to rigorous instruction, materials, and academic choices. We will ensure equity for English learners while maintaining their cultural and linguistic identity."

Sources: Adapted from Anne Arundel County Public Schools (n.d.), Bellevue School District (n.d.), Summit Hill School District 161 (n.d.).

APPLICATION ACTIVITY 1.4: REFLECTION QUESTIONS, PART 1

To create your vision, consider these questions:

1. Which aspects of your core beliefs from Figure 1.12 resonate the most with you?

    _____

    _____

2. What content from your core beliefs can you synthesize into succinct key ideas and values regarding equitably educating MLs?

    _____

    _____

Step 3. Referring to your vision for equitably educating MLs, outline a brief elevator speech that defines your role in the process.

One way for ELD and content teachers to reflect upon their roles and effectively explain them to others is to develop an *elevator speech, which is a concise summary of a topic—so concise that it can be delivered during a short elevator ride* (Staehr Fenner, 2014b). We recommend limiting your elevator speech to about 30 seconds. ELD and content teachers can also use it as a tool to clearly define the expertise they bring in serving MLs in their school within their school vision and explain it to administrators. The elevator speech you develop corresponds to your core beliefs and grade-level team, department, school, or district vision for educating MLs. It should outline how you see your role and the unique skills you leverage in supporting your MLs' equitable and excellent education. To develop your elevator speech, consider these questions:

APPLICATION ACTIVITY 1.4: REFLECTION QUESTIONS, PART 2

1. Which aspects of your department, school, or district's vision resonate the most with you?

   _____

   _____

2. In which aspects can you take a lead role to equitably educate MLs so that they excel? You may want to highlight these aspects in your elevator speech.

   _____

   _____

online resources Available for download at **resources.corwin.com/FennerUnlocking2E**

Once your elevator speech draft is complete, compare yours with that of your colleagues to ensure you're leveraging your expertise to support MLs. You may need to revise your elevator speech periodically as your skills with working with MLs evolve. Figure 1.14 provides an example of elevator speech.

FIGURE 1.14   EXAMPLE ELEVATOR SPEECH

In order to support MLs in becoming integral members of our school community and to support them in building the content knowledge and language skills needed to be successful in school and beyond, I am a strong advocate for MLs' equitable and excellent education. I collaborate with colleagues to integrate research-based practices that foster MLs' language development and content learning. I build relationships with ML families to provide both social-emotional support and goal-setting opportunities for MLs. I speak up when I hear deficit language being used about MLs and when I see barriers that are standing in the way of MLs' access to school academic and extra-curricular programs.

My Elevator Speech

Conclusion

In this chapter, we shared why it is crucial to equitably instruct MLs to unlock their potential for excellence. We began with a brief discussion of who MLs are and shared why there is such an urgent need to equitably educate MLs. The bulk of the chapter was devoted to our five core beliefs. For each core belief, we described relevant research, as well as provided practical tools for you to use to apply the principles. Finally, we gave you the opportunity to draw from our five core beliefs to create your own set of core beliefs; a grade-level team, department, school, or district vision; and a personalized elevator speech that outlines your crucial role in supporting MLs. In the next chapter, we focus on creating a culturally responsive learning environment for MLs.

CHAPTER 1 REFLECTION QUESTIONS

1. Which core beliefs resonated the most with you? Why?

2. What are your three takeaways from this chapter? Why?

 Available for download at **resources.corwin.com/FennerUnlocking2E**

USING A CULTURALLY RESPONSIVE FRAMEWORK TO LEVERAGE THE STRENGTHS AND MEET THE NEEDS OF MLs

2

During parent–teacher conference time, four elementary teachers are eating lunch together. They begin to complain that many of the parents of the multilingual learners (MLs) in their class do not attend conferences, show up late, attend the conference with a younger child in tow, or do not actively participate in the conference. Conferences are scheduled over the course of three afternoons between 12:00 p.m. and 3:30 p.m. The teachers feel that, in general, ML families are less invested in their children's education than non-ML parents. They decide they will share their frustrations with the English language development (ELD) teacher.

REFLECTION QUESTIONS

1. What role might culture be playing in this scenario?

2. What other factors might be at play?

3. As an advocate for MLs in this scenario, what might you do to encourage stronger relationships between the elementary teachers and the ML families?

 Available for download at **resources.corwin.com/FennerUnlocking2E**

There are many factors that might be at play in this scenario, both cultural and situational. First and foremost, ML families might not have experience with parent–teacher conferences in their home countries. Also, families might not have availability from work during the conference times, might not have access to childcare, or might not have transportation to the school. The school may not have communicated expectations around the importance of conferences and the tight conference schedule. They also might not have arranged for interpreters who speak the families' home languages to be available during the conference times. Additionally, some families might not feel safe or comfortable in the school.

As the opening scenario shows, culture can significantly impact teacher and ML family expectations as well as school and family relationships. While the teachers in this scenario did nothing wrong, there is more that they could do in order to be responsive to the needs of the ML families. For example, the educators involved might begin from a place of empathy and belief in the good intentions of families with the knowledge of how important it is to learn about ML families' backgrounds and build relationships with these families in support of their students. With these considerations in mind, the teachers in the scenario could then take steps to learn about the barriers that might be preventing ML families from attending conferences or arriving on time. For example, the teachers might work with their school administrators and ELD teacher(s) to consider whether alternative conference time slots are needed and how childcare might be provided on site. They could also ask families about what times might work best for them and whether transportation is a barrier. The teachers could also take steps to ensure that interpreters who represent the families' home languages are available for all conferences.

Because of the significant impact that culture can have on the work we do with MLs, we have positioned our discussion of strategies in this book within a framework of culturally responsive teaching. It is our intention that as you work through Chapters 3–9 in this book, you will refer back to this chapter and consider the cultural implications for your instruction, assessment, and general interactions with MLs as well as their families. We recognize that those of you who are choosing to read this book may be more informed and more passionate about the instruction of MLs than others that you work with. It is our hope that this chapter will also provide you with some strategies and talking points that you can use to strengthen your role as an ML advocate and help shift your colleagues' mindsets if needed.

In this chapter, we will define culture and the characteristics of culture, discuss the importance of cultural understanding for your work with MLs, and provide strategies to support culturally responsive and culturally sustaining teaching framed around five guiding principles. We will also ask you to step outside your comfort zone and think critically about your own culture and how it shapes your instruction, your classroom expectations, and your interactions with students. We would like you to consider areas of potential bias in your work with MLs based on your cultural background and experiences.

What Is Culture?

REFLECTION QUESTIONS

1. How do you define culture?

2. Why is an understanding of culture important for your work with MLs?

 Available for download at **resources.corwin.com/FennerUnlocking2E**

While there are many, varied definitions of culture, it is generally understood that **culture is "the customary beliefs, social forms, and material traits of a racial, religious, or social group"** (Merriam-Webster, 2023). In thinking about different aspects of culture, social scientists generally believe that it is not the cultural artifacts, tools, or other tangible aspects of culture that are the essence of a culture but rather how members of a cultural group understand and relate to these tools or artifacts (Banks & Banks, 2019).

In order to understand the importance of culture in your work with MLs, in Application Activity 2.1, we have highlighted some considerations when thinking about aspects of culture and the potential impact that culture may have on teaching and learning for MLs. For each consideration, make note of the potential impact for MLs in your context. The first example has been completed for you.

APPLICATION ACTIVITY 2.1: POTENTIAL IMPACT OF CULTURE ON TEACHING AND LEARNING FOR MLs

CONSIDERATIONS	IMPACT ON TEACHING AND LEARNING FOR MLs
Variability: There is great variability of cultures within social groups. We are each a member of various cultural groups. These smaller cultural groups are part of the larger, mainstream culture (Banks & Banks, 2019). Our connection to specific cultures and how the culture manifests itself in our ideas and behaviors can change throughout our lives (Erickson, 2007).	MLs' culture(s) may be different from their parents' or caregivers' culture(s). This may be particularly true for MLs who were born in the United States. Second-generation immigrants are often pulled between the culture of their families and the culture that they learn at school or in the community. This means that it's important to avoid overgeneralizing aspects of culture (e.g., "Mexicans like to . . .") or asking one student to speak on behalf of their culture or nationality.

(Continued)

CONSIDERATIONS	IMPACT ON TEACHING AND LEARNING FOR MLs
Distinction between individualist and collectivist cultures: One aspect on which a culture can be measured is the degree to which individualism versus collectivism is prioritized. Individualist cultures prioritize independence and individual achievement. Collectivist cultures prioritize interdependence and cooperation. The United States is the most individualistic culture worldwide. In contrast, 80 percent of world cultures prioritize collectivism (Dubner, 2021; Hofstede, 2016; Hofstede et al., 2010).	
Levels of culture: There are three different levels of culture. An analogy is often made between these three levels and an iceberg (Hall, 1976). The elements of culture that are visible (at the surface level), such as food, clothing, and language, are understood to carry a low emotional load. The invisible elements of culture that include both shallow and deep culture, such as beliefs about time and notions of justice, are much more likely to lead to misunderstandings and frustration when there are cultural differences (Z. Hammond, 2015).	

In her description of the levels of culture, Z. Hammond (2015) uses an analogy of a tree that highlights the dynamic nature of culture. Hammond argues that surface culture (the branches, leaves, and fruit) and shallow culture (the trunk) can change over time through migration, intermarriage, and generational changes. However, deep culture (the roots of the tree) is more fixed and is what grounds and sustains individuals and informs their sense of self and group belonging. Figure 2.1 provides more details about the three levels of culture. As you look at Figure 2.1, consider how culture is discussed in your context. At which level of culture do you feel most of the conversations occur? How might you integrate more considerations of shallow and deep culture into your work with MLs?

FIGURE 2.1 THREE LEVELS OF CULTURE

LEVEL OF CULTURE	DEFINITION	EXAMPLES
Surface	• Comprises concrete elements of culture that can be seen • Carries low emotional load	Food, clothing, celebrations, music, literature, and dance
Shallow	• Comprises the cultural rules for everyday communication and behavior • Carries strong emotional charge • Differences can lead to misunderstandings and disagreements	Beliefs about time, concepts of personal space, nonverbal communication patterns, and relationship to authority
Deep culture	• Comprises the unspoken knowledge and unconscious understandings in how we relate to others and the world • Carries substantial emotional charge • Differences at this level can lead to culture shock	Ideas about cooperation and collaboration, notions of justice, and concepts of self

Source: Adapted from Hammond, Z. (2015). Culture tree (p. 24).

Now that we have discussed different aspects of culture, we would like you to take a little time to reflect on the cultural groups to which you belong and how they shape your sense of self and belonging.

APPLICATION ACTIVITY 2.2: MY MULTICULTURAL SELF

1. Make a list of all of the cultural groups that you belong to (e.g., Asian-American, female, Jewish, gay, person with a disability). Then, consider which ones you identify with most, and put a star next to those.

(Continued)

(Continued)

2. Describe a time that you felt proud to be a member of one of these cultural groups.

3. Describe a time that you found it challenging to be a member of one of these cultural groups.

4. What made the difference between the two times?

Source: Adapted from Gorski, P. (2015). *Circles of my multicultural self.* http://www.edchange.org/multicultural/activities/circlesofself.html

 Available for download at **resources.corwin.com/FennerUnlocking2E**

In this activity, we hope you recognized the complexity and emotional charge that can come with being a member of a specific cultural group, especially when confronted with the norms, values, and beliefs of a different cultural group. It is important to consider such distinctions because variability in norms and values across social groups can cause cultural misunderstandings or conflict (Banks & Banks, 2019). How we are able to navigate such differences will shape our relationships with individuals from other cultures.

Why Does Culture Matter for MLs' Teaching and Learning?

APPLICATION ACTIVITY 2.3: MS. MONTROSE'S CLASSROOM

Read the scenario that follows, and then, answer the reflection questions.

Scenario: Ms. Montrose is a sixth-grade language arts teacher in a rural school with few MLs. The MLs in her class are from the Democratic Republic of Congo, India, and South Korea. She regularly includes discussion activities in her lessons and expects students to be active participants in these discussions. She selects discussion prompts that she hopes will encourage debate, as well as close analysis of the texts that the class is reading. Ms. Montrose has worked with the ELD teacher to develop the language scaffolding that her MLs may need to participate, including vocabulary instruction, sentence stems, and word banks. However, she has been frustrated by her MLs' participation patterns in these discussions. Some of her MLs contribute very little, and in general, they tend to avoid controversial topics. Ms. Montrose thinks that some of the MLs aren't very motivated to be successful in her class, and she is at a loss for what more she can do to encourage these students to be more active in the discussions.

APPLICATION ACTIVITY 2.3: REFLECTION QUESTIONS

1. What impact might culture have on MLs' participation in classroom discussions in general?

   _____

   _____

2. What might be preventing Ms. Montrose's MLs from being more active participants in the class discussions?

   _____

   _____

3. What might Ms. Montrose do to support greater participation on the part of her MLs? Consider linguistic supports, student groupings, and other types of support she could offer.

   _____

   _____

Culture impacts students' and teachers' beliefs about education and learning. It can have an effect on MLs' ways of communicating, their classroom participation and behavior, and their expectations for the role of the teacher, among other areas. Similarly, culture has an effect on educators' expectations for students, their ways of communicating with students, and their classroom management. This means that the expectations for student behavior, communication, and patterns of language use at home could be significantly different than the expectations for student behavior, communication, and patterns of language use at school (Banks & Banks, 2019; Delpit, 1995; Heath, 1983, 2012; Ogbu, 2003). When teachers and students do not share the same cultural and linguistic background, the differences may influence their relationship and also student learning. Accordingly, teachers need to recognize these potential differences and validate MLs' students and families' expectations of teachers and the school (Staehr Fenner & Teich, in press). They also need to support students in learning the expectations of the teacher and the school (Delpit, 1995). All students need guidance in learning how to function within and across cultures in order to build their sociocultural consciousness while also feeling proud of their home cultures. **Sociocultural consciousness is understanding that your worldview is not universal and believing that your worldview is not superior to the worldviews of others.**

For example, in the scenario discussed earlier, Ms. Montrose had specific expectations for what student engagement and participation looked like, and when her MLs did not meet those expectations, she questioned their motivation, placing blame on the students. There are several barriers that might be standing in the way of student participation from a linguistic perspective, including students having sufficient understanding of the content and the structure of the discussion activities. However, Ms. Montrose should also explore cultural differences that may be preventing some MLs from participating in ways she expects. She can be explicit with her students about expectations for academic discussions in her classroom while at the same time validating experiences from MLs' cultures. For example, Ms. Montrose could engage in a discussion with her students about how norms for discussions and debate vary from culture to culture and even within cultures. She should also provide models of academic discussions via video clips that students can use to inform their understanding of her expectations. It would be important for Ms. Montrose to make sure that she does not call out, stigmatize, or make MLs feel unwelcome during these discussions and that she also affirms expectations from students' home cultures.

REFLECTION QUESTIONS

1. How do you think your cultural beliefs and expectations around teaching and learning may differ from those of MLs that you teach or work with?

2. How might you address these differences in your context?

online resources   Available for download at **resources.corwin.com/FennerUnlocking2E**

What Is Culturally Responsive Teaching?

Once you have begun to recognize how culture impacts who you are as an educator, as well as learned more about the backgrounds and experiences of your MLs, you can apply this new or more nuanced understanding to your teaching. Culturally responsive educators draw on the cultural knowledge, backgrounds, and experiences of their students in order to make the learning more meaningful. Ladson-Billings (1994) developed the term *culturally relevant teaching* to describe "a pedagogy that empowers students intellectually, socially, emotionally, and politically by using cultural referents to impart knowledge, skills, and attitudes" (p. 18). Gay and other researchers began using the term *culturally responsive teaching*, which is the term more widely-used today. Gay (2010) defined culturally responsive teaching as "using the cultural knowledge, prior experiences, frames of reference, and performance styles of ethnically diverse students to make learning encounters more relevant to and effective for [students]" (p. 31).

It can also be helpful to think about what culturally responsive teaching is not. Nieto (2016) explains that "culturally responsive teaching is not

- A predetermined curriculum

- A specific set of strategies

- A watering down of the curriculum

- A 'feel-good' approach

- Only for students of particular backgrounds" (p. 1)

Instead, Nieto (2016) describes culturally responsive pedagogy as a mindset that respects and builds on students' backgrounds and experiences through the use of materials and specific teaching approaches. Culturally responsive educators strive to learn what makes each student unique in order to appreciate the diverse perspectives and insights they can bring to their classroom. Culturally responsive educators are also able to confront their own biases.

Paris and Alim (2017) have built on the idea of culturally responsive teaching in their work on culturally sustaining practices. They describe the urgent need for schools to be places that nurture the cultural practices of students of color. Culturally sustaining practices are instructional practices that meaningfully integrate students' languages and ways of being into classroom learning and across curricular units (Paris & Alim, 2017). Paris and Alim (2017) describe the importance of identifying which aspects of culture and language students and their families want to sustain through schooling.

What Are the Guiding Principles of Culturally Responsive Teaching?

While educators and researchers describe varying characteristics of culturally responsive teaching, we have attempted to synthesize these ideas into five overarching guiding principles. Figure 2.2 highlights how the five guiding principles connect to one another. The guiding principles are as follows:

- Guiding Principle 1: Culturally responsive teaching is assets-based.

- Guiding Principle 2: Culturally responsive teaching simultaneously supports and challenges students.

- Guiding Principle 3: Culturally responsive teaching places students at the center of the learning.

- Guiding Principle 4: Culturally responsive teaching leverages students' linguistic and cultural backgrounds.

- Guiding Principle 5: Culturally responsive teaching unites students' schools, families, and communities (Snyder & Staehr Fenner, 2021).

In the sections that follow, we will provide an explanation of each guiding principle, its relationship to MLs, and some classroom "look-fors" that indicate these criteria are at work in the classroom and school.

FIGURE 2.2   THE GUIDING PRINCIPLES OF CULTURALLY RESPONSIVE TEACHING

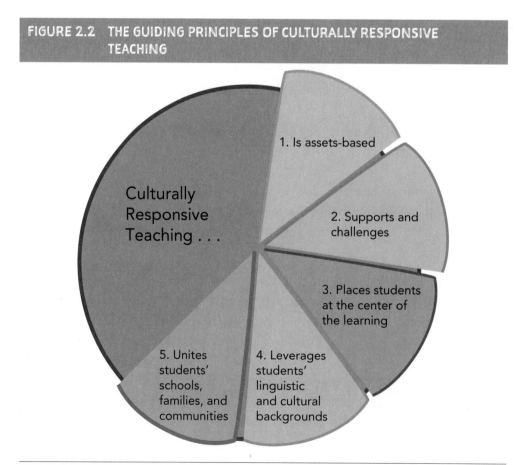

Guiding Principle 1: Culturally responsive teaching is assets-based.

When we consider the obstacles that MLs must surmount in order to acquire a new language while, at the same time, learning academic content, it can be easy to approach our work with MLs from a deficit perspective. **A deficit perspective is one in which we focus on MLs' challenges and frame our interactions with them in terms of these challenges.** Using a deficit lens, educators tend to view MLs' home language(s) and culture(s) as hindrances to overcome. In addition, they may attribute performance or achievement that falls below expectations to MLs' linguistic abilities in English, motivation, lack of parental involvement, or other such factors (Adair et al., 2017; González, 2005; Matthiesen, 2017; Valencia, 1997; Valenzuela, 1999). In contrast, **an assets-based perspective is one that values students' home languages and cultures and sees them as foundations for future learning** (González, 2005; Valencia, 1997; Valenzuela, 1999; Zacarian & Staehr Fenner, 2020). Similarly, an assets-based perspective recognizes that parents of MLs are engaged in their children's education and support their children in varied and perhaps unrecognized ways (Staehr Fenner, 2014a).

Essential to having an assets-based view of MLs and their families learning about them, their backgrounds, and experiences. We have included some suggestions for how to learn about them in the list that follows. Figure 2.3 provides a tool that you can complete as you learn more about each ML you work with.

- Look for opportunities for students to comfortably share about themselves, their families, and their backgrounds and experiences. You can build activities into instruction that provides a space for students (if they feel comfortable) to share about their families, their backgrounds, their responsibilities, how they spend their time outside of school, and their interests (Staehr Fenner, 2014a; Snyder & Staehr Fenner, 2021). When you are asking students to describe their backgrounds and experiences, it is important to be clear that you are not asking students to speak for an entire cultural group.

- Take opportunities to talk with students informally (e.g., at lunch, after school, or on field trips), and get to know more about them.

- Collaborate with other educators to find out relevant background information on MLs (e.g., home language or educational experiences).

- Attend school and community events that your MLs and their families attend.

- Conduct home visits with MLs and their families (if families are comfortable and have an opportunity to decline). It can be effective to visit in the beginning of the year as a get-to-know-each-other activity to build relationships and limit discussions about behavior and academic progress.

- Research general information about your MLs' home cultures and important features of their home languages (Staehr Fenner, 2014a).

- Conduct a community walk. A community walk is a student or family-member led tour of a community that allows educators to have a better understanding of students, families, and their communities (L. Markham, personal communications, November 25, 2019; Safir & Dugan, 2021; Snyder & Staehr Fenner, 2021).

FIGURE 2.3   WHAT I KNOW ABOUT MY ML

Name: 	Country of birth or family's country of birth: 
Home language(s): Comments related to strengths in home language (e.g., oracy and literacy in home language, identity as a speaker of home language):	If applicable English proficiency level: English language proficiency scores from _____ (date) Composite (the combined score): _____ Speaking: _____ Reading: _____ Listening: _____ Writing: _____

Relevant educational experiences (e.g., amount of time in U.S. schools, educational experience in home country, areas of strength in current school):

Cultural connections with schooling (e.g., individualist vs. collectivist, nonverbal communication preference, interactions with teacher):

Family background (e.g., who student lives with, what family likes to do together, family interests):

Student interests (e.g., sports, animals, video games, musical artists):

Student plans and/or goals (e.g., high school graduation, career and technical education courses, college):

Inequities student may face (e.g., microaggressions, access to technology, childcare duties):

Source: Snyder and Staehr Fenner (2021); adapted from Staehr Fenner and Snyder (2017). Icons by iStock.com/nuiiun, iStock.com/bubaone, iStock.com/IuliiaBagautdinova, iStock.com/ilyaliren, iStock.com/bsd555, iStock.com/Dmytro_Vyshnevskyi.

online resources | Available for download at **resources.corwin.com/FennerUnlocking2E**

The process of learning about MLs and differences between your cultures and theirs might bring up some feelings of discomfort or uncertainty. It is important to acknowledge these feelings and even be open and transparent about them. Keep this idea of discomfort in mind as you read the scenario in Application Activity 2.4.

APPLICATION ACTIVITY 2.4: MR. GERARD'S CLASSROOM

Read the scenario and answer the discussion questions that follow.

Scenario: Mr. Gerard, an elementary school music teacher, has a new student in his class from Indonesia. He looks at her name on the attendance list, and then he asks her what her name is. She responds, "Cinta Hartono." Mr. Gerard immediately feels uncomfortable with this unfamiliar name and asks, "Can I call you Cindy?" Cinta agrees that would be fine.

APPLICATION ACTIVITY 2.4: REFLECTION QUESTIONS

1. What is the underlying message that Mr. Gerard is sending to Cinta about her home language and culture?

   _____

   _____

2. What steps could Mr. Gerard take to become more comfortable learning and using the names of students that might be unfamiliar to him?

   _____

   _____

online resources — Available for download at **resources.corwin.com/FennerUnlocking2E**

In order to envision how an assets-based perspective plays out in the classroom, review the classroom look-fors in Figure 2.4. Consider which of these practices are already in place in your context and which you might wish to prioritize for improvement.

FIGURE 2.4   GUIDING PRINCIPLE 1 LOOK-FORS

✓ Administrators, teachers, and staff pronounce MLs' names correctly.

✓ Administrators, teachers, and staff show interest in MLs' home languages by learning a few words or phrases.

✓ Administrators, teachers, and staff are aware of MLs' interests outside of the classroom or school setting.

✓ The school puts supports in place to help MLs and their families overcome obstacles that may get in the way of student learning or family participation.

✓ MLs' cultural, linguistic, and community backgrounds are incorporated into instruction.

An assets-based perspective requires that you approach the work you do with MLs with respect and empathy. Respect and empathy will grow when you try to put yourself in the shoes of MLs and their families and imagine what it is like to assimilate into an unfamiliar culture, learn a new language, and figure out a new school system (Staehr Fenner, 2014a). For example, if you happen to catch yourself blaming MLs or their families, try to "shake up" your thinking so that you start by assuming the best about the student or the family members involved and consider their perspective, as well as challenges or obstacles that they might be facing. Application Activity 2.5 provides you with an opportunity to think about how you might reframe a deficit perspective into actions that come from a place of grace for MLs and their families.

APPLICATION ACTIVITY 2.5: ASSETS-BASED PERSPECTIVE SCENARIOS

We present three scenarios in this application activity.

1. Read the first scenario. Also, read the second and third columns, which present another way of understanding the scenario.

2. For the second and third scenarios, complete the second two columns. First, approach the MLs and their families in each scenario from a respectful and empathetic perspective, and then determine what steps the teacher(s) in the scenarios might take to change their deficit perspectives.

3. In the final row, write a scenario that is relevant to your context.

SCENARIO	RESPECTFUL AND EMPATHETIC PERSPECTIVE	STEPS YOU MIGHT TAKE TO SUPPORT MLs AND THEIR FAMILIES
1. The members of an elementary school parent-teacher association (PTA) are complaining that despite there being a significant number of MLs in the school, none of the ML parents attend the PTA meetings. They feel that families of MLs are not interested in supporting the school.	There are many reasons why the families of MLs may not be involved in the PTA. For example, ML families may come from countries where parent associations do not exist or information about the PTA meeting may not be clearly shared with families in a language they can understand. The PTA meetings may not be welcoming or comfortable for ML families. Additionally, family members may have such constraints as having to work, not having childcare, or not having transportation.	• Consider what steps you have taken to build relationships with ML families and make them feel welcome. Consider what more might need to be done. • Make sure meeting information is clear and delivered in families' home languages. • Reach out to families and explain what the PTA does and how their participation would benefit the group. • Be welcoming to ML families who attend meetings, making sure that they understand what is being discussed and that there is a comfortable way for them to contribute (if they wish). • Offer childcare during PTA meetings. • Offer support with transportation if needed.

(Continued)

(Continued)

SCENARIO	RESPECTFUL AND EMPATHETIC PERSPECTIVE	STEPS YOU MIGHT TAKE TO SUPPORT MLs AND THEIR FAMILIES
2. A fifth-grade science teacher has students work in groups on various assignments. He has three emergent MLs in his class who are at a low-to-intermediate English proficiency level, and he has tried to group them with emergent MLs at higher English proficiency levels. However, he finds that when they are grouped together, they like to speak Spanish. He feels uncomfortable because he doesn't know what they are saying, and he is worried that they are off task or talking about him.		
3. A ninth-grade math teacher feels frustrated when a new emergent ML from Afghanistan is added to her class mid-year. She complains to the ELD teacher that the student doesn't speak any English and isn't able to follow the lessons, can't understand the word problems, or take part in small-group discussions. The math teacher feels that the student doesn't appear very motivated to be a part of the class and hasn't asked for help in understanding the assignments.		
Scenario from my context:		

Guiding Principle 2: Culturally responsive teaching simultaneously supports and challenges students.

The second guiding principle is based on the importance of having high expectations for the MLs in your classes while at the same time giving them the support that they need to achieve. MLs should have access to the same grade-level content and texts as their non-ML peers, but they should receive sufficient instructional support for this work (August, 2018). Kleinfeld (1975), in her work with Inuit and Yupik students in Alaska, coined the term *warm demander* to represent the need to have high expectations for students as a way to foster student autonomy in their learning while at the same time providing adequate assistance (Z. Hammond, 2015). We have expanded this term to be *warm and informed demander*. **A warm and informed demander understands students' multifaceted past histories and present contexts and uses this knowledge to both support and challenge students in their learning** (Snyder & Staehr Fenner, 2021).

Guiding Principle 2 is also framed around the idea that within our society, certain groups of people have unearned privileges based on traits such as race, ethnicity, gender, or sexual preference that are not granted to individuals outside these groups. Culturally responsive teachers develop lessons that include the history and experiences of diverse groups and provide instruction about structures that reinforce power, privilege, and discriminatory practices in society. In addition, culturally responsive teaching provides opportunities for students and educators to think critically about institutionalized inequity, how inequity and injustice impact their lives or the lives of others, and the steps needed to address this inequity (National Center for Culturally Responsive Educational Systems [NCCREST], 2008).

Figure 2.5 offers some suggestions for how to apply this guiding principle in your classroom. An example of what Guiding Principle 2 might look like in practice is a unit that is taught at a diverse urban high school in California. The ninth-grade English teachers at the Nelson Mandela Academy have developed a unit called

FIGURE 2.5   GUIDING PRINCIPLE 2 LOOK-FORS

✓ MLs are taught grade-level content and texts. Instructional texts include a balance of grade-level texts and texts at students' reading levels.

✓ Instruction and materials are appropriately scaffolded so MLs are able to access and engage with grade-level content and texts.[1]

✓ Instruction includes activities that require students to make connections with their prior learning.

✓ Instruction includes activities that require students to consider alternative ways of understanding information and push students to challenge the status quo.

✓ Instruction includes activities that foster critical thinking and reflection (e.g., open-ended discussion prompts and student monitoring of their learning).

✓ MLs have access to and the support needed to be successful in gifted, honors, and college preparatory classes.

[1]For more on scaffolded instruction strategies, see Chapter 3.

"Linguistic Biographies" in which students reflect on their own experiences of using language in different contexts and engage in collaborative academic tasks designed to foster students' appreciation for linguistic diversity and strategies for responding to negative comments about their home language(s) or dialects (California Department of Education, 2015). During this unit, students take part in a variety of collaborative activities, including reflecting on their own multilingual or multidialectal experiences, analyzing poetry and contemporary music to understand the connections between language choices and cultural values and identity, and producing writing and multimedia pieces that examine the connection between language, culture, and society.

Guiding Principle 3: Culturally responsive teaching places students at the center of the learning.

Student-centered learning is not new in the field of education, and there are a variety of approaches that fit within this model (e.g., collaborative learning, inquiry-based learning, or project-based learning). **Student-centered learning can be defined as an instructional approach in which the students in the classroom shape the content, instructional activities, materials, assessment, or pace of the learning.** Student-centered learning also prioritizes peer learning with the goal of providing students opportunities to learn from one another rather than solely from the teacher. We dive into peer learning opportunities for MLs in Chapter 4 and also discuss peer learning activities to support reading and writing in Chapter 8.

In order to incorporate student-centered learning practices in your classroom, review the classroom look-fors in Figure 2.6.

FIGURE 2.6   GUIDING PRINCIPLE 3 CLASSROOM LOOK-FORS

✓ Classroom activities frequently include structured pair and small-group work.

✓ Students and teachers develop the classroom norms and expectations together.

✓ MLs are given choice in their learning.

✓ MLs are given opportunities to speak and write about their lives and people and events that are important to them.

✓ MLs are involved in goal setting and assessment through the use of student goal sheets, checklists, peer-editing activities, and teacher–student or student–student conferencing.

✓ ML student work is displayed in the classroom.

✓ Lessons include intentional groupings of students to support student learning and to allow for grouping that considers language backgrounds.

One step toward student-centered learning is engaging students in self-assessment and goal setting related to learning goals and language development. For MLs, this could be an unfamiliar experience. Figure 2.7 is a document that you could use to help emergent MLs set goals for their language development. We have also included a student example.

FIGURE 2.7   STUDENT GOAL SETTING FOR LANGUAGE DEVELOPMENT

Name _____   Date _____

MY SCORE	1.0	2.0	3.0	4.0	5.0	6.0
Listening						
Reading						
Speaking						
Writing						

To exit the ELD program, I need an overall score of 4.5.[2]

From the data, I know that I am really good at _____.

From the data, I know I need to improve _____.

I can improve my _____ by _____.

Source: Rebecca Thomas. Icon by iStock.com/Zham.

[2]The English language proficiency score that students need to be reclassified and exit the ELD program varies by state.

In this goal-setting document, the student identifies that he wants to improve his speaking skills by using complete sentences.

Guiding Principle 4: Culturally responsive teaching leverages students' linguistic and cultural backgrounds.

The fourth guiding principle focuses on ways that teaching and learning can elevate students' home language, cultures, and experiences. This guiding principle builds on the idea of Guiding Principle 1, being assets-based, and asks educators to create multicultural and multilingual learning environments for students as a way to use MLs' linguistic and cultural backgrounds as foundations for all learning. In their work on culturally sustaining practices, Paris and Alim emphasize the need to support students in making meaningful connections between their learning and the languages, practices, and histories of their communities (Ferlazzo, 2017; Paris & Alim, 2017).

In order to think about what this guiding principle looks like in practice, read the classroom look-fors in Figure 2.8, and then complete Application Activity 2.6.

FIGURE 2.8   GUIDING PRINCIPLE 4 CLASSROOM LOOK-FORS

✓ Lessons include multicultural materials and resources.

✓ Lessons and units include perspectives of individuals that come from MLs' home cultures (e.g., literature written by non-U.S. American authors).

✓ Lessons include activities that draw on MLs' backgrounds and experiences.

✓ Lessons include opportunities for MLs to use bilingual resources (e.g., dictionaries, books, or glossaries) and home languages.

✓ ML families and communities are included in the learning (e.g., community members are invited to speak in class).

APPLICATION ACTIVITY 2.6:
MR. WASHBURN'S CLASSROOM

Read the scenario that follows, and consider how Mr. Washburn might make his unit on immigration more culturally responsive to the MLs whom he is teaching. Answer the discussion questions that follow.

Scenario: Mr. Washburn is a middle school social studies teacher at an urban middle school with a large population of MLs from Mexico and Central America. He has seven emergent MLs in one of his social studies classes. Three of the MLs have been in the country for less than a year. The other MLs have been in the United States for two to six years. Mr. Washburn is currently teaching a unit on U.S. immigration, focusing on the experiences of immigrants who came to the United States in the early 1900s. As part of this unit, students will take a virtual tour of Ellis Island, read excerpts from *Island of Hope: The Story of Ellis Island and the Journey to America* (Sandler, 2004), and give an oral report on one aspect of the immigrant experience during this time (e.g., travel to the United States or life in the tenements).

APPLICATION ACTIVITY 2.6:
REFLECTION QUESTIONS

1. In what ways is the unit plan relevant to the lives of the students in the class? In what ways could the unit be made more relevant to their lives?

_____

_____

(Continued)

(Continued)

2. What steps could the teacher take to build on the backgrounds and experiences of the MLs in the class?

_____

_____

3. What might he need to be cautious about related to students' own experiences with the topic?

_____

_____

4. What additional recommendations do you have for activities that would strengthen students' engagement with the unit and bring in diverse perspectives?

_____

_____

online resources 🔍 Available for download at **resources.corwin.com/FennerUnlocking2E**

As you probably concluded, a unit on immigration is most likely very relevant to the lives of MLs. However, rather than focusing only on immigration in the early 1900s, the teacher could also discuss current immigration. There are many young adult novels that address issues of immigration (e.g., *American Street* [Zaboi, 2017], *Inside Out & Back Again* [Lai, 2013], *We Are Not From Here* [Sanchez, 2021], *Messy Roots: A Graphic Memoir of a Wuhanese American* [Gao, 2022], and *Shooting Kabul* [Senzai, 2011]). Students could also read and discuss editorials about current immigration from a social justice lens. They could make connections between why immigrants came to the United States in the early 1900s and why they come now. There are many resources for teaching about immigration that support a multicultural perspective on the topic, such as *Learning for Justice*'s "The Human Face of Immigration" (Costello, 2011). You can also find text sets on a particular topic, such as immigration, that offer materials at varied reading levels (in addition to providing scaffolded instruction of grade-level texts on the topic). As you plan lessons, even on those topics that may seem far removed from the lives of the MLs you work with, keep looking for opportunities to make meaningful connections to MLs' own experiences while at the same time being sensitive to possible trauma that students may have experienced and topics that may be difficult for them to discuss.

What About Home Language Use and Translanguaging?

With the increase in online translation tools, there has also been an increase in the use of translation to support MLs' understanding and learning of new content. Research indicates that MLs can draw from their home language when acquiring knowledge and skills in English. Instruction that incorporates and builds on MLs' home language will support them in developing literacy in English (August, 2018; August et al., 2009; Carlo et al., 2004; Dressler & Kamil, 2006; Liang et al., 2005; Restrepo et al., 2010). In addition, by providing MLs opportunities to use their home language through using translanguaging practices, you are validating MLs' cultural and linguistic backgrounds and honoring the benefits of being multilingual. **Translanguaging is the use of more than one language for communication, and it allows students to make full use of their linguistic resources** (Creese & Blackledge, 2010; O. García et al., 2017).

In our work, we recommend intentionally and strategically using translation and opportunities for translanguaging. We specify being intentional and strategic because we know that MLs benefit when they are taught to use their home language as a resource for new content learning and language development. However, translation should not be the primary or only scaffold used to support student understanding and engagement. Let's take a look at two examples. Consider which example provides a model of intentional and strategic use of home language.

- Example #1: A science teacher presents a lesson in English on energy transfer. She pauses her instruction every couple of minutes so the bilingual paraprofessional can interpret the lesson in Spanish for a group of emergent MLs at lower levels of proficiency. After the lesson, students work independently to answer a set of questions that the paraprofessional translated into Spanish. The students use Google Translate to translate their responses into English. During this activity, the emergent MLs rely heavily on Spanish and make minimal use of English in describing terms and concepts associated with energy transfer.

- Example #2: A science teacher presents a short lesson in English on energy transfer. She embeds visuals, hands-on examples, and instruction of key terms in English. Emergent MLs at lower levels of proficiency are provided a bilingual glossary that includes short definitions in English and students' home languages as well as images to support understanding. After the lesson, students work in home language groups to answer discussion questions. Students are able to discuss in any language they choose and then use their glossary and sentence stems to write responses in English.

REFLECTION QUESTION

Which scenario is a better example of intentional and strategic use of MLs' home languages? Why?

 Available for download at **resources.corwin.com/FennerUnlocking2E**

While it is important to honor and draw from MLs' home languages, the overuse of translation and interpretation as we see in Example #1 can result in missed opportunities, such as a waste of valuable teaching time, a lack of opportunity for language development, and a reluctance by students to take risks with language use as they acquire language. Instead, translation should be understood to be just one of many types of instructional supports that can be used to foster students' acquisition of language and content learning.

There are many different ways to incorporate home language use and translanguaging into instruction, even if you do not speak students' home languages. When providing students opportunities to work in their home language or use home language resources, it is essential that you have a clear understanding of their literacy skills in that language. Students who do not have strong home language literacy skills are not likely to benefit from written resources in their home languages, and they might also be embarrassed if they do not feel comfortable reading and writing in their home language. Consider the following strategies:

- **Home language resources:** School librarians are often wonderful resources for finding translated or home language texts to support the content you are working on (e.g., a translated copy of a short text about types of energy).

- **Bilingual assignments:** You can provide students with opportunities to do bilingual work on their assignments such as using a bilingual glossary, writing a story in both English and their home language, or having them interview a family or community member in their home language. You can also encourage students to make connections between their home language and English as a tool for language development.

- **Multilingual discussions:** Another strategy for supporting home language development is intentionally grouping students to allow opportunities for them to use their home language during group work (as appropriate). It is understandable that if you don't speak the home language, you may be uncomfortable with this strategy because you don't know what is being discussed in the group. However, if you set up concrete tasks for the group, you will be able to identify whether or not students are engaged in the activity. You can also have students record their discussions and seek support from a colleague who speaks the home language (if you have one) to interpret the conversation for you.

Guiding Principle 5: Culturally responsive teaching unites students' schools, families, and communities.

The final guiding principle highlights the importance of collaborating with MLs' families and communities. There are strong positive connections between family engagement and student outcomes such as higher rates of high school graduation, higher grades and test scores, higher levels of language proficiency, and increased enrollment in higher education (Ferguson, 2008; Henderson & Mapp, 2002; Lindholm-Leary, 2015; National Academies of Sciences, Engineering, and

Medicine [NASEM], 2017). Additionally, the 2015 Every Student Succeeds Act (ESSA) requires family engagement as a critical step toward improving ML student outcomes. Schools are required to solicit recommendations from families related to school programming and share information with families about supporting their children's education.

In *Culturally Responsive Teaching for Multilingual Learners: Tools for Equity* (Snyder & Staehr Fenner, 2021), we suggest five strategies for strengthening ML family engagement and collaboration with ML communities.

1. **Create a welcoming environment for ML families.** Consider what it might feel like to be an ML family entering your school for the first time. How might they be greeted and to what extent would they see themselves represented in the visual images that are displayed around the school? This strategy is framed around the idea of creating a space where ML families feel comfortable and that they are valuable members of the school community. Take a look at this picture of a welcome sign that greets families as they enter Whittier Primary in Findlay, Ohio. Educator Chrystal Whipkey shared that the purpose of this sign is to support a welcoming environment for all students.

This welcome sign at Whittier Elementary includes the languages of all the students who attend the school. Additional languages will be added as the population grows and changes.

Source: Chrystal Whipkey.

2. **Build relationships with ML families.** In order to build strong partnerships with MLs' families and communities, it is essential to get to know families' backgrounds, experiences, and goals for their children. Spending time, both informally and formally, in ML families' communities is a wonderful way to learn more about ML families and their assets. For example, take time to participate in community events and consider hosting a school event in families' communities if possible.

3. **Communicate effectively with ML families.** It's important to determine families' preferred ways of communication and set up a system that also makes it easy for families to communicate with the school. Many schools are now using messaging apps that include translation options. It is also critical to have interpreters who represent ML families' home languages at all school events and meetings.

4. **Overcome barriers to ML family engagement.** This strategy calls on educators to work with families to determine barriers that might be preventing family engagement and then brainstorm possible solutions to those barriers. Possible barriers might include language, transportation, time, childcare, understanding the school system and role of families, and fear related to immigration status. Surveys, focus groups, and discussion with community leaders are some possible ways to learn more about potential barriers.

5. **Empower ML families.** The final strategy is empowering ML families. When ML families develop a stronger voice, they are better positioned to advocate for the needs of their children and provide an often-missing perspective to schools. Some ways to empower families include providing English classes or other support services in the school to help families in becoming more comfortable at the school, strengthening representation of ML family members on district committees and advisory groups, and asking ML families to share their perspectives on such topics as school policies and procedures (Snyder & Staehr Fenner, 2021). It is essential that ML families have an opportunity to talk about the issues that matter most to them.

**SYRACUSE
CITY SCHOOL
DISTRICT VIDEO**

resources.corwin
.com/FennerUnlocking2E

If you would like to see one way Syracuse City School District strives to unite students' schools, families, and communities, please watch the video *Building Relationships with Multilingual Families Through Family Engagement Events*. As you watch the video, consider what strategies the district uses to build strong partnerships with ML families. The video can be found on the online companion website. To access the companion website, please visit resources.corwin.com/FennerUnlocking2E.

Figure 2.9 provides a list of look-fors related to the strategies for uniting students' schools, families, and communities.

FIGURE 2.9   GUIDING PRINCIPLE 5 LOOK-FORS

✓ The school visually demonstrates a commitment to multicultural families and students (e.g., flags from students' home countries, signs posted in multiple languages, student work displayed on walls).

✓ Interpreters are provided at all school events.

✓ Educators use a variety of tools to communicate with ML families (e.g., emails, phone calls, texts in home languages, flyers in home languages).

✓ School administration looks for ways to remove barriers that might prevent ML families from participating (e.g., timing of events, childcare, transportation).

✓ ML family members are actively involved with school committees or organizations that are open to parents (e.g., PTA).

Now that we've explored the five guiding principles for culturally responsive teaching, let's apply this lens to our work with ML newcomer students and students with limited or interrupted formal education (SLIFE), as well as to our work around collaboration, equity, advocacy, and leadership.

ML NEWCOMER STUDENTS AND SLIFE CONSIDERATIONS

What Are Key Considerations for Culturally Responsive Teaching for ML Newcomer Students and SLIFE?

While all MLs benefit from schools and classrooms that embrace a culturally responsive school climate, culturally responsive teaching is particularly critical for students who are new to the country or who enter the school system with gaps in formal education. We want to acknowledge that the very language that we use to describe these groups of students is framed from a deficit viewpoint. Shouldn't we instead use an acronym that highlights their strengths of resiliency, perseverance, motivation, problem-solving skills, family and community bonds, and cultural and linguistic capital?

While we use the terms *ML newcomer students* and *SLIFE* for the sake of shared understanding, we advocate for a classroom and school climate that values and creates space to build on the assets that these students bring as well as opportunities to share their assets and perspectives with other students. In each chapter, we will highlight specific considerations that are relevant to our work with ML newcomer students and SLIFE related to the strategies discussed in that chapter. Specific considerations related to culturally responsive teaching follow.

(Continued)

(Continued)

Considerations:

- Cultural dissonance: ML newcomer students and SLIFE may experience a sense of disharmony, confusion, and even alienation because they do not understand the expectations and requirements of North American schools (DeCapua et al., 2020). We need to provide a safe space for students to learn the expectations of their new schools and classrooms and give them the tools and resources to make connections with teachers and peers as well as language for asking for support. It is also important to note that these students may be arriving throughout the school year, and it is crucial that whenever they arrive, they be welcomed and provided essential information.

- It's also important to recognize that ML newcomer students and SLIFE may be coming from collectivist cultures. As you design group work, consider how you can build in both individual and group accountability. For example, you can have students work in groups but assign them individual roles within the group or individual pieces of the project that they are accountable for. In addition, ML newcomer students and SLIFE will benefit from explicit modeling of expectations.

Source: iStock.com/AJ_Watt.

Example: Joseph is a seventh-grade student from the Democratic Republic of Congo. He recently arrived in the United States after spending several years at a refugee camp where his opportunities to attend school were irregular. Joseph has come to the United States with his mother and two younger sisters. He speaks Swahili, Lingala, and French. He is mechanically minded and is often able to repair small electronic devices. He also loves to play soccer.

Joseph arrived in November, well after the school year had started. His ELD teacher, Ms. Frank, paired him up with Bernadette, a willing ML buddy who had been at the school since fifth grade and also speaks Swahili. Bernadette was given a note to share with her teachers so she could get to class a little late and leave a little early in order to help Joseph find his new classes. Ms. Frank also took the time to introduce Joseph to all his teachers and let them know about the languages he spoke and his love for soccer. She shared this information to support her colleagues in thinking about the assets that Joseph brings and to provide a possible way to connect with him. She also gave him a laminated resource that had questions and corresponding visuals that Joseph might need. She practiced the questions and statements with him, so he could either ask questions to his teachers or point to a question that he had. Here are a couple of examples from the resource:

- Can you please repeat?

- Can you show me an example?

What Is the Role of Collaboration in Developing a Culturally Responsive Classroom?

Collaboration is at the heart of a culturally responsive classroom. The task of learning more about the cultures of others while, at the same time, reflecting on your own culture requires risk taking, openness, flexibility, and occasional feelings of discomfort. There will be times that you will make mistakes, and there will be times that you may feel angry or frustrated. However, the relationships that you build and the knowledge that you gain can be incredibly rewarding. We make the following recommendations for collaboration with colleagues and ML families:

- Collaborate with colleagues to learn more about the backgrounds, experiences, and cultures of MLs and their families. You can share what you know about specific instructional strategies that have worked well with certain students and strategies for building on students' linguistic and cultural backgrounds. You can also share ways that you have for communicating with and engaging ML families. ELD teachers, classroom teachers, and administrators may want to visit ML communities together.

- Collaborate with colleagues to share resources. Building a multicultural library and/or developing online file sharing can be effective ways to support culturally responsive teaching. A multicultural library can include resources related to particular themes (e.g., peacebuilding or the civil rights movement), books written by authors from MLs' home countries, books that share perspectives that may be traditionally overlooked, bilingual books, and more. Your school librarian might be an excellent person to collaborate with on this work. In addition, online file sharing can be a way to share resources or online tools connected to a particular unit or theme. It can also be a way to share information about student backgrounds, goals, and achievement.

- Collaborate with families of MLs to support MLs' engagement and achievement. Be flexible about the times you are available to meet with families and consider what steps you might take to meet in families' communities. In addition, look for opportunities to invite families into the classroom and participate in classroom activities in ways that they might feel comfortable.

What Is the Role of Equity, Advocacy, and Leadership in Developing a Culturally Responsive Classroom?

Having a culturally responsive classroom that builds on the strengths of your students, encourages sharing diverse English perspectives and experiences, and ultimately supports each ML in acquiring language proficiency and mastering content knowledge is at the core of equity and advocacy for MLs. However, a climate of cultural awareness and inclusivity is something that must be cultivated not only in your classroom but throughout the entire school. If your school currently does not offer a welcoming environment for MLs and their families or if you feel interactions with MLs are often framed from a deficit perspective, you can take on a leadership role in order to advocate for these students. We suggest that you prioritize an area where you have the greatest opportunity to make an impact, rather than focusing on an area in which there is little chance for change (Staehr Fenner, 2014a). Then, find an ally or two who can help you promote an assets-based perspective of MLs. Next, plan out some steps you will take to make positive changes and advocate for equity for MLs.

APPLICATION ACTIVITY 2.7: MS. MONAHAN'S CLASSROOM

Read the scenario, and answer the discussion questions that follow.

Scenario: Ms. Monahan is an ELD teacher at a suburban high school with a growing number of emergent MLs. She felt that the school administration, in general, and the assistant principal, Mr. Yarrow, in particular, did not have a strong understanding of the strengths and needs of the MLs in the school or respect for these students and their families. At one point, when advocating for more professional development for the teachers working with emergent MLs at the school, Mr. Yarrow commented to her that the students didn't seem to be making much progress and that he found them hard to understand. Ms. Monahan decided to invite Mr. Yarrow into her class as a guest. She had her students prepare short presentations on some of their favorite things about the high school (e.g., particular classes, friendships they had, and school activities), and she also encouraged them to speak about some of the challenges that they had (e.g., navigating the lunchroom, understanding some of their teachers, and making new friends). Ms. Monahan also asked Mr. Yarrow to prepare some questions that he could ask the students in order to learn more about their interests, goals, and challenges.

APPLICATION ACTIVITY 2.7: REFLECTION QUESTIONS

1. What do you think was Ms. Monahan's goal in inviting the assistant principal into her classroom?

   _____

   _____

2. What else might Ms. Monahan do to advocate for the MLs in her school?

   _____

   _____

This scenario and the teacher's response demonstrate the need for teachers to take a lead in advocating for better understanding of MLs at all levels within the school. In some situations, complex planning and collaboration will be necessary.

 Available for download at **resources.corwin.com/FennerUnlocking2E**

Next Steps

We have provided a lot of information in this chapter, and we will explore many of these topics in greater depth throughout the remaining chapters of the book. However, in order to start down the path of culturally responsive teaching, use the Culturally Responsive Tool Checklist and Goal Setting Tool in Appendix D in the online companion website to determine priorities for culturally responsive teaching in your context. This checklist can be a helpful tool as you collaborate with colleagues around this important topic. To access the companion website, please visit resources .corwin.com/FennerUnlocking2E.

UNLOCKING RESOURCES

resources.corwin .com/FennerUnlocking2E

Conclusion

In this chapter, we have given you an opportunity to reflect on your own culture and how it impacts your beliefs about teaching and learning. We have also shared some insight into how MLs who come from different cultural backgrounds may have varying beliefs about and approaches to education. Finally, we presented five guiding principles for culturally responsive teaching, along with some tools for using these guiding principles in your classroom. In the next chapter, we will provide some strategies for scaffolding instruction to recognize the strengths and meet the needs of MLs of varying proficiency levels. Chapter 3 correlates directly with Guiding Principle 2: culturally responsive teaching simultaneously supports and challenges students.

SupportEd TOOLBOX

For ready-to-use, practical tools to support culturally responsive teaching, please visit SupportEd.com/ unlocking-toolbox.

CHAPTER 2 REFLECTION QUESTIONS

1. What new understandings do you have about how your own culture shapes who you are as an educator?

2. What are two ideas that you have for drawing on students' cultural backgrounds and experiences to make connections to content in your classroom? Or what ideas do you have for building on MLs' cultural and linguistic assets in your school or district?

 Available for download at **resources.corwin.com/FennerUnlocking2E**

SCAFFOLDING INSTRUCTION FOR MLs

3

During an end-of-unit assessment, students in Mr. Lee's seventh-grade math class work to solve word problems in which they make comparisons between decimals. As the students solve the problems, they are also expected to explain their thinking in writing. During the assessment, the principal, Ms. McNally, visits the class. She notices that the MLs in the classroom receive various types of scaffolds to support their work. For example, emergent MLs of lower proficiency levels are given sentence frames and word banks, and emergent MLs at higher proficiency levels use sentence stems to support their work.

During her post observation discussion with Mr. Lee, Ms. McNally asks him about these supports and questions whether it is unfair to the non-MLs in the class. Mr. Lee explains that he is assessing students' skills in mathematics and mathematical thinking. The scaffolds, or temporary supports, that he provides MLs give them the language assistance needed in order for them to more accurately demonstrate what they know and can do. He also explains that as the students are given these types of scaffolds during instruction, it would be a significant disadvantage to the students to remove the scaffolds during the assessment. He further explains that his language objective for the unit leading up to the assessment was for students to be able to explain the steps that they used to solve a word problem using key academic vocabulary. As the MLs in his class gain greater language proficiency (including the acquisition of mathematical vocabulary and expressions), he will remove the scaffolds, and the students will be able to complete the work independently. In fact, three emergent MLs in the class took the assessment without any scaffolds because they had demonstrated during instruction that they could explain their thinking without the additional language support.

As we describe in the prior scenario, in order for MLs to meet the challenging demands of content-based instruction and acquire the academic language required to do so, they need instructional supports in the form of scaffolds. Findings by the National Literacy Panel on Language Minority Children and Youth illustrate that effective instructional practices designe for English-proficient students may be insufficient to meet the learning needs of MLs (August & Shanahan, 2006). This means that MLs require additional types of supports in order to benefit from instruction to the same extent as their English-proficient peers (Goldenberg, 2008). August (2018), in her synthesis of research-based practices for supporting MLs, described the importance of providing both visual supports (e.g., pictures, short videos, graphic organizers) and verbal supports (e.g., glossaries, sentence and paragraph frames) to help MLs learn core content and access the same grade-level content of non-MLs.

This chapter will provide a definition of scaffolds, categories and examples of scaffolds, and strategies for selecting and developing scaffolds based on the academic task and MLs' proficiency levels, as well as other ML background factors. You will also have an opportunity to think about how to select and use scaffolds in your own context. As using scaffolds is a nonnegotiable component of supporting MLs' content and language development, each chapter in this book also includes a variety of scaffolding practices. Throughout this chapter, we indicate specific chapters or pages in the book that you can refer to in order to find out more information on a particular strategy.

What Is a Scaffold?

A scaffold is a temporary support a teacher provides to a student that enables the student to perform a task they would not be able to perform alone (Gibbons, 2015; National Governors Association for Best Practices, CCSSO, 2010). This support could come from the instructional materials and resources provided to the student, the instructional practices the teacher uses, or how students are grouped during instruction. de Oliveira and Westerlund (2023) explain that scaffolding is a dynamic process that is (1) targeted and responsive to learners' performance and needs, (2) involves gradual withdrawing of support as students develop essential knowledge and skills, and (3) is framed around a transfer of responsibility designed to increase student independence and autonomy (van de Pol et al., 2010, as cited in de Oliveria & Westerlund, 2023). The goal of scaffolding is for students to be able to engage with rigorous grade-level content and ultimately to be able to perform academic tasks independently, no longer requiring scaffolds.

Scaffolding includes both **macro (planned scaffolding)** and **micro (in-the-moment, spontaneous scaffolding)** (de Oliveira & Westerlund, 2023). WIDA (2022) describes macroscaffolding practices as occurring "when teachers develop a long-term vision with clear learning goals for their students and sequence lessons that build students' cumulative and coherent body of knowledge" (p. 3). In contrast to macroscaffolding, microscaffolding practices are those that happen spontaneously during interactions between teachers and students (WIDA, 2022).

In support of macroscaffolding practices, J. Hammond (2023) emphasizes that, for MLs, the cumulative nature of scaffolding that results from strategic "selection and sequencing of tasks within and between lessons" is critical (p. 16). In other words, intentionally planning lessons and academic learning tasks that systematically build on one another and provide targeted support related to the content and language skills that MLs need is an essential component of scaffolding. These strategically planned scaffolds will move students toward greater independence in their learning.

Returning to our opening scenario, an example of a macroscaffolding practice is the decision that Mr. Lee made in advance as he was unit planning to brainstorm with students the language that they could use to explain their thinking and to co-create an anchor chart with this language. Mr. Lee also intentionally planned to have students use the anchor chart when they explained how they found solutions to problems. Following the co-creation of the anchor chart, he embedded opportunities for students to practice with this language during whole-group and small-group discussions and also provided opportunities for students to use this language in their math journals. These thoughtfully planned opportunities for academic language use built on each other and allowed Mr. Lee to gradually remove the scaffolds for some MLs. Mr. Lee based the word bank, sentence stems, and sentence frames provided as scaffolds during the assessment to some MLs on the anchor chart that they had co-created in class. However, as not all students needed the anchor chart, he removed it during the assessment. As the other MLs in his class acquire the language used to explain their mathematical thinking, Mr. Lee plans to remove all scaffolds related to this learning goal.

In contrast to the strategically planned scaffolds described above, microscaffolds are scaffolding practices that teachers instinctively provide during instruction. Examples of microscaffolding practices include a teacher revoicing what a student said, asking for clarification, building on what students say, or clarifying information (de Oliveira & Westerlund, 2023; National Academies of Sciences, Engineering, and Medicine [NASEM], 2018). These types of "teacher moves" (Michaels & O'Connor, 2015) can strengthen ML participation and understanding. For example, imagine that a student in Mr. Lee's class is explaining how she solved the problem but is not using the specific academic language that students have been practicing in class. Mr. Lee might ask clarifying questions of the student and also direct her attention to the anchor chart in order to support her in strengthening her response.

Let's turn our attention now to consider the different types of scaffolding strategies that you can use to support MLs' understanding of content and academic language development. In Application Activity 3.1, jot down a list of the scaffolds that you use in your classroom or that you see others using. We've added an example to get you started. Then, answer the reflection questions that follow.

APPLICATION ACTIVITY 3.1: SCAFFOLDS IN MY CONTEXT

Graphic organizers

APPLICATION ACTIVITY 3.1: REFLECTION QUESTIONS

1. What are some scaffolds that work best for the MLs in your classroom or context?

   _____

   _____

2. What factors do you (or your colleagues) take into consideration when selecting appropriate scaffolds for MLs (e.g., prior schooling, home language literacy), and why?

   _____

   _____

3. How do you (or your colleagues) differentiate the scaffolding that you provide in order to leverage the strengths and meet the needs of MLs of varying language proficiency levels?

_____

_____

4. What steps do you take to plan for the gradual removal of scaffolds?

_____

_____

online resources ⬊ Available for download at **resources.corwin.com/FennerUnlocking2E**

What Are Different Types of Scaffolds?

Instructional scaffolds can be grouped into three main categories: (1) instructional materials, (2) instructional practices, and (3) instructional groupings. **Instructional materials are visual and hands-on teacher-created or teacher-curated resources that students can use to understand content and support language production** such as pictures, sentence stems, or graphic organizers. **Instructional practices are the actions that a teacher takes to support student understanding and engagement** such as modeling language and clarifying concepts. **Instructional groupings are the ways that a teacher can intentionally group students in order to provide peer support, teacher support, and/or differentiated resources.** In discussions of scaffolds, educators often focus on the instructional materials that they use, but it can be very helpful to consider how the three types of scaffolds can work hand-in-hand to strengthen MLs' access to content and language use. Return to the list of scaffolds that you wrote down in Application Activity 3.1. Now, group these scaffolds into the three categories. What do you notice about the types of scaffolds that you listed?

APPLICATION ACTIVITY 3.2: CATEGORIZING SCAFFOLDS

INSTRUCTIONAL MATERIALS	INSTRUCTIONAL PRACTICES	INSTRUCTIONAL GROUPINGS

FIGURE 3.1   CATEGORIES OF SCAFFOLDS

CATEGORIES OF SCAFFOLDS	EXAMPLES
Instructional Materials Audio, visual, or hands-on resources created or curated by an educator used to support MLs' engagement with content and language acquisition 	• Amplified texts (texts with embedded supports such as visuals and vocabulary) • Anchor charts • Audio versions of texts • Bilingual dictionaries and glossaries • English dictionaries and glossaries • Graphic organizers • Home language materials • Sentence frames and paragraph frames • Sentence stems • Visuals and manipulatives • Word banks and word walls
Instructional Practices Actions an educator takes to support MLs' understanding of content and engagement during instruction 	• Activating and concisely teaching background knowledge • Clarifying and paraphrasing key concepts • Embedding instruction of vocabulary and academic language structures • Interactive modeling (teacher or student models an activity, language, or skill and all students reflect on what was modeled) • Multimodal and translanguaging opportunities (using a variety of modes to practice content, such as speaking, drawing, hands-on activities; using more than one of MLs' languages for communication) • Practicing academic language with non-academic topics (e.g., practicing language for comparison using a familiar topic) • Reduced linguistic load

CATEGORIES OF SCAFFOLDS	EXAMPLES
Instructional Groupings Intentionally grouping students to provide peer support, teacher support, or differentiated resources aligned to lesson objectives	• Structured pair work • Structured small-group work • Teacher-led small-group work • Examples of intentional groupings: academic skills grouping, home language grouping, language proficiency grouping, mixed proficiency grouping for language modeling and relationship building

Source: Adapted from Table C–1. Supports and Scaffolding Recommendations by Level in the U.S. Department of Education, Office of Career, Technical and Adult Education (2016).

 Available for download at **resources.corwin.com/FennerUnlocking2E**

Figure 3.1, "Categories of Scaffolds," provides examples of each type of scaffold. We have also left space for you to add in your own ideas to the list. In determining which scaffolds to use for a particular unit, lesson, or instructional task, consider which scaffolds would be most effective in each category to leverage the strengths and support the needs of your MLs in meeting content and language objectives. Next, we provide more information on the three categories and examples of scaffolds in each category.

What Types of Instructional Materials Can I Use to Scaffold Instruction?

Instructional materials are the visual and hands-on tools that you can provide to MLs to support them in accessing content, sharing their understanding of content orally or in writing, and developing language.

Amplified texts are instructional materials that can help MLs gain access to essential content knowledge and support their understanding of academic language. While MLs need opportunities to grapple with challenging grade-level texts, there are also times when they will benefit from an amplified text that supports their understanding of content. **An amplified text has embedded supports such as headers and subheaders to chunk texts, embedded definitions of challenging vocabulary, visuals to support understanding, and key information highlighted** (Billings & Walqui, 2021). For more on developing amplified texts, see Chapter 8.

Anchor charts that include examples of target language and language structures that align to your language objectives can support MLs in using this language when speaking and writing. Anchor charts can also support comprehension. As MLs become more familiar with a particular language structure or text structure that is

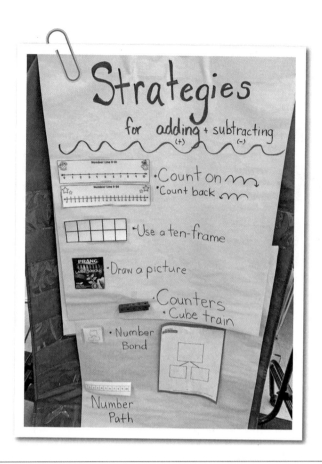

First-grade students use this anchor chart when explaining the strategy that they used to solve a math problem.

Source: Susan Bitler.

being practiced (e.g., cause-and-effect language), they will also be better prepared to break down or deconstruct complex sentences or texts. Co-creating anchor charts with your class can be an effective way to tap into students' prior knowledge and demonstrate modeled language. In the picture, you can see an anchor chart used by first-grade teacher Susan Bitler to support students in explaining the strategy that they used to solve an addition or subtraction problem in math.

Audio versions of texts can be especially helpful for MLs at lower levels of proficiency and MLs who are emergent readers. Listening to audio versions of texts while following along with the text and looking at accompanying visuals can support comprehension and development of listening and literacy skills.

Bilingual dictionaries and glossaries can be beneficial for students who are literate in their home language. In order to most effectively support MLs, bilingual glossaries should include a translation of each word, student-friendly definitions of key terms, and visual representations of each word, whenever possible. For more information on creating student-friendly definitions, see Chapter 5. Bilingual glossaries can also provide opportunities for students to build their knowledge of **cognates, words in different languages that have the same linguistic derivation** (e.g., *membrane* and *membrana*). Figure 3.2 provides an example of a bilingual glossary. To use a bilingual glossary during instruction, students can be asked to add underlined words in a text to the glossary. The teacher can provide a student-friendly definition or the class can develop a definition together. The student can be asked to provide the example from the text, include a picture or

---

FIGURE 3.2   BILINGUAL GLOSSARY EXAMPLE

GLOSSARY				
WORD AND TRANSLATION	**ENGLISH DEFINITION**	**EXAMPLE FROM TEXT**	**PICTURE OR PHRASE TO REPRESENT THE WORD**	**COGNATE (YES OR NO)**
diagnosis *diagnóstico*	*Identifying an illness or problem*	*"All she did was give me some stupid 'diagnosis'" (p. 5).*		*Yes*
soul *alma*	*spirit*	*"The Place Without a Soul—that's what my best friend, Bree, and I decided to call this neighbourhood" (p. 1).*		*No*

Source: Adapted from August, D., Staehr Fenner, D., & Snyder, S. (2014). *Scaffolding instruction for English language learners: Resource guide for ELA*, p. 70. Reprinted with permission of American Institutes for Research. Text quotes from Marquardt, M. (2016). Photographs by iStock.com/FatCamera and iStock.com/recep-bg.

---

phrase that will support their understanding, and note whether or not the word is a cognate in their home language.

English dictionaries and glossaries can be an effective scaffold for MLs to support them in learning academic vocabulary and engaging with complex texts. English dictionaries (online or paper) are appropriate resources for students who possess literacy skills in English or in their home language. Using an English dictionary is suitable for students who may not be literate in their home language but who have literacy skills in English. It is critical that MLs using an English or bilingual dictionary be provided explicit instruction and guided practice to use the dictionary. The recommendations for creating and using English glossaries are similar to the recommendations for developing bilingual glossaries, but English glossaries do not include translations or cognates.

Graphic organizers can support MLs in a variety of ways, including helping them to organize new information and verbalize the relationships between concepts. You should select which graphic organizer to use based on the task students are being asked to complete. For example, you would use one type of graphic organizer to introduce a new topic (e.g., concept map) and another type of graphic organizer to support students in discussing the development of a story (e.g., story map). Graphic organizers most likely will need to be used in conjunction with other scaffolds, especially for MLs at lower proficiency levels. The graphic organizer in Figure 3.3 could be used as part of a vocabulary sorting activity to reinforce key vocabulary. Students could then use the scaffold to compare and contrast the experiences of colonists and Indigenous Americans (e.g., both colonists and Indigenous Americans grew corn) orally and in writing.

FIGURE 3.3   GRAPHIC ORGANIZER: EXAMPLE OF VENN DIAGRAM

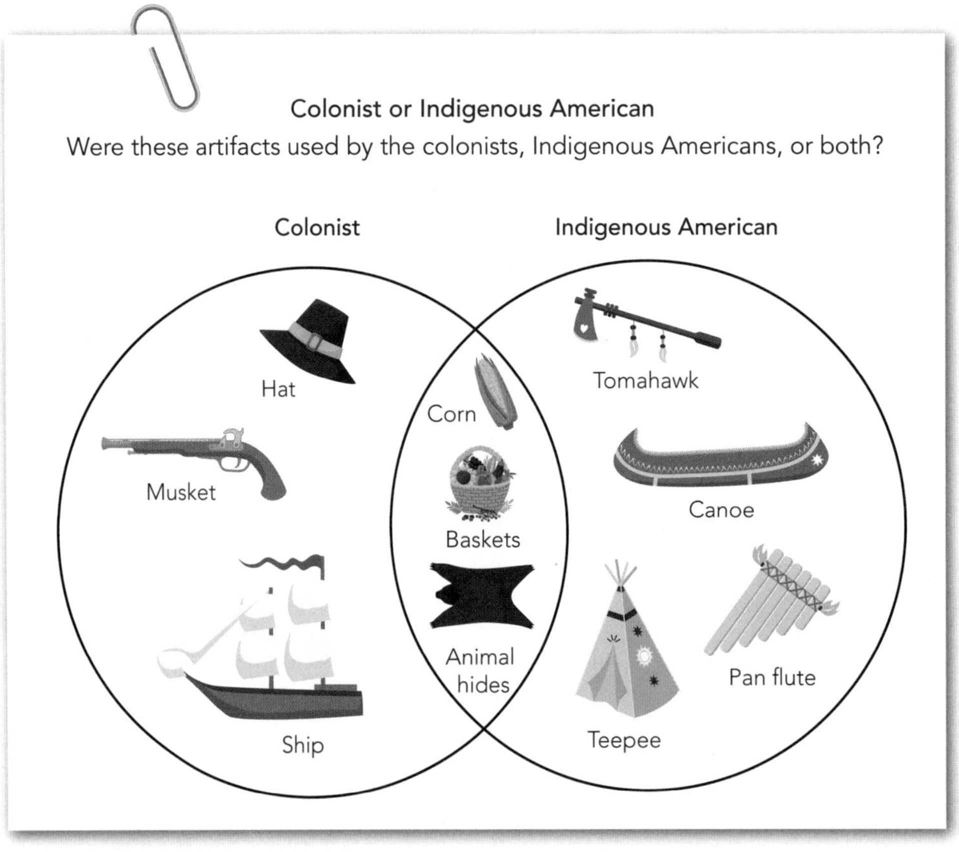

Colonist or Indigenous American
Were these artifacts used by the colonists, Indigenous Americans, or both?

Source: Adapted from a Venn diagram graphic organizer created using Kidspiration®. Illustrations by iStock .com/Teneresa, iStock.com/Soloveva2686, iStock.com/deepfuze.

Home language materials can be an effective scaffold for some MLs. Instructional practices and materials that capitalize on MLs' home language knowledge and skills have been shown to support them in developing literacy and content knowledge in English (August et al., 2009; Escamilla et al., 2022; Francis et al., 2006; Restrepo et al., 2010). Home language support can be provided in various ways, but you should have a sense of MLs' home language literacy skills in order to determine how to best build on MLs' home language knowledge and skills. Examples of supporting materials in the home language include bilingual dictionaries (online or print), supplementary texts in the home language, home language translations, home language videos, and appropriate bilingual home-work activities. For more information on home language use and resources, see Chapter 2.

Sentence frames and paragraph frames can be useful for MLs at lower levels of language proficiency. **Sentence frames (a complete sentence with spaces for students to fill in missing words)** can be used with word banks to support emergent MLs in responding to content-based questions and partici-pating in oral pair and group work

To support students in producing larger amounts of text, you can provide students with paragraph and essay frames. These longer frames can also be one way to provide a gradual release of support. More structured support can be provided at the beginning of the paragraph or essay frame with the idea that students will need less support as they progress in their writing. In Figure 3.4, you can see how different color fonts are used to distinguish between the sentence frames and the directions for what to include in the blanks. Paragraph frames can also be used in conjunction with graphic organizers, glossaries, or word banks, as appropriate.

FIGURE 3.4   PARAGRAPH FRAME EXAMPLE

Text Analysis Essay

In _____ a central theme was _____.

The author developed the central theme through the use of _____

_____ (insert literary device). _____ (literary device) is

_____ (define literary device used).

For example, _____.
(Include an example of the use of the literary device in the text). *In this example, the*

author _____.
(Explain, in your own words, how the author used the device to support the theme).

Another example is when _____.

In conclusion, _____. (Restate your
main argument about the central theme of the text and how the author developed
the theme).

Sentence stems are similar to sentence frames, but they include only the beginning few words of a sentence. As emergent MLs develop language proficiency, you can transition away from providing sentence frames during instruction and allow for more open-ended responses using sentence stems. Examples of sentence stems are provided in Figure 4.9 in Chapter 4. Both stems and frames can be codeveloped with students as a way to support authentic language use and increase student autonomy in their learning.

Using visuals and manipulatives to support the understanding of key ideas and vocabulary is another effective tool for MLs. You can use visuals when introducing or reinforcing new vocabulary, when providing concise background knowledge to support understanding of a text, and when learning about a new content topic. Examples of visuals include pictures, videos, and concrete objects (i.e., realia). Figure 3.5 demonstrates how a simple visual can provide a lot of information that students might need when solving a math problem including the name of the coin, what to count by when adding, what it looks like, and different ways to represent the amount.

FIGURE 3.5   VISUAL EXAMPLE FOR MATH

Source: Adapted from a visual created by Amanda Brudecki. Coin image by iStock.com/janzwolinski.

Manipulatives are physical or virtual items that students can touch or move to support learning such as taking part in a card sort activity (e.g., sorting events on a timeline), using counters or base ten blocks for math, or creating a foldable graphic organizer (see the picture of the science foldable). Manipulatives can be effective in helping students conceptualize challenging concepts. Buckley (2023) recommends using "atypical manipulatives" that allow students to share something of themselves. Students can be asked to bring in small objects that they have a connection to, and these manipulatives can be used during a lesson. She encourages educators to listen to the stories that students tell about their objects. Foldables, a student-created manipulative, can incorporate student-created definitions, visuals, and home language translations (if appropriate). They can also provide an easy way for a student to review key concepts.

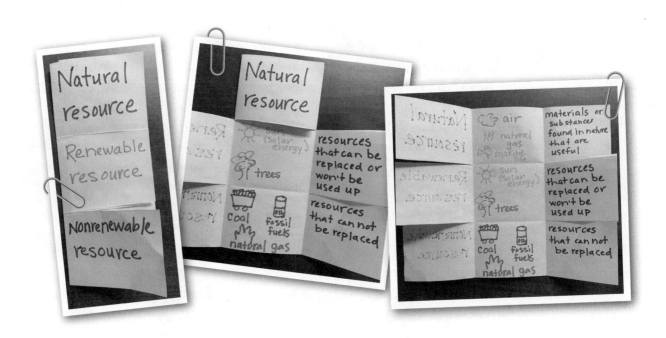

This science foldable on natural resources is a tool to help students build and practice their understanding of different types of resources. The resource includes a student-friendly definition and some visual examples.

Word banks and interactive word walls can be an effective scaffold for MLs in a variety of tasks. For example, MLs might use word banks or word walls when responding to content questions (orally or in writing). MLs might also refer to word walls or word banks when engaging in other content-based tasks, such as completing a graphic organizer, writing a summary of their understanding of a topic, or engaging in an academic conversation. Word banks and word walls can be developed to be used either with a specific task or in conjunction with a content-based unit. However, they should be developed in tandem with vocabulary instruction and practice. A word wall that is interactive is co-created with students and can also be accompanied by visuals and home language translations whenever possible. Word banks and word walls should not be so lengthy as to overwhelm MLs and prevent their use.

What Instructional Practices Can I Use to Scaffold Instruction?

In addition to providing scaffolded materials, you can also scaffold instruction for MLs through specific instructional practices that are both planned and in-the-moment.

Activating and concisely teaching background knowledge needed for the lesson is an essential scaffold to support MLs in learning new content and engaging with complex texts. MLs may differ from their non-ML peers in terms of the type of content knowledge that they bring to the classroom. Teachers of MLs should determine what background knowledge is necessary for an academic task and how to concisely teach the information needed or draw on students' previous learning and experiences to help set the context for the lesson. Chapter 7 provides in-depth guidance in determining which background knowledge is essential to teach as well as concrete steps for concisely teaching background knowledge.

Clarifying and paraphrasing key concepts is another important instructional scaffold for MLs. While teaching, educators naturally check in with students to confirm understanding. However, MLs can sometimes be overlooked during these comprehension checks and are often hesitant to speak up when they don't understand. As you are teaching, consider how you can build in comprehension checks that will give you a sense of what your MLs understand. For example, whiteboards can be a tool for providing a quick formative assessment with MLs. You should also intentionally build in wait time for students to process and produce language.

Embedded instruction of vocabulary and academic-language structures is a component of effective instruction for MLs (August, 2018). Instruction that includes an intensive focus on a few key vocabulary words across several days and using varied instructional practices has been shown to be highly effective in supporting MLs' understanding of new content (Baker et al., 2014). It is also important for MLs to receive explicit language instruction that goes beyond a focus on words (NASEM, 2018). For example, giving students opportunities to deconstruct challenging academic-language structures and then practice producing similar language structures will support MLs' engagement with complex texts while promoting their language development. Chapters 5 and 6 delve into what academic language is and suggest strategies for teaching and practicing academic language at the word/phrase, sentence, and discourse levels.

Interactive modeling is a highly effective strategy to support ML understanding. We specify "interactive" because we want students to have an active role in reflecting on what was modeled for them. Teachers can model thought processes, language skills, content skills, and learning activities. Imagine during a read-aloud a teacher comes across a challenging word that she thinks many of the students will not know and is important to understanding the text. This teacher might do a think-aloud to talk through what she could do to identify the meaning of the word. For example, she might first sound out the word and say it aloud. She then might look at the word parts to see if those give any clues to understanding the meaning of the word. Next, she might think aloud about the sentence as a whole and what types of words would make sense in the context. After this think-aloud, the teacher could ask the class to share what they noticed about the strategies that she used. She might even use that opportunity to co-create an anchor chart of strategies that students could refer to when doing independent reading. The vignette of Ms. Alvi's

ELD classroom provides an example of how you might model a skill that students will then reflect on and practice.

Ms. Alvi's ELD Classroom: Paragraph Writing

Ms. Alvi teaches a beginner ELD class to fifth- and sixth-grade emergent MLs. In her class, students have been studying community issues and working on developing claims and counterclaims in their writing. In order to help them prepare to write on a community issue of their choice, she has the class construct an idea web, based on an example of littering in local parks. She asks the students to make connections to their experiences with littering in their home countries, explain why littering is an important issue, and discuss how the problem might be addressed by the community. She also asks students to provide challenges that the community could face in trying to address this issue. Once the class has collaboratively developed the idea web, Ms. Alvi models for students how they can transition from a graphic organizer to writing a paragraph. She asks for students to identify the main idea from the web, and she also asks them to identify similar ideas in the web. As a class, they write a sample paragraph on the board. Then, Ms. Alvi asks her students to work in pairs to complete a similar task about their own community issue.

REFLECTION QUESTION

Which strategies do you use to model activities, academic strategies, or skills with your students?

 Available for download at **resources.corwin.com/FennerUnlocking2E**

Multimodal and translanguaging opportunities benefit MLs by giving them the opportunity to explore content using multiple modalities and all languages available to them (Grabe, 1991; Grapin, 2018; McLaughlin, 1987; NASEM, 2018). **Modalities refer to the different ways that communication takes place and include nonlinguistic modalities** (e.g., pictures, graphs, symbols, gestures) **and linguistic modalities** (e.g., talk and text) (NASEM, 2018). The WIDA ELD Standards Framework (WIDA, 2020a) states that "multimodality allows all students to use multiple means to engage, interpret, represent, act, and express their ideas in the classroom. For example, as students read, they also might refer to illustrations or diagrams, and as students write, they might also represent their ideas numerically or graphically" (p. 19).

Translanguaging, as described in Chapter 2, **is the use of more than one language for communication.** Incorporating translanguaging opportunities into lessons allows for students to draw on all their linguistic resources when exploring a topic (Creese & Blackledge, 2010; O. Garcia et al., 2017). To engage students in using multiple modalities and translanguaging in learning about causes of the U.S. Civil War, for example, students might be asked to:

- watch a video on the Civil War (in English or their home language) and answer questions,

- do a carousel walk to discuss different images from the U.S. Civil War, and jot down their reflections on sticky notes (which could be discussed in English or their home language),

- take part in a jigsaw reading in which each group member reads and shares about a short passage related to the topic, and

- work in peer groups to develop a poster presentation on one cause of the war.

Practicing academic language with non-academic topics is an excellent way to support MLs' language development and use of academic language. For example, if you are working on sequencing language to describe the events of a story, consider teaching a mini language lesson on sequencing words (e.g., first, next, finally) and have students practice by describing a sequence of events in their own life. By focusing explicitly on academic language during the mini lesson, you will provide students a structured opportunity to practice the language that you will later ask them to apply to the academic content.

A reduced linguistic load is a scaffold that can benefit MLs at lower proficiency levels. In order to decrease the linguistic load, paraphrase key concepts using simple and direct language, and write down essential ideas so that emergent MLs can review this information later, as needed. When giving directions, be cognizant of vocabulary or language structures that may be confusing to emergent MLs, and look for opportunities to appropriately reduce the linguistic load while not watering down content. Always try to provide clear directions in writing as well. We are cautious when talking about a reduced linguistic load because we don't want to remove MLs' opportunities to engage with rigorous, academic language. However, adjusting your vocabulary, rate of speech, and sentence complexity based on MLs' levels of proficiency when giving directions, providing examples, and clarifying ideas will support MLs' comprehension (Goldenberg, 2008).

What Instructional Groupings Can I Use to Scaffold Instruction?

In addition to instructional materials and instructional practices, student groupings can be an effective scaffold (Mackey & Gass, 2006; WIDA, 2013). In order to ensure that MLs are benefiting from group work, students will need sufficient structure and guidance in engaging in the pair or group task. Depending on their level of language proficiency, MLs will most likely need other types of scaffolds to facilitate the task. Further, educators should intentionally group students based on the lesson or unit's learning objectives (Brooks & Thurston, 2010; WIDA, 2013). As you think about how to group students, consider the questions in Figure 3.6 and possible ways of grouping students. We would like to note that these are merely possibilities and are not prescriptive. You know your students best, and we encourage you to use your professional expertise when grouping MLs. You will also want to provide some opportunities for students to choose who they would like to work with.

FIGURE 3.6 CONSIDERATIONS IN INTENTIONALLY GROUPING STUDENTS

CONSIDERATION: DO I WANT TO . . .	POSSIBLE GROUPING
Use this time to support emergent MLs in negotiating meaning and building academic language through interactions with English-proficient peers?	Heterogenous grouping of mixed English language proficiency levels and English-proficient students
Provide students with differentiated materials or differentiated learning tasks?	Homogenous grouping based on language proficiency levels, academic skills, or home languages—each group of students will get a different set of materials based on their strengths and needs
Use this time to work with a small group of students on specific content or language skills?	Homogenous grouping based on language proficiency levels and/or academic skills
Provide an opportunity for translanguaging or home language support for MLs?	Homogenous grouping based on home languages
Use students' strengths as a way to support group roles?	Heterogenous grouping based on individual students' strengths to support such group roles as leader, scribe, and reporter
Consider students' background knowledge, interests, personalities, or other factors that may impact group work?	All types of groupings

REFLECTION QUESTIONS

1. What are your takeaways from these considerations in ML student groupings?

2. What other considerations do you use when grouping students?

3. What is a new way of grouping students that you would like to try?

online resources Available for download at **resources.corwin.com/FennerUnlocking2E**

All of these considerations are valid reasons to group students. What is most important is that you be intentional about how you group students and that your groupings align to your learning and activity objectives and the needs of your students. For example, you could group MLs with the same home language to work together, thus bringing in home language support that you personally may not be able to provide. Alternatively, you may create mixed-ability or language proficiency pairs or groups in which some students are providing additional support to others or providing language modeling. You can also choose to group students in homogeneous groups in order to provide directed support to students with similar strengths and needs. For example, you could provide targeted mini lessons (e.g., features of academic language or specific language functions) based on the needs of the group. It is important that you draw on students' strengths so that all students can have an opportunity to demonstrate what they can do. You will want to mix up your groups every so often so that students have opportunities to work with different students, practice different skills, and get new perspectives. For more on strategies to support MLs in small groups, please see Chapter 4.

REFLECTION QUESTIONS

Review the list of scaffolds in Figure 3.1, then answer these reflection questions:

1. Which category of instructional scaffolding (i.e., materials, practices, groupings) would you like to strengthen in your context? Why?

2. What step will you take next?

 Available for download at **resources.corwin.com/FennerUnlocking2E**

What Steps Should I Take to Scaffold a Unit?

Planning and preparing to teach differentiated scaffolded units that leverage the strengths and meet the needs of MLs of varying proficiency levels can seem like a daunting task. However, once you gain practice and familiarity with these steps, the process will become an intuitive part of planning. Also, if the thought of differentiating a unit for MLs of varying proficiency levels seems overwhelming, begin by trying one or two scaffolds that will support all of the MLs in your classroom on a particular task or working toward a specific learning goal. As you experiment with different types of scaffolds, your ability to meet the varied needs of the MLs that you work with will grow. Figure 3.7 highlights the six steps we recommend when scaffolding a unit. These same steps can be used when scaffolding an individual lesson or activity. The process is cyclical in order to support ongoing implementation and reflection on scaffolding. This cycle is most effective when implemented within a framework of collaboration (with colleagues and students) and when MLs' assets are used as a foundation for learning.

FIGURE 3.7   SIX STEPS FOR SCAFFOLDING A UNIT

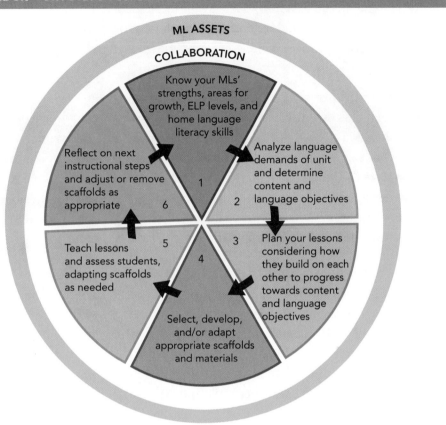

Steps for Developing Scaffolded Units

1. **Know your MLs' strengths, areas for growth, English language proficiency (ELP) levels, and home language literacy skills.** Scaffolding must be responsive to the particular needs of students and provide the right level of support (Walqui & Schmida, 2023). Before you begin scaffolding units for MLs, you must have an understanding of their backgrounds, strengths, and areas for growth, just as Mr. Lee did in the opening scenario. It may be helpful to keep an index card or use an online tool provided by your school or district to keep track of information on each student that will help you to appropriately scaffold instruction. You could also use the template provided in Chapter 2, Figure 2.3, "What I Know About My ML." In determining appropriate scaffolds, you will want to know the student's home language, level of literacy in their home language and English, educational background, and ELP level. You will also want to consider your student's strengths and needs related to their understanding of the content and language development in order to best determine what supports to provide and how to help students progress toward meeting content and language objectives. Additionally, it is important to consider how you will know when it is time to remove a specific support. You can give a brief preassessment to your students before beginning each unit in order to gauge your students' understanding of content, vocabulary, and language skills. Effective preassessments can

help you determine specific scaffolds that you will need to support student understanding and also how to effectively implement scaffolded units to advance MLs' language development. Chapter 9 provides more information on types of formative assessments that you can use.

2. **Analyze the language demands of the unit and determine the content and language objectives for the unit.** For each unit that you will teach, it is essential that you analyze the academic-language demands of each task. In other words, what will MLs have to do during the unit, and what challenges might they face? Chapter 6 provides specifics on how to analyze the language demands of a text or academic task. Once you understand the language demands of the unit (e.g., academic vocabulary, complex sentences, expectations for language use), you can begin to determine how you will support the MLs in your classroom.

As you consider how to scaffold a specific activity, lesson, or unit, think about the three categories of scaffolds that you may wish to include. It is important to remember the specific needs of your MLs and recognize that their needs will vary depending on the academic task that they are working on. For example, an emergent ML may be testing at an intermediate English proficiency level over-all but may need the scaffolded support that is more appropriate for a student at a high beginner level when completing writing tasks because the student needs a greater degree of support in organizing their ideas.

There are no hard and fast rules for selecting appropriate scaffolds for MLs of varying proficiency levels. However, it is important to keep in mind that the goal of scaffolding is to gradually remove scaffolds after providing sufficient structure and support. Ultimately, your MLs should be able to complete academic tasks with the same instructional tools and practices provided to their non-ML peers. That is to say, some scaffolds might be developmentally appropriate for all students (e.g., graphic organizers or pair work) and may be used as supports for the whole class. It is also important to note that an ML's need for a particular scaffold will vary depending on the familiarity of the content and the complexity of the task. For example, a student may be able to draw comparisons between two sports teams the student is familiar with using only sentence stems as a scaffold. However, when asked to draw comparisons between two content-based, grade-level texts read in class, the student may need sentence stems, a word bank, and a graphic organizer in order to be able to successfully complete the task.

Figure 3.8, "Suggested Scaffolds at Each Proficiency Level," provides some general guidelines for selecting scaffolds for MLs at different language proficiency levels. However, it is always important to take into consideration the strengths and needs of your individual MLs when making decisions about scaffolding. For example, students' grade level, amount of background knowledge on a particular topic, and proficiency level within a particular domain (i.e., listening, speaking, reading, and writing) will all influence the need for a particular scaffold.

FIGURE 3.8 SUGGESTED SCAFFOLDS AT EACH PROFICIENCY LEVEL

Key	
Icon	**Description**
●	Scaffold **is critical** for MLs to access language and content dependent on task and individual student needs.
◑	Scaffold **may be necessary** for MLs to access language and content dependent on task and individual student needs.
○	Scaffold **may be appropriate** for MLs to access language and content dependent on task and individual student needs.

Scaffold	Beginning ELP Level	Intermediate ELP Level	Advanced ELP Level
Activating and concisely teaching background knowledge	●	●	◑
Amplified texts	●	●	○
Anchor charts	●	◑	○
Audio versions of texts	●	◑	○
Bilingual dictionaries and glossaries	●	●	◑
Clarifying and paraphrasing key concepts	●	●	◑
Embedding instruction of vocabulary and academic-language structures	●	●	○
English dictionaries and glossaries	●	◑	○
Graphic organizers	●	◑	○
Home language materials	●	●	○
Intentional student grouping	●	◑	◑
Interactive modeling	●	◑	○
Multimodal and translanguaging opportunities	●	●	◑
Practicing academic language with non-academic topics	●	◑	○
Reduced linguistic load	●	◑	N/A
Sentence and paragraph frames	●	○	N/A
Sentence stems	●	●	○
Visuals and manipulatives	●	◑	○
Word banks and word walls	●	●	○

Source: Adapted from August, D., Staehr Fenner, D. & Snyder, S. (2014). *Scaffolding instruction for English language learners: Resource guide for ELA*, p. 25. Reprinted with permission of American Institutes for Research.

REFLECTION QUESTIONS

Review Figure 3.8, and answer the following questions:

1. What takeaways do you have about how to gradually remove scaffolds based on Figure 3.8?

2. Are there any recommendations that you disagree with? Why?

online resources — Available for download at **resources.corwin.com/FennerUnlocking2E**

3. **Plan your lessons considering how they build on each other to progress toward your content and language objectives.** Once you have determined the academic-language demands of a unit, you will need to account for these language demands when planning your individual lessons. Keeping your learning objectives in sight, consider the scaffolds that are going to most effectively support your MLs in working toward those objectives. Figure 3.9, the Scaffolded Unit Planning Checklist, provides areas to consider as you are planning your unit.

    As an example of how lessons can build incrementally with scaffolded support, imagine that you are going to teach a fourth-grade science unit in which students will be asked to identify the structures of a plant and explain their functions using targeted academic language. You would want to consider how you will introduce and give students opportunities to practice both the specific terminology associated with plant structures as well as the language needed to explain their functions (e.g., a function of roots is to absorb water and minerals from the soil). In order to build incrementally toward your content and language goals, you might first practice identifying the different parts of plants. Then, you might introduce language for describing the functions. Students could do a sort in which they match the structure with the function and orally make a connection between the two. Finally, you might ask students to write picture captions to describe plants and their functions using a word bank (if needed).

4. **Select, develop, or adapt appropriate scaffolds and materials.** Once you have determined a plan for your unit you will need to select, develop, or adapt the scaffolds and other materials that you will use. Examples of scaffolds and materials that you might develop or select include the following:

    *   Graphic organizers
    *   Home language supporting materials
    *   Manipulatives
    *   Sentence stems, sentence frames, and paragraph frames
    *   Visuals
    *   Word banks

FIGURE 3.9   SCAFFOLDED UNIT PLANNING CHECKLIST

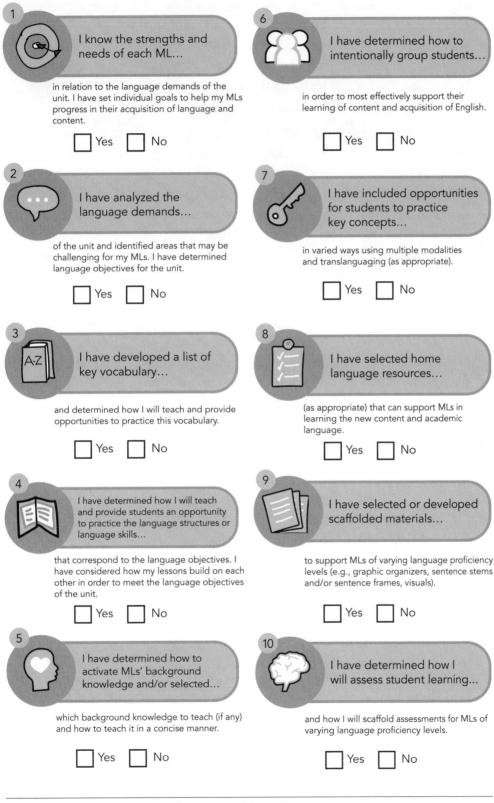

1 I know the strengths and needs of each ML...

in relation to the language demands of the unit. I have set individual goals to help my MLs progress in their acquisition of language and content.

☐ Yes   ☐ No

2 I have analyzed the language demands...

of the unit and identified areas that may be challenging for my MLs. I have determined language objectives for the unit.

☐ Yes   ☐ No

3 I have developed a list of key vocabulary...

and determined how I will teach and provide opportunities to practice this vocabulary.

☐ Yes   ☐ No

4 I have determined how I will teach and provide students an opportunity to practice the language structures or language skills...

that correspond to the language objectives. I have considered how my lessons build on each other in order to meet the language objectives of the unit.

☐ Yes   ☐ No

5 I have determined how to activate MLs' background knowledge and/or selected...

which background knowledge to teach (if any) and how to teach it in a concise manner.

☐ Yes   ☐ No

6 I have determined how to intentionally group students...

in order to most effectively support their learning of content and acquisition of English.

☐ Yes   ☐ No

7 I have included opportunities for students to practice key concepts...

in varied ways using multiple modalities and translanguaging (as appropriate).

☐ Yes   ☐ No

8 I have selected home language resources...

(as appropriate) that can support MLs in learning the new content and academic language.

☐ Yes   ☐ No

9 I have selected or developed scaffolded materials...

to support MLs of varying language proficiency levels (e.g., graphic organizers, sentence stems and/or sentence frames, visuals).

☐ Yes   ☐ No

10 I have determined how I will assess student learning...

and how I will scaffold assessments for MLs of varying language proficiency levels.

☐ Yes   ☐ No

Source: Adapted from Snyder & Staehr Fenner (2021), p. 143.

 Available for download at **resources.corwin.com/FennerUnlocking2E**

5. **Teach the lessons and assess students, adapting scaffolds and materials as needed.** As is common in teaching, you may realize during the course of a lesson that you need to adjust your instruction or materials to better leverage your students' strengths and meet their needs. Perhaps your students have mastered a key concept, and you need to spend less time on it than you thought. Maybe some students are struggling with a particular aspect of the lesson, and you need to develop some additional opportunities for students to practice that skill or concept.

    Formative assessments can help guide your decision-making in this area. See Chapter 9 for more information on designing formative assessments for MLs. You will also need to consider how to scaffold any assessment that you create. For example, it is not reasonable to expect that an emergent ML (particularly an ML at beginner or intermediate levels of proficiency) who has been completing tasks using scaffolds, such as sentence stems, word banks, and graphic organizers, will be able to successfully complete an assessment without these supports.

6. **Reflect on next instructional steps and adjust or remove scaffolds as appropriate.** After teaching the unit, take the time to reflect on its effectiveness with your MLs. Consider whether the scaffolds that you provided were effective in supporting MLs in meeting the language and content objectives. We also encourage you to ask students what worked well for them and what could be improved. Often, we do not ask students to provide their input in our instruction as this may put us in a more vulnerable position as teachers. Decide how you might modify the scaffolds you provide in your next unit as well as which scaffolds may no longer be needed for specific MLs.

APPLICATION ACTIVITY 3.3: SELECTING APPROPRIATE SCAFFOLDS

Read the scenario. Then, complete the template in Figure 3.10 to explain which scaffolds you would choose to use for the unit. Provide a reason for your selected scaffolds in the "Rationale" column. We have completed the instructional materials scaffolds and rationale for emergent MLs with beginning-level proficiency to get you started.

Scenario: A ninth-grade class will begin a unit on conservation. In the class, nine of the 24 students are emergent MLs. They range in proficiency level from beginner to advanced. Students will read and discuss several texts that explain why conservation is necessary and include strategies for conserving natural resources. The students will work in groups to select one conservation strategy that they will present to the class. They will be asked to use persuasive language to explain why their conservation strategy is important. Students will create a poster that they will use to present their strategy to the class. If you were the teacher of the class, which scaffolds would you use, and why? Refer to the scaffolds in Figure 3.8 to guide your work.

FIGURE 3.10 SELECTING APPROPRIATE SCAFFOLDS		
PROFICIENCY LEVEL	**SELECTED INSTRUCTIONAL SCAFFOLDS**	**RATIONALE**
Beginner	*Materials:* Word bank with visuals *Practice:* *Grouping:*	A word bank with visuals will support beginner MLs in learning and using the key academic vocabulary needed for the unit.
Intermediate	*Materials:* *Practice:* *Grouping:*	
Advanced	*Materials:* *Practice:* *Grouping:*	

Let's now explore specific considerations for scaffolding instructional content for ML newcomer students and students with limited or interrupted formal education (SLIFE) and the role that collaboration, equity, advocacy, and leadership can play in fostering scaffolded instruction for MLs.

ML NEWCOMER STUDENTS AND SLIFE CONSIDERATIONS

What Are Key Considerations for Scaffolding for ML Newcomer Students and SLIFE?

ML newcomer students and SLIFE need instruction that is highly scaffolded to support their understanding of new content.

Considerations:

- Many ML newcomer students, and SLIFE in particular, will benefit from educators being explicit about the relevance of a particular topic or learning task to their long-term goals (DeCapua et al., 2020). In other words, share with students why the learning is important for them in order to build a sense of relevancy.

(Continued)

(Continued)

- In planning lessons for ML newcomer students and SLIFE, there is an urgent need to embed scaffolds that will support students' understanding of and engagement with content learning and also support language development. When introducing new academic skills or tasks, have students practice all skills and tasks with familiar language and content first before having students apply the skills and language to more decontextualized content. For example, if you want students to use cause-and-effect language to describe outcomes of scientific experiments, consider first having them practice that language using images of everyday events that represent a cause-and-effect scenario (DeCapua & Marshall, 2013; DeCapua et al., 2020).

- Many ML newcomer students and SLIFE come from collectivist cultures with strong oral traditions (in which they focus on sharing traditions and histories orally rather than writing) and benefit from opportunities to discuss content orally with peers before writing (DeCapua & Marshall, 2023; DeCapua, et al., 2020).

Example: Let's return to Joseph, the seventh-grade student who we introduced in Chapter 2. In Joseph's art class, students will be required to write a short essay comparing the works of two different artists. Joseph is worried about the assignment, and he is also not clear on its relevance. His art teacher, Ms. Zielinska, explains that being able to make comparisons and use comparative language is an important skill that is needed in all subjects. In order to support Joseph and other MLs in the class with this assignment, Ms. Zielinska brainstorms with the class ways that pieces of art can be alike or different. They develop a list of words and phrases that can be used to describe artwork. The word wall includes images to represent each word and phrase. Ms. Zielinska also has students work in pairs to compare two pieces of art using sentence stems that she has introduced and practiced with students. For the final writing assignment, Ms. Zielinska gives students a graphic organizer to use to organize their ideas. Students are given the opportunity to complete the graphic organizer in pairs, but then they are asked to complete the final assignment individually. Ms. Zielinska gives Joseph a paragraph frame to support his writing and meets with him one-on-one to assist him in using the scaffolds that she has provided (i.e., word wall with visuals, graphic organizer, paragraph frame). After completing the assignment, Joseph feels proud of his final product, and he has a better understanding of the process and language to use when making comparisons.

What Is the Role of Collaboration in Scaffolding Instruction for MLs?

As you add to your scaffolding repertoire, look for other educators who can support you in this work. Content teachers can turn to the ELD teachers in their school for resources and advice on how to scaffold a particular lesson or unit.

ELD teachers could work with content teachers to make sure they know the critical vocabulary and language structures that MLs need to master as well as the objectives and key understandings for each unit of instruction. The Scaffolding Self-Assessment Checklist found in Appendix E in the online companion website can be a helpful tool for collaborating around scaffolding. Teaching teams can review the checklist and prioritize scaffolds that they want to strengthen in their contexts. To access the companion website, please visit resources.corwin.com/ FennerUnlocking2E.

UNLOCKING RESOURCES

resources.corwin .com/FennerUnlocking2E

What Is the Role of Equity, Advocacy, and Leadership in Developing Scaffolded Materials?

An essential component of advocacy for MLs is equitable educational opportunities and access to effective instruction (Staehr Fenner, 2014a). In order for MLs to have access to content to the same extent as their non-ML peers and to minimize the achievement gap that exists between MLs and non-MLs, MLs need instructional practices and materials that are adapted to meet their specific needs (Goldenberg, 2008). Advocating for equity for MLs requires that educators go beyond providing high-quality instructional practices and think critically about what the specific MLs in their classroom will need to acquire language and master content while providing them access to challenging grade-level content.

Next Steps

Throughout this book, we have provided you an opportunity to develop a unit plan that is comprehensive in implementing research-based practices for MLs. Appendix A is the complete unit planning template. Appendix B is a model of a completed template. These two appendices can be found on the online companion website. To access the companion website, please visit resources. corwin.com/FennerUnlocking2E. In each chapter of this book, we'll give you an opportunity to reflect on one piece of the unit plan and share supporting tools with you. In this chapter, we suggest you begin by identifying the unit you would like to implement, the standards you wish to address, and your content and language objectives. If you teach more than one class or content area, select one to focus on. We encourage you to be as specific as possible related to the learning objectives. Then, describe the MLs in your class including their strengths, needs, and interests. Additionally, consider possible scaffolds that you might provide MLs at different levels of English language proficiency. If you are not currently in the classroom, consider a classroom that you observed or the classroom of a peer.

UNLOCKING RESOURCES

resources.corwin .com/FennerUnlocking2E

APPLICATION ACTIVITY 3.4: UNIT PLANNING, STEP 1

Complete the *Unit Overview* and Step 1 in the *Unit Preparation* sections of the Unlocking MLs' Potential Unit Planning Template (the portion of Appendix A reproduced in Figure 3.11).

FIGURE 3.11 PORTION OF THE UNLOCKING MLs' POTENTIAL UNIT PLANNING TEMPLATE (APPENDIX A)	
UNIT OVERVIEW	
Timeframe:	**Topic:**
Subject:	**Grade Level:**
Standard(s) ☐ **Content:** ☐ **English Language Development:**	**Objective(s)** ☐ **Content:** ☐ **Language:**
UNIT PREPARATION	
Describe Your MLs (e.g., home language literacy, English language proficiency level, interests) *Figure 2.3 What I Know About My ML*	

UNIT DELIVERY	

Scaffolds

Figure 3.1 Categories of Scaffolds

Figure 3.8 Suggested Scaffolds at Each Proficiency Level

Figure 3.9 Scaffolded Unit Planning Checklist

What **scaffolds** will you provide to MLs of varying proficiency levels?

ELP LEVEL(S)	SCAFFOLDS
Beginning	
Intermediate	
Advanced	

APPLICATION ACTIVITY 3.4: REFLECTION QUESTIONS

1. What specific language objectives do you have for your MLs for this unit? What are the language or language skills that you will be focusing on during the unit?

   _____

   _____

(Continued)

(Continued)

2. What are the strengths that your MLs have? How can you build on these strengths during this unit?

_____

_____

3. As you think about the scaffolds discussed in this chapter, what is one scaffold that is new to you, or that you would like to use more effectively that you plan to incorporate into this unit?

_____

_____

online resources Available for download at **resources.corwin.com/FennerUnlocking2E**

SupportEd
TOOLBOX

For ready-to-use, practical tools to support scaffolding instruction, please see SupportEd .com/unlocking-toolbox.

Conclusion

In this chapter, we have shared descriptions and examples of different types of scaffolds, general recommendations for scaffolding instruction, and guidelines to use in determining which scaffolds to use in order to leverage the strengths and meet the needs of MLs of varying proficiency levels in your classrooms. Throughout the remainder of the book, we provide additional strategies for scaffolding materials and examples of scaffolded materials that correspond to each instructional practice. As you work through the exercises in the remaining chapters, it may be helpful to refer back to this chapter for scaffolding ideas and considerations. In the next chapter, you will learn more specifics on how to incorporate peer learning activities into your instruction in order to support MLs' language development and understanding of new content.

CHAPTER 3 REFLECTION QUESTIONS

1. If you are teaching in a collaborative setting, how might you divide the work to plan and prepare for teaching scaffolded units?

2. What steps will you take to strengthen scaffolded instruction for MLs in your upcoming instructional units?

online resources Available for download at **resources.corwin.com/FennerUnlocking2E**

PEER LEARNING: FOSTERING MLs' ORAL LANGUAGE DEVELOPMENT AND CONTENT UNDERSTANDING

4

Mr. Hernandez's eighth-grade science class, which is about 20 percent emergent multilingual learners (MLs) of varying proficiency levels, is working on a unit on

the relationship among organisms within an eco-system. They have learned key vocabulary, read a short text on the topic, and answered open-ended questions about the text they are using. In order to reinforce the material before their next activity, Mr. Hernandez has prepared a set of discussion questions that require students to use the new vocabulary and provide evidence to support their thinking on the topic. Students are seated in groups of four with their desks facing each other.

Source: iStock.com/asiseeit

Before beginning the activity, Mr. Hernandez reviews with students that the purpose of the lesson is for students to gain a deeper understanding of the topic but also to practice their discussion skills. He asks students what it looks like to actively listen to another student. A couple of students respond, saying that they should be facing the speaker and making eye contact with the speaker. Mr. Hernandez also refers students to the word bank of unit vocabulary that they have as a handout and sentence stems on the wall that they can use when having a discussion (e.g., I agree with _____ because _____). As the students engage in their discussion of the questions, Mr. Hernandez walks around the room with a checklist (Figure 4.1). He takes notes of the types of skills students are using in their discussions (e.g., supporting ideas with evidence, clarifying, and building on one another's ideas), and he records which skills the students need to work on. He also copies down some key ideas that students share. He will present these to the whole group as a way of reviewing important ideas and recognizing the contributions students have made during the discussion.

Mr. Hernandez knows that content standards require that students be able to effectively participate in different types of conversations and with diverse partners. Students are expected to build on others' ideas and express their own ideas clearly and persuasively. Mr. Hernandez also knows that including peer learning opportunities, such as academic conversations, regularly in instruction can benefit both his MLs and non-MLs in terms of their academic language and literacy development, content understanding, and critical-thinking skills (Zwiers, 2019). He recognizes that supporting MLs' oral language development will provide a foundation for their literacy development (Escamilla et al., 2022). However, in order to have MLs effectively participate in peer learning, they need explicit preparation, scaffolded support, and instruction in what it means to participate including an understanding of their teachers' expectations for participation, as well as validation of what participation may look like in their home culture (e.g., rote learning, limited opportunities for discussion) (Staehr Fenner & Teich, in press).

REFLECTION QUESTIONS

Reflect on the scenario from Mr. Hernandez's science classroom.

1. How did Mr. Hernandez prepare the emergent MLs in his class to participate in the small-group discussion?

2. What additional scaffolds or supports might you add to this activity? Why?

online resources   Available for download at **resources.corwin.com/FennerUnlocking2E**

In this chapter, we discuss the importance of including peer learning opportunities in instruction, explain why peer learning is important for MLs, and provide guidelines for developing effective peer learning activities. We then describe four student practices that will foster MLs' engagement in peer learning activities in order to support their oral language development and their engagement with challenging content material. We include tools that you can use when planning and implementing peer learning activities and give you some recommendations for

FIGURE 4.1 DISCUSSION CHECKLIST

STUDENT NAME	SCAFFOLDS USED WITH MLs	USES EXPECTED NONVERBAL COMMUNICATION			SUPPORTS IDEAS WITH EVIDENCE			ASKS CLARIFYING QUESTIONS			MAKES CONNECTIONS TO WHAT OTHERS HAVE SAID			NOTES
		1	2	3	1	2	3	1	2	3	1	2	3	

Key: (1) needs additional support in achieving expectations, (2) meets expectations, and (3) exceeds expectations

different types of peer learning activities to use with MLs. We also include recommendations for using peer learning activities with ML newcomer students and students with limited or interrupted formal education (SLIFE).

Why Is It Important to Focus on Peer Learning for MLs?

Most teachers understand that partner or small-group peer learning activities provide excellent opportunities for MLs' oral language development because each student has more time to talk than in a large-group discussion. In addition, students often feel more comfortable sharing their ideas in a small-group setting, increasing student engagement. However, if appropriately structured, pair and small-group discussions can also be highly beneficial to MLs for other reasons. Figure 4.2 highlights some of the key benefits of peer learning for MLs.

FIGURE 4.2   BENEFITS OF PEER LEARNING FOR MLs

 Oral language development supports literacy development in a second language, particularly in the area of comprehension.

 Academic discussions are a powerful way for MLs to learn content as they provide meaningful opportunities to hear and practice content-specific language and vocabulary.

 Peer learning activities support MLs in developing stronger social emotional skills, academic identity, agency, and voice.

 Peer learning activities provide opportunities for formative assessment.

Sources: August & Shanahan (2006); Escamilla, Olsen, & Slayik (2022); National Academies of Sciences, Engineering, & Medicine [NASEM] (2017); Zwiers (2019).

In the 2017 NASEM report *Promoting the Educational Success of Children and Youth Learning English: Promising Futures*, peer learning is identified as a promising and effective practice for emergent MLs at all grade bands: K–5, 6–8, and 9–12. However, despite the many benefits of peer learning for MLs, opportunities for MLs to engage in academic speaking remain limited. In her work shadowing K–12 MLs across the county, Soto (2021) estimated that MLs appeared to be spending approximately 5 percent to 10 percent of their school day engaged in academic speaking. However, Gibbons (2015) notes that the percentage of time students engage in conversations should be closer to 30 percent. Additionally, even in instances where a teacher includes peer learning activities, MLs may find the work too challenging if they do not understand their expected role in the task they are working on, if they do not feel confident in using the level of language required for the task, or if the task differs greatly from their cultural expectations.

REFLECTION QUESTIONS

Reflect on student speaking time in your context.

1. How often do MLs have the opportunity to engage in discussion with their peers about what they are learning?

2. If opportunities for MLs to engage in discussions are limited, why might this be?

3. Where do opportunities exist to build in more time for ML peer interaction?

 Available for download at **resources.corwin.com/FennerUnlocking2E**

How Do I Develop Effective Peer Learning Activities for MLs?

A critical step in supporting ML engagement in academic conversations is developing peer learning activities that will encourage their participation. To begin exploring this topic, read the following classroom scenarios, and then answer the discussion questions that follow.

APPLICATION ACTIVITY 4.1: GRADE 4 LESSON COMPARISON

Ms. Michael's Lesson: Ms. Michael's fourth-grade class has been learning about the ways that colonists interacted with Indigenous Americans in the New World. They have watched a short video on the topic and completed written questions about the video. Ms. Michael wants to build more peer learning opportunities into her lessons, so before transitioning to a new topic, she asks students to turn and talk. She tells the students that each person in the pair should share one way colonists interacted with Indigenous Americans. As the students talk, Ms. Michael walks around the room. She notices that many of her emergent MLs, even those at intermediate and advanced levels of language proficiency, are saying very little or giving one- or two-word answers. She also notices that other pairs are off task, talking about what they want to do after school or what they did during music class. Ms. Michael feels frustrated and stops the activity after about three or four minutes.

(Continued)

(Continued)

Mr. Thomas's Lesson: Mr. Thomas's fourth-grade class has been learning about the ways that colonists interacted with Indigenous Americans in the New World. They completed a graphic organizer while watching a short video on the topic. Mr. Thomas strategically paused the video to discuss key ideas and provide time for students to add information to their graphic organizers. Mr. Thomas wants to build more peer learning opportunities into his lesson, so before transitioning to a new topic, he instructs students to turn and talk. He writes the prompt on the board, "Which action by the colonists do you believe was the most impactful to Indigenous Americans in the New World? Why?" He provides sample sentence stems for students to use during their turn and talk and models the activity with a student volunteer prior to asking students to engage in discussion with their partner. He also informs students that he will be circulating the room, listening for key ideas and evidence students share. As the students discuss their ideas, Mr. Thomas walks around the room taking notes on key ideas he hears and providing additional support to pairs as needed. He notices that the emergent MLs at the beginning to intermediate levels of language proficiency are referencing their graphic organizers and sentence stems throughout the activity. To conclude the activity, Mr. Thomas displays his notes and highlights several key ideas he heard students discussing.

APPLICATION ACTIVITY 4.1
REFLECTION QUESTIONS

Compare Ms. Michael's and Mr. Thomas's lessons.

1. Which teacher, Ms. Michael or Mr. Thomas, more effectively prepared their emergent MLs to participate in the pair discussion? Explain why.

    _____

    _____

2. What recommendations would you make to Ms. Michael about how to improve the peer learning task she provided to her students?

    _____

    _____

Ms. Michael's lesson described above is a cautionary tale. Just providing students opportunities to talk will not necessarily lead to the desired results. As we can see in this scenario, despite Ms. Michael's good intentions there were several missed opportunities, as her peer learning activity did not meet her expectations, nor did it benefit students to the extent that it might have. Mr. Thomas strategically planned his peer learning activity to more appropriately support his emergent MLs, including providing time for students to prepare for the discussion using a graphic organizer, modeling expectations for the discussion, sharing optional sentence stems, and providing an open-ended discussion prompt. Zwiers (2014, 2019) makes several recommendations for supporting the development of oral language skills. Walqui and Heritage (2018) provide six guidelines for promoting quality interactions for MLs during peer learning activities. We have made connections between these researchers' suggestions and synthesized them, along with contributing our own understanding of their importance for MLs.

1. **Adapt activities to include authentic talk and scaffold ML participation and growth.** This strategy requires that, during peer learning activities, students do not merely read a prepared sentence or two from a piece of paper. They must have opportunities to speak authentically about the topic (Zwiers, 2014, 2019). This can be a challenge for emergent MLs who may not yet have the English language skills or confidence to do so. Be sure to include appropriate scaffolds to support ML participation and growth (Walqui & Heritage, 2018), such as sample sentence stems that increase in complexity and a word bank with visual supports. For more on helping MLs prepare for opportunities for authentic talk, see Practice 1 later in this chapter. In developing peer learning activities, think about how you might structure an activity in order to help prepare students to speak authentically. For example, you might have students discuss a question in small groups and write down their responses. Then, they could practice sharing their responses with each other without their notes. After they have had this opportunity to practice, students could change groups and share their responses with someone new.

2. **Use activities that develop meaningful and robust language.** As was described in the earlier example, students need opportunities to practice, refine, and deepen their oral language responses. Such practice is especially beneficial to MLs, as they are able to hear and use key vocabulary and academic language several times. It also provides MLs, as well as other students, with opportunities to hear the content explained in varied ways and to think about the content from multiple perspectives. Peer learning activities that allow MLs opportunities to practice expressing their ideas in clearer and more compelling ways will support their oral language development and content understanding. Walqui and Heritage (2018) highlight that oral language activities are most effective when they challenge MLs and are designed to incrementally build students' language and content understanding. Examples of these types of activities include the 1-3-6 protocol and debrief circles. For an explanation of these activities, see Figure 4.12.

3. **Be selective in addressing errors and intentional in providing feedback.** Walqui and Heritage (2018) highlight that during peer learning activities MLs may produce language that is comprehensible but that

contains errors. They recommend focusing on providing feedback on errors related to making sense of the academic content, rather than focusing on correcting errors of language production. For instance, if a student uses a technical vocabulary word in a way that interferes with understanding, the teacher can directly explain how to use the word in context in order to support understanding. Teachers should consider the strengths and needs of the individual MLs in their class (e.g., English language proficiency levels, language goals, personality) when making decisions about how much feedback to provide.

4. **Use engaging discussion prompts that create a need to talk and contain clear expectations and directions.** Zwiers (2014, 2019) recommends discussion prompts that require students to share information and build one or more ideas. The prompts should align with clearly defined lesson goals and integrate reading and writing (Walqui & Heritage, 2018). If you ask students to reshape, choose, or do something with ideas, it is likely to foster greater discussion and debate among students than if you ask them merely to identify. Zwiers (2019) identifies the following verbs to use when developing engaging prompts: *agree on, create, clarify, argue, decide, rank, prioritize, come up with, solve, evaluate, combine, compare, choose, fortify, build, weigh,* and *transform.* As we saw in the scenario in Application Activity 4.1, Ms. Michael's discussion prompt was insufficient to garner much student interest in the topic as it simply asked students to identify. Students in Mr. Thomas' class had more to say because he used a discussion prompt that asked students to both prioritize and explain.

FIGURE 4.3   ENGAGING DISCUSSION PROMPT

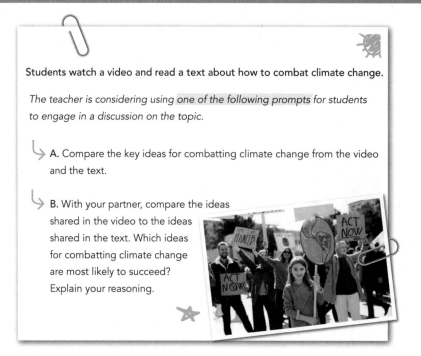

Students watch a video and read a text about how to combat climate change.

The teacher is considering using one of the following prompts *for students to engage in a discussion on the topic.*

A. Compare the key ideas for combatting climate change from the video and the text.

B. With your partner, compare the ideas shared in the video to the ideas shared in the text. Which ideas for combatting climate change are most likely to succeed? Explain your reasoning.

Source: iStock.com/Halfpoint

REFLECTION QUESTION

Which prompt related to combatting climate change in Figure 4.3 is more effective? Why?

online resources ⟋ Available for download at **resources.corwin.com/FennerUnlocking2E**

The types of questions and prompts teachers develop are important for fostering student participation and engagement (Ward Singer, 2018; Zwiers, 2010). Figure 4.4 provides examples of these types of prompts and questions that will encourage meaningful communication and student learning. We have adapted this table (Zwiers, 2010) to include specific considerations for MLs.

FIGURE 4.4	TYPES OF QUESTIONS, CONSIDERATIONS FOR MLs, AND EXAMPLES	
CREATE QUESTIONS THAT . . .	**ML CONSIDERATION**	**EXAMPLE QUESTION**
Focus students on key content concepts.	Ensure MLs have the proper scaffolding (e.g., visuals, glossaries, and home language support) to focus on key content concepts.	Discuss the purpose of the *Bill of Rights*. Agree on why it is important.
Allow for divergent and personalized responses, as long as they connect back to evidence in the material being studied.	Ensure that MLs' background experiences and cultures are valued and drawn from during instruction.	With your partner, come up with a list of all the ways your school manages waste. Rank your list from most effective to least effective.
Emphasize one or more thinking skills being developed in the lesson and unit. Such skills include questioning, interpreting, classifying, persuading, evaluating, analyzing, comparing, and synthesizing.	Provide supports so that MLs can engage in these higher order thinking skills, including modeling the skill, posting sentence stems and frames, and providing time for MLs to practice the skill.	Consider the character's actions throughout the story. What can you infer about the character's relationship with his grandmother based on his actions?
Deepen understandings and emphasize the essential objectives of the text, lesson, or unit.	Ensure that MLs understand the essential objectives and that instruction of academic language is intertwined with instruction of the content.	Think about today's activity. What does the activity have to do with our goal of learning how plants get the materials they need to grow?

Source: Adapted from Think-pair-share tips by Jeff Zwiers. Retrieved from http://jeffzwiers.org/tools

What Practices Can MLs Engage in to Support Their Participation and Engagement in Peer Learning Activities?

In order to support MLs' participation and engagement in peer learning, we have developed four practices for supporting this engagement as well as instructional tools that can support these practices. These practices were synthesized and adapted from Zwiers and Crawford's (2011) work to account for the specific strengths and needs of MLs. The four practices are shown in Figure 4.5.

FIGURE 4.5   FOUR PRACTICES FOR SUPPORTING MLs IN PEER LEARNING ACTIVITIES

Come to the discussion prepared

Be aware of nonverbal communication

Participate by taking turns

Make connections

We will be discussing each of these practices in depth, providing example scenarios to illustrate the practices and tools that can support the practices. In addition to focusing on these practices, it is also important for teachers to create a classroom climate that supports sharing diverse ideas, respectful listening, and active participation. Students need to understand that academic conversations during peer learning activities are an opportunity for them to think more deeply and critically about a topic, and they will be able to do this deeper-level thinking when they take the opportunity to share their ideas and listen to the ideas of others. In fact, research indicates that peer interaction provides an opportunity for scaffolding language learning as MLs receive feedback from one another on language forms, which supports future learning and use of language (Blum-Kulka & Snow, 2004; Kibler, 2017).

Practice 1: Come to the discussion prepared.

In order for MLs to successfully participate in an academic discussion, they must have sufficient preparation in the content they will be discussing. It is unfair to expect MLs to engage in pair or small-group tasks in which they feel unprepared to contribute. In order to support MLs in being prepared for the peer learning activity, you can draw on many of the strategies that we address in this book, including the following:

- Using scaffolded materials (Chapter 3)

- Modeling (Chapter 3)

- Explicit vocabulary instruction (Chapter 5)

- Developing academic language at the sentence and discourse levels (Chapter 6)

- Instruction of essential background knowledge (Chapter 7)

- Strategies for supporting reading and writing (Chapter 8)

This doesn't mean that peer learning activities should only be used to summarize what students already know but rather that MLs should have sufficient content and language knowledge and support in order to be able to take their understanding of the content to a deeper level. For example, in the opening vignette about Mr. Hernandez's eighth-grade science class, prior to the discussion, students had learned key vocabulary, read a short text on the relationships among organisms in an ecosystem, and answered open-ended questions about the text. Students were also given a word bank containing the list of vocabulary that they had been studying and sentence stems to support their participation in discussions.

In structuring group and pair discussions, it can be helpful for MLs to have written ideas or notes for reference. However, it is also important to help students transition to being able to speak without the use of notes so as to support more authentic conversations. For example, students could use sticky notes to write down ideas that they have that they want to share with the class as they are reading. In this way, students can remember their big ideas but not be overly dependent on written notes in a discussion.

Part of supporting MLs in being prepared is also helping them build their confidence to participate in academic conversations. For example, you might first have students think about their responses to a text individually and take notes on their responses (as was described above with the use of sticky notes). Then, they can share their responses with a partner. This structure allows them to practice in a lower anxiety-producing context. Finally, you can ask students to share their responses with the whole group. In addition to building confidence, this method also allows MLs to process the academic content and language from reading about it, writing notes about it, saying it to one person as a rehearsal, and then saying it confidently to the whole group as a more polished product. It is important to note that some MLs (those with lower levels of language proficiency or those who are less confident speaking in front of a group) may need more time before they are ready to speak in front of the whole class.

Practice 2: Be aware of nonverbal communication.

In order to effectively participate in peer learning activities, students must understand that there are certain cultural expectations for how they should conduct themselves when participating in a discussion. Zwiers and Crawford (2011) identify the following nonverbal communication behaviors as those valued in an academic setting:

- "Appropriate" eye contact (which can mean not constantly staring at the other person but also not always looking down, away, or past the other person)

- Facing one another with the entire body

- Leaning toward the person speaking

- Showing understanding through head nodding

- "Appropriate" gesturing (not rolling eyes, sighing, or folding arms)

- Showing interest by laughing and smiling appropriately

- Using encouraging language to promote continued conversation (e.g., uh huh, hmm, interesting, yes, okay)

- Interrupting to ask for clarification if needed (pp. 41–42)

It is likely apparent from reviewing this list that these behaviors are the expectations of teachers from the dominant culture, and it is important to note that nonverbal communication may be incongruent across cultures (Staehr Fenner & Teich, in press). It is also worth noting that the rise of online communication through social media and its acceleration during the COVID-19 pandemic may have had an impact on all students' use of and understanding of nonverbal communication (Paradisi et al., 2021). Explicitly teaching and practicing these skills is essential to supporting students' understanding of the role of nonverbal communication during peer learning activities.

Expected nonverbal communication in U.S. culture may not be appropriate in other cultures or for neurodivergent students, and you should exercise caution in how you use nonverbal communication when interacting with students from diverse backgrounds (Staehr Fenner & Teich, in press). You can provide students with some examples of how expectations of nonverbal communication vary among cultures as a way of getting the discussion started, and you can also ask students to provide their own examples. For example, in the United States, making eye contact with a speaker shows that you are interested in what they have to say. However, in other cultures, eye contact may be perceived as a challenge, or extended eye contact between members of the opposite sex may be considered taboo. As you explain what is considered expected nonverbal communication in U.S. culture, be sure to demonstrate respect for your MLs' cultures and validate them.

REFLECTION QUESTION

How might the MLs in your classroom have different understandings or expectations for what a conversation looks like (e.g., both in terms of nonverbal communication and communication patterns)?

 Available for download at **resources.corwin.com/FennerUnlocking2E**

Another strategy for teaching MLs about expected nonverbal communication for conversations is to model nonverbal communication that does not align with what is valued in U.S. academic settings. To do so, you could find video clips to share or do a role-play with a coteacher (if you have one) while the class observes. Then, you could discuss what reactions the students observed and what alternative nonverbal communication could look like. You could also use this opportunity to discuss how cultural expectations for nonverbal communication vary among cultures (e.g., in some cultures, students stand up when the teacher enters the room).

In order to reinforce understanding of nonverbal communication, you could use an observation checklist to monitor student communication (see Figure 4.1 as an example). You could also have students complete a self-assessment in which they reflect on their own nonverbal communication during discussions (see Figure 4.6 as an example).

FIGURE 4.6   PARTICIPATION PROTOCOL SELF-ASSESSMENT CHECKLIST

Directions: Reflect on today's partner activity. Next, read each statement, and check the box that reflects how you engaged with your partner.

DURING TODAY'S ACTIVITY, I . . .	ALWAYS	SOMETIMES	NEVER
1. Looked at my partner(s)			
2. Leaned toward my partner			
3. Used my quiet conversation voice			
4. Listened attentively			
5. Used evidence and examples			
REFLECTION			
Something I did well was . . .			
Something I would like to improve next time is . . .			

Source: Adapted from Teaching Channel (2014).

Practice 3: Participate by taking turns.

It is important for students to take turns speaking. In pairs, it is likely that turn-taking will occur naturally. However, in a small or large group, it can be challenging for MLs to have their turn. A tool such as a talking rock or talking stick (a rock or a stick that students hold to "give them the floor" to talk) can encourage all members of the group to take part in the discussion. Students can pass the talking rock or talking stick around in a circle, and the student who has the rock or stick can take the opportunity to say something or pass. The rock or stick can also be placed in the center of the group, and students can take it as they have something to say. Another take on a talking rock or talking stick is to use talking chips. Each student is provided with a set number of talking chips. As they share an idea, they add a chip to the center of the table. Once a student's chips are gone, they cannot add an idea until others have contributed chips. This encourages participation by all, not just those who are the most outgoing. Of course, some students are quieter than others and may not feel comfortable sharing aloud, especially emergent MLs at the beginning stages of language proficiency. Additionally, in many cultures students aren't expected to speak in pairs or small groups, and in some cultures, people speak over each other. To account for these variations, students may add their chips to the center when they hear an idea that they agree with or have also thought of.

Here you see an example of talking sticks that can be used to encourage turn-taking. Students use these sticks while working in pairs as a reminder of who is the speaker and who is the listener.

How you set up your activity and the supports you provide can encourage greater participation by all students, including MLs. Some examples of visual tools that would support participation include graphic organizers (e.g., story map, timeline, or Venn diagram), manipulatives, and objects connected to the unit. For example, you might have students complete a timeline to sequence key historical events from the unit. In small groups, they can be required to take turns sharing which events they believe have enough significance to place on the timeline and why. In this example, both the structure of the activity and the tool (timeline) would support participation by all members of the group. Similarly, you could have students work in pairs to use manipulatives to explain how they solved a particular math problem. They could discuss how they could take different approaches to solve the same problem or how they might use a similar approach to solve different problems.

Figure 4.7 provides an example of an activity that you can use to have students speak to several different students. Students will have short conversations with three to four students in the class and summarize each person's response, first orally and then in writing, in an interview grid. The teacher could ask the students to write down three names in the column under "Name" that the teacher assigns as interviewees to one student. The teacher may want to consider assigning interviewees who speak the same home language as the interviewer or perhaps assigning a native English speaker who is supportive to an emergent ML at the beginning stages of language proficiency.

FIGURE 4.7   INTERVIEW GRID FOR HIGH SCHOOL BIOLOGY CLASS

Name	Contrast the differences between prokaryotic and eukaryotic cells	Explain how mitochondria convert energy in cells	Argue why cells must be small in size
Marcelo			
Sofia			
Amadou			

You could also adapt this activity to develop an information gap activity (see Figure 4.8). For example, you could have two different sets of one to two questions and assign each student to either Group A or Group B. Each group first meets together to discuss their question(s) and plan their response. Then, in pairs, students from Group A would meet up with Group B members in order to ask their questions. At the end of the activity, the class could compile a list of possible responses. Emergent MLs of lower proficiency levels may need word banks or sentence stems as support for this activity.

FIGURE 4.8   GAP ACTIVITY FOR HIGH SCHOOL BIOLOGY CLASS

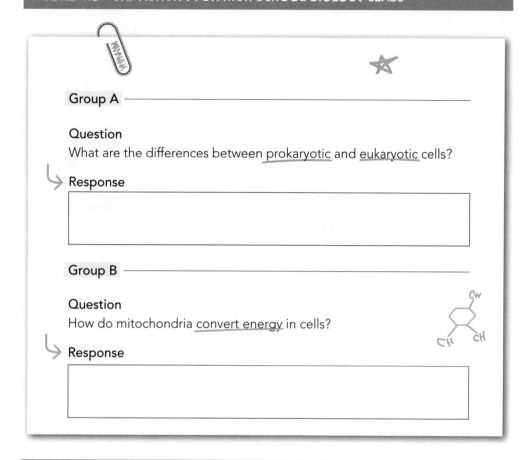

Group A

Question
What are the differences between prokaryotic and eukaryotic cells?

Response

Group B

Question
How do mitochondria convert energy in cells?

Response

An additional way to encourage turn-taking is to teach and model strategies for inviting someone into the conversation (e.g., Farah, what do you predict the girl in the story will do next?). You can model these strategies, and you can also teach students to use these strategies in their small group. Emergent MLs of lower language proficiency levels or those who may feel particularly uncomfortable speaking in a group should be given confidence-building opportunities to practice speaking and hearing their own voice in both small groups and whole groups. For example, this could mean asking students to read the learning objective for the day or directions that are written on the board. It might also mean wrapping up a whole-group discussion by asking a question that all students who haven't yet contributed to the conversation are invited to answer (e.g., What was one idea you found most interesting from today's discussion?). If you plan to ask students who haven't yet contributed to answer a question, it is helpful to tell students that you will be doing that, so they know to expect it. These types of opportunities to speak will help build students' confidence in their abilities.

Practice 4: Make connections.

Not only do students need to be able to share their own opinions by using evidence from texts or content material being studied, but they also need to interact with others' ideas. Modeling and providing MLs with key phrases can support them in their efforts to build on others' ideas. Some educators use the term *talk moves* to describe the discourse actions that students need to practice in order to effectively engage in a discussion. Such actions include restating what was said, agreeing and disagreeing, asking clarifying questions, adding to or piggybacking on what someone has said, and making connections between ideas.

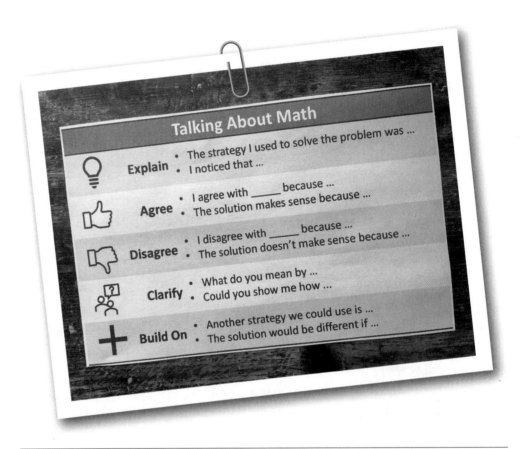

Here you see an example of math talk moves that can be taped to students' desks as a resource for them to access during discussions.

You can post sentence stems that correspond to the various talk moves on the wall or provide the stems at students' desks. You can encourage students to use them as they monitor small-group discussions or during whole-group discussions. Depending on your MLs' language abilities, you could give them simpler or more complex language to use. Figure 4.9 includes some possible sentence stems for specific types of talk moves.

A game that you can play to help your MLs practice using different types of talk moves is Conversation Bingo. Each student receives a Conversation Bingo card with sentence starters on it. Over the course of a week, when students use one of the sentence starters, they get to cross it off. Once students have crossed off

FIGURE 4.9   TALK MOVES WITH SENTENCE STEMS AND FRAMES

TALK MOVE	SENTENCE STEM OR FRAME
Restating	• So you are saying . . . • What I understood you to say is . . .
Agreeing	• I agree with (Yuri) because . . . • (Emma's) point about . . . was important because . . .
Disagreeing	• I disagree because . . . • I see it differently because . . .
Asking a clarifying question	• Could you give an example of . . . ? • I'm confused when you say . . .
Adding to an idea	• I'd like to add to (Tram's) point. I think that . . . • I agree with (Woo Jin), and furthermore I think that . . .
Making connections between ideas	• When (Albert) said . . . , it reminded me of . . . • I see a connection between what (Laura) said and what (Karolina) said. The connection is . . .

Source: Staehr Fenner, D., & Snyder, S. (2015b). Icons by iStock.com/Ros4Jesus

a complete horizontal, vertical, or diagonal line, they can use it to be a listener for another group, win a prize, or earn bonus points for getting bingo and using five different conversation starters (L. Kuti, personal communication, September 22, 2016).

A conversation mini lesson is a way for teachers to introduce a conversation skill to students and then have them practice it in a relatively short time period. Examples of possible mini lessons could include asking each other for supporting examples, building on a partner's idea, and paraphrasing conversation themes. Mini lessons should include opportunities for students to watch and analyze strong models of the conversation skill being focused on and opportunities to practice and build independent skills.

In Figure 4.10, we have developed a checklist to account for the four practices for supporting MLs' participation and engagement in peer learning. Use this checklist as a guide for developing peer learning activities that will support MLs' active participation and engagement.

FIGURE 4.10   PEER LEARNING ACTIVITY CHECKLIST

CRITERIA	YES	NO	FOLLOW-UP STEPS
1. Have I developed a peer learning activity that will provide my MLs with • authentic opportunities to speak, • time to strengthen and deepen their responses, and • an engaging discussion prompt or task? *(Practice 1)*			
2. Have my MLs had sufficient exposure to the content and academic language needed to participate in the activity? *(Practice 1)*			
3. Have my MLs been taught expected nonverbal communication to support peer learning activities (e.g., looking at people when speaking, nodding understanding)? *(Practice 2)*			
4. Do I have a way of monitoring students' nonverbal communication? *(Practice 2)*			
5. Have I provided sufficient structure to the activity (including the use of supporting tools) and clear evaluation criteria so as to encourage all of my MLs to participate in the activity? *(Practice 3)*			
6. Have I thought about how to intentionally group students? *(Practice 3)*			
7. Have I considered assigning roles to students? *(Practice 3)*			
8. Have I given sufficient thought to how to structure the classroom so that students can effectively interact and work together? *(Practice 3)*			
9. Have I provided MLs sufficient practice and support in making connections to others' ideas before and during the activity? *(Practice 4)*			
10. Have I considered how I might use the activity to assess MLs' acquisition and use of academic language or understanding of content? *(Practice 4)*			

Source: Adapted from Snyder & Staehr Fenner (2021), p. 172–173.

 Available for download at **resources.corwin.com/FennerUnlocking2E**

APPLICATION ACTIVITY 4.2: MS. RAWLINGS SCENARIO REFLECTION

Before we move on to describe some different types of peer learning activities, read the following vignette about a cotaught elementary English language arts class. As you read it, reflect on the following questions:

APPLICATION ACTIVITY 4.2: REFLECTION QUESTIONS

1. The class described in the vignette is composed of six emergent MLs at the low intermediate level of language proficiency. How might you differentiate the instruction to meet the needs of emergent MLs of varying language proficiency levels?

    _____

    _____

2. How might a classroom teacher without the benefit of an English language development (ELD) coteacher adapt some of the strategies Ms. Rawlings uses during her small-group lesson to meet the needs of emergent MLs?

    _____

    _____

online resources Available for download at **resources.corwin.com/FennerUnlocking2E**

Scenario: Ms. Rawlings is an ELD teacher in a school with a growing ML population. She coteaches with third-grade teacher Ms. Tomas. Their primary goal as coteachers is to ensure that all MLs in the class can access the grade-level curricula. There are six emergent ML students in the class, and they are all at a low intermediate level of language proficiency, which means they know and use some social and academic language with visual support.

Students are learning about folktales in their English language arts unit. During a coplanning session, Ms. Tomas shares that the emergent MLs in the class need to develop more background knowledge around key elements of folktales and the specific content vocabulary involved in discussing them. She also notes that they are working on getting more comfortable with speaking in class in general. Ms. Rawlings uses this information to plan for a teacher-led small-group lesson that will take place within the grade-level classroom during small-group rotations.

(Continued)

(Continued)

In previous classes, Ms. Tomas and Ms. Rawlings worked with the whole class to establish discussion norms that included the following:

- Listen carefully to others

- Explain my ideas

- Ask questions when I am confused

- Participate

- Connect my ideas to others' ideas

They also created an anchor chart of key sentence frames for giving examples (e.g., *An example of this is _____*), agreeing or disagreeing (e.g., *I agree with _____ because* and *I respectfully disagree*), and supporting claims with evidence (e.g., *I think _____ because _____*). In a previous small-group session with the emergent MLs in the class, Ms. Rawlings has modeled using the frames and has set up simple practice activities using social topics to get students more comfortable with using this academic discussion language in a more familiar context. For example, they have discussed whether or not they should be allowed to chew gum in school.

During this teacher-led small-group lesson, Ms. Rawlings and her students review their discussion norms and frames chart. Then, she reads her students *Martina, the Beautiful Cockroach (A Cuban Folktale)* and introduces key vocabulary for folktale elements. Each vocabulary word is accompanied by a visual and a sample sentence containing the new vocabulary items. Then, as a group, the students identify the elements in the folktale they just read on a graphic organizer. As they respond, Ms. Rawlings uses probes to encourage more language use. A phrase such as "say more" elicits more language and encourages them to go into more detail in a nonthreatening way. It also communicates her interest in what they have to say. At times, she asks her students to clarify their thinking by rephrasing what they've said: "So are you saying _____?" This again communicates her desire to understand what they are trying to say and gives them the opportunity to better explain their ideas.

Ms. Rawlings continues, "Can you find an example of _____ in the book?" As she prompts students, she gestures toward their sentence frame chart to encourage their use of the academic discussion language they've been practicing in previous whole-group lessons. A student flips through the book and describes the example using the sentence frame she's been learning. Ms. Rawlings turns to one of her other students, "Can you rephrase or repeat what _____ just said?" This seemingly simple act encourages careful listening by all. She then follows up, "Do you agree with _____? Why, or why not? What's your evidence for _____?"

As a whole class, they continue discussing the different elements of a folktale. Their whole-class follow-up lesson later in the week is to read a new, unfamiliar folktale, record the elements together, and discuss it using their folktale elements and language charts. Eventually, all students read and analyze a folktale independently using a graphic organizer to record their responses. They then come together and have a discussion around what they have found. This final activity offers several opportunities for peer learning.

What Are Some Effective Peer Learning Activities for MLs?

There are many different peer learning activities that you can use in your classroom to support MLs' oral language development and content understanding. As you are deciding what activity to use, reflect on your learning objectives for the activity and what type of activity will best help your students meet those objectives. Also, remember, the activity should accomplish the following goals:

- Provide students opportunities to hear and practice key academic language

- Be structured in such a way so that all students will have an opportunity (and sufficient support) to share their ideas

- Push student understanding of content to deeper levels

We have described a few of our favorite activities to support MLs' oral language development and content understanding here, beginning with a more in-depth description of Socratic circles. You can adapt these activities to meet the specific needs of the MLs in your classroom by providing various types of scaffolding, such as sentence frames, sentence stems, word banks, and strategic student grouping. You can also encourage (or require) students to use specific vocabulary in their conversations.

Socratic Circle

We would first like to explain an activity that may take a bit more preparation to use successfully with MLs but one that can be highly effective for all students once they are familiar with the process. It is most commonly used with middle and high school students. A **Socratic circle, also known as Socratic seminar, is a teaching strategy used to support deep understanding of a specific piece of writing, music, or art**. It is based on Socrates's belief in the importance of developing students' ability to think critically and independently through the use of dialogue. The focus of the Socratic method is on giving students questions rather than answers. By posing and responding to questions, students examine and reevaluate their beliefs on a particular topic. In addition to fostering critical thinking, Socratic circles are designed to support student collaboration, creativity, and intellectual curiosity.

Prior to the Socratic circle activity, students read, analyze, and take notes on a common "text" (e.g., novel, poem, song, or painting). Students are then typically divided into two groups—an inner and an outer circle. The activity begins with the inner circle of students engaging in dialogue about the text and the outer circle observing. After a specified period of time, the outer circle provides feedback to the inner circle on their conversation, and the two groups of students switch roles. Throughout the activity, the teacher acts as a facilitator. The activity is not meant to result in a winning argument, as opposed to debates. Students are expected to use the text to support their ideas, ask questions, share their opinions, and build on the ideas of others.

Although they present great potential to engage students in discussions around complex text, Socratic circles can be especially challenging to MLs. First of all, the mere thought of having to speak about a nuanced topic in front of the entire class without linguistic support could be especially nerve racking for emergent MLs who are at lower levels of proficiency (or quiet students in general). In order to effectively participate in this type of discourse, MLs need to have a deep understanding of the text being discussed.

Also, the pace and language of the discussion may prove a challenge for some MLs who need time and support to "digest" what others are saying and frame their ideas before presenting them orally. In addition, without specific support, MLs may not have the academic language necessary to orally summarize, refute, or support the ideas of others. Figure 4.11 provides specific strategies to help MLs prepare for and participate in Socratic circles.

FIGURE 4.11   HELPING MLs PREPARE FOR A SOCRATIC CIRCLE

STRATEGY	RECOMMENDATIONS FOR MLs
Preparing for Socratic circles: MLs need deep understanding of the text.	• Be sure that students are adequately prepared for the activity by giving them sufficient scaffolding to understand the text (e.g., concise background knowledge, glossaries, and scaffolded text-dependent questions). • Provide students with graphic organizers to help them frame their thinking about the text in writing. • Give students practice and support in developing open-ended questions about a particular text. • Give students practice in anticipating the types of open-ended questions that other students might ask about a text.

Modeling: MLs need to know what high-quality responses and questions sound like.	• Model a successful Socratic circle by first practicing the following steps with a familiar text at a lower level of complexity.
	    ○ Provide MLs with opportunities to practice questioning and responding in small groups before expecting them to participate in a whole-class discussion.
	    ○ Provide sentence stems that students can use in asking and responding to questions, clarifying others' ideas, and commenting on the ideas of others. Give students practice in using these stems.
	    ○ Highlight questions or responses that are particularly effective. Explain why those particular questions or responses are of high quality.

Balancing Participation: Help support MLs' participation in the discussion.	• If some students are dominating the discussion, limit all participants to a certain number of questions and responses. • Guide students to invite those who are less active to participate (e.g., "Marisol, what do you think about what Sam said?"). • As the facilitator, use the last few minutes of the discussion to invite those students who haven't asked a question to take part in the discussion. • Be comfortable with silence. The time will allow those who need more time to think more opportunities to participate.

Source: Staehr Fenner & Snyder (2015a).

In Figure 4.12, we outline eight additional peer learning activities for supporting MLs' oral language development and content understanding. As you read each one, consider how you might use the activity in your classroom or suggest to a colleague how it could be used in their classroom.

FIGURE 4.12	PEER LEARNING ACTIVITIES AND RESOURCES	
ACTIVITY	**DESCRIPTION**	**CONSIDERATIONS FOR USE IN MY CLASSROOM**
Barometer: Take a Stand	• Select a statement that students can have an opinion about and is connected to your lesson. • Ask students who agree with the statement to go to one end of the classroom and students who disagree to go to the other end. • Students who are neutral or undecided can go to the center of the room. • Have students find a partner in their group and share why they went where they did. Or, have students find someone in a different group to discuss why they went where they did. • Invite several students to share their ideas with the large group. • Ask if any students have changed their minds after hearing the discussion.	
Carousel	• Write questions connected to the unit of study on poster paper and hang them up around the room (one piece of poster paper per question). • Divide students into small groups so that there is one question per group. • Give each group of students a different color marker and assign them a question to start with. • Instruct students to discuss and write their responses on the poster paper. • Have the groups rotate to another question after several minutes. • Encourage the groups to add on to and provide additional evidence to the responses that are already written. • Debrief each question as a whole class, providing appropriate scaffolds for your MLs.	
Debrief Circles (also known as Reel Activity or Parallel Lines)	• Give each student an index card, and ask them to answer two questions (one on each side of the card). • Have students count off by twos. • Have students form two concentric circles, with one student facing another student (e.g., number ones in the inner circle and number twos in the outer circle). • Instruct students to share their responses to one of the questions with each other.	

(Continued)

(Continued)

ACTIVITY	DESCRIPTION	CONSIDERATIONS FOR USE IN MY CLASSROOM
	• Have students in the inner circle move one or two students to the left and then share their responses to the second question. • Consider having students move multiple times, each time sharing their responses and hearing other students' responses. You can also have students put away their index cards as they gain increasing confidence in speaking about the topic. • Ask students to compare how their responses differed from those of their peers or to share whether their responses changed based on listening to their peers.	
Gap Activity	• Put students in pairs. • Provide each student in the pair different information. • Have students ask each other questions in order to complete a task. • For example, one student might have a math word problem to solve. However, the partner's handout has all the numbers that are needed to solve the problem. Partner A must ask Partner B questions in order to solve the problem.	
Numbered Heads Together	• Set up student desks so that they are clustered in groups facing each other. • Assign each group member a number. • Pose a question or challenge to the class. • Instruct each group to discuss their ideas and come to a consensus on a response. • Identify a number and ask the group member assigned that number to share their group's response.	
Role Play	• Students might feel intimidated or strange using academic language to discuss an issue. Role-playing can be a good way to have students tackle these issues under the guise of another persona. • For example, during a science unit focused on conservation, you might ask students to take on specific roles (e.g., a scientist and a businessperson) and discuss, in pairs, the pros and cons of renewable energy sources, such as wind or solar energy.	
World Café	• Put students in groups of three to four. • Give each group a different topic or a question to discuss. All topics and questions should share a common theme. • Have each group select a leader to take notes on the discussion on a piece of poster paper. • Instruct all students, except for the leader, to move to another discussion group. Students do not have to stay in the same groups. • Have the leader provide highlights of the previous discussion to the new group. • Assign a new leader in each group. The new group discusses the same topic or question and adds to the notes. • Debrief the activity, by hanging the posters in front of the class and having students share highlights from their discussion.	

ACTIVITY	DESCRIPTION	CONSIDERATIONS FOR USE IN MY CLASSROOM
1-3-6 Protocol	• Provide students with a discussion question or task to work on individually. • Have students move to a group of three where they discuss their responses to the question. • Have two groups of three combine to form a group of six. With the group of six, instruct students to finalize their answers to the question and present these to the large group.	
Suggested scaffolds: Anchor charts, graphic organizers, home language materials, intentional student grouping, modeling, pretaught vocabulary, sentence frames and stems, visuals and manipulatives, word banks, and word walls		

Source: Adapted from Snyder & Staehr Fenner (2021), p. 182–185.

REFLECTION QUESTIONS

1. Which peer learning activity would you like to try in your context?

2. What scaffolds will you embed in the activity to support the MLs in your classroom?

 Available for download at **resources.corwin.com/FennerUnlocking2E**

Now that we've explored specific strategies to foster MLs' oral language development and content understanding, let's take a look at some considerations for ML newcomer students and SLIFE and the role of collaboration, equity, advocacy, and leadership when engaging in peer learning activities.

ML NEWCOMER STUDENTS AND SLIFE CONSIDERATIONS

What Are Key Considerations for Supporting ML Newcomer Students and SLIFE During Peer Learning Activities?

ML newcomer students and SLIFE need targeted supports for successful participation in peer learning activities.

Considerations:

• As we pointed out in Chapter 2, it is important to recognize that ML newcomer students and SLIFE may be coming from collectivist cultures. Students from collectivist cultures may prefer to work in groups rather than individually. This

(Continued)

(Continued)

is an area of strength MLs bring to the classroom that can be built on. When possible, group students that share the same home language and encourage them to use the language of their choice during peer learning activities.

- Recognize the importance of developing listening skills as part of the second language acquisition process. When ML newcomer students and SLIFE work in pairs and small groups, they may initially feel more comfortable listening than producing language. Teachers can use this as a learning opportunity and build active listening into peer learning activities. For instance, ML newcomer students and SLIFE can be tasked with listening for and noting or highlighting key words during a discussion.

- Background knowledge plays a critical role in students understanding a lesson or task. Get to know your ML newcomer students and SLIFE and the background knowledge they bring to the classroom. Whenever possible, tap into their background knowledge to help prepare them to participate in a peer learning activity. Leveraging the experiences and knowledge MLs bring to the classroom can help to create a safe space in which students feel more comfortable taking risks using their new language.

Example: Joseph, the seventh-grade student from the Democratic Republic of Congo who was introduced in Chapter 2, is in a physical education and health class with his teacher Mr. Engel. In the current unit, students are exploring personal fitness. As an introduction to the unit, Mr. Engel has set up a carousel activity in which students work in small groups to view and discuss various examples of personal fitness. During their discussions, students are expected to identify and analyze different activities and exercises they notice in terms of their potential fitness benefits (e.g., cardiovascular endurance, muscular strength and endurance, flexibility, and body composition). Mr. Engel embeds a number of scaffolds into the activity to support Joseph's active participation. First, he intentionally places Joseph in a group with another student, Ambar, who speaks Swahili. He also provides Joseph with sentence frames and a word bank that includes visual support. During a warm-up activity, Mr. Engel works individually with Joseph to model using the sentence frames and word bank. Throughout the carousel activity Mr. Engel checks in on Joseph's group and provides additional support, as needed, including encouraging Joseph to share ideas in Swahili and act things out to explain his thinking.

How Can I Collaborate Around Peer Learning for MLs?

The inclusion of peer interaction in lessons is an excellent opportunity for ELD teachers and content teachers to collaborate. Figure 4.13 illustrates the different roles teachers might fill in preparing for and teaching lessons that incorporate peer learning. Please note that these are recommendations and should be adapted to your context.

FIGURE 4.13   POTENTIAL ROLES FOR TEACHING ACADEMIC CONVERSATIONS IN A COLLABORATIVE SETTING

CONTENT TEACHERS	ELD TEACHERS	BOTH
• Develop peer learning activity and prompt to support student understanding of content. • Be explicit with students about why they are practicing oral language skills and what academic conversations include. • Develop checklists and other assessments to monitor student progress (including self-assessments for students).	• Determine supports needed for MLs to effectively participate in a peer learning activity. • Share cultural expectations that may impact MLs' participation. • Develop scaffolds to support MLs' understanding of content and participation in activity (e.g., background knowledge instruction and sentence stems). • Work with small groups of MLs to provide targeted language instruction.	• Model expectations for discussions. • Teach mini lessons on skills used during discussions (e.g., agreeing, disagreeing, and adding on). • Model language for encouraging deeper thinking on a topic (e.g., Can you say more about that?). • Monitor student participation and language development.

What Is the Role of Equity, Advocacy, and Leadership in Supporting Peer Learning for MLs?

The focus on oral English language development that is included in most ELD programs is insufficient to meet the needs of MLs (August & Shanahan, 2006). By developing lessons that support MLs' participation and engagement in peer learning activities, you are advocating for MLs' equal access to content, supporting high academic expectations for MLs, and providing MLs with opportunities to develop their academic identity. You are also creating a classroom climate that encourages the sharing of diverse perspectives and the development of critical-thinking skills. As students acquire the skills to take part in peer learning activities, they learn the ways in which hearing diverse perspectives can broaden their own thinking. They also can recognize the feeling that comes from being really listened to and having their ideas valued. Thus, as you focus on the often underused area of peer learning, you are fostering MLs' equitable and excellent education and advocating for MLs' voices to be heard in their classrooms.

Next Steps

In order to help you get started thinking about how you might incorporate peer learning activities into your unit plan, we have developed a planning template that uses the four-practices framework.

APPLICATION ACTIVITY 4.3: PEER LEARNING ACTIVITY PLANNING

For the final application activity of this chapter, use the Peer Learning Activity Planning Template (Figure 4.14) to plan for building opportunities for peer interaction into your unit plan. Note that the Peer Learning Activity Template can also be used as a standalone tool.

FIGURE 4.14　PEER LEARNING ACTIVITY PLANNING TEMPLATE

Unit or lesson topic:

_____

_____

Content objective(s):

_____

_____

Language objective(s):

_____

_____

Oral language task:

_____

_____

PRACTICE 1: COME TO THE DISCUSSION PREPARED.	PRACTICE 2: BE AWARE OF NONVERBAL COMMUNICATION.
How will you help MLs prepare for the discussion?	How will you support MLs in using expected nonverbal communication during the discussion?
_____ _____	_____ _____

_____   _____

_____   _____

_____   _____

PRACTICE 3: PARTICIPATE BY TAKING TURNS.	PRACTICE 4: MAKE CONNECTIONS.
How will you support MLs in taking turns during the discussion?	How will you support MLs in making connections to what others have said and what they have previously learned?

_____   _____

_____   _____

_____   _____

_____   _____

_____   _____

online resources ☞ Available for download at **resources.corwin.com/FennerUnlocking2E**

Now, add your plans to the *Unit Delivery: ML Strategies*; and *Sequence and Activities* sections of the Unlocking MLs' Potential Unit Planning Template (the portion of Appendix A reproduced as Figure 4.15). Appendix A can be found in the online companion website. To access the companion website, please visit resources.corwin.com/FennerUnlocking2E.

UNLOCKING RESOURCES

resources.corwin .com/FennerUnlocking2E

FIGURE 4.15 PORTION OF THE UNLOCKING MLs' POTENTIAL UNIT PLANNING TEMPLATE (APPENDIX A)

UNIT DELIVERY		
ML Strategies Included (Check all that apply)		
☐ Activate prior knowledge	☐ Peer interaction	☐ Word/phrase-level strategies
☐ Teach new background knowledge	☐ Collaborative reading strategies	☐ Sentence-level strategies
☐ Formative assessment strategies	☐ Collaborative writing strategies	☐ Discourse-level strategies

(Continued)

(Continued)

Unit Sequence and Activities

Figure 4.14 Peer Learning Activity Planning Template

How will you ensure there are **opportunities for language practice in all domains**?

How will you ensure that **lessons build upon each other to progress towards mastery** of content and language objectives?

For **co-teaching partnerships**, identify the role of the ELD teacher and content teacher.

LESSON OBJECTIVES	LEARNING ACTIVITIES (INCLUDING TEACHER ROLES AS APPLICABLE)

(Continued)

Conclusion

In this chapter, we have explained why peer interaction can be an excellent way to foster MLs' oral language development and understanding of new content. We have also highlighted that, in order for MLs to get the most out of these types of discussions and actively contribute to them, they need adequate support and structure to prepare for and participate in each activity. We presented four student practices and strategies connected to each of the four student practices that can support MLs in benefiting from academic conversations and oral language activities. In the next two chapters, we offer insights and strategies to provide MLs with the instruction they need to develop the academic language that is necessary for them to access and meaningfully take part in challenging content instruction.

SupportEd TOOLBOX

For ready-to-use, practical tools to support peer interaction, please see SupportEd.com/unlocking-toolbox.

CHAPTER 4 REFLECTION QUESTIONS

1. How do you plan to incorporate peer learning activities for MLs into your instruction in more systematic and intentional ways?

2. What is one peer learning activity that you would like to try next in your class? What steps will you take to ensure that your MLs are prepared to participate?

---

online resources Available for download at **resources.corwin.com/FennerUnlocking2E**

TEACHING ACADEMIC LANGUAGE TO MLs AT THE WORD/PHRASE LEVEL

5

Mrs. Saunders is an English language development (ELD) teacher in an urban school district[1] who works at the elementary and middle school levels. She shared the following description of how she addresses vocabulary development with her ML students. As you read, we encourage you to take notes in the margins on strategies Mrs. Saunders uses to teach, practice, and assess her MLs' vocabulary development.

*To begin, I **identify words** that are content specific that my MLs will need to understand to interact fully with a text. We begin our learning by activating schema about our topic of study to see what vocabulary comes up as terms that students are already familiar with and know how to use. To gauge what vocabulary students already know, I might create true/false sentences with our vocabulary words for an anticipation guide.[2] Students read each statement, and based on their prior knowledge, they indicate whether the statement is true or false. After reading, students validate or refute their responses on their anticipation guide. I also use preassessments (selected response, fill in the blank) of the chosen vocabulary to gauge students' understanding of key terms. I would then give the same vocabulary assessment after the unit in order to measure growth and determine next steps.*

*Next, we move into **explicit teaching of the selected key vocabulary**. I provide an abridged definition and find a pertinent image to accompany the vocabulary word. To introduce the word, I read it aloud and ask students to repeat it to*

---

[1]*Source:* The description of the vocabulary development activities was shared with us by Jennifer Saunders, a K–5 ELD teacher.

[2]See Chapter 7 for more on using anticipation guides.

Mrs. Saunders introduces key vocabulary using an image, definition, and example sentence of the word used in context.

Source: Jennifer Saunders. Illustration by iStock.com/RomanEgorov.

rehearse pronunciation. During explicit instruction of vocabulary, I also include an example sentence so students can see it used in context. If a home language single-word translation is helpful, I also provide it or co-construct the translation with students. As an additional support, I often print and use these vocabulary presentations as personal visual dictionaries for my ML students to reference in their content-area classrooms. As we learn together, students often complete a "quick draw" of an icon, a doodle, or a symbol that may help them to remember the word. I have found that Frayer Models[3] for the term, definition, example/ nonexample, and image are especially helpful for content-specific vocabulary. We might also add a motion to accompany the term. Co-construction of motions to accompany words has proven to be more memorable (and fun) for students. We may use arm motions, whole-body movement, or American Sign Language.

*After explicitly teaching vocabulary, we move into **reading the text** for which the vocabulary was taught. During the first reading of the text, I might use a cloze reading strategy whereby I read the majority of the text aloud and pause for students to chorally say those pretaught vocabulary words aloud. This ensures all-pupil response and higher engagement levels throughout the reading. It calls students' attention to the pretaught words and gets them to utilize them in context. Their choral response (or lack thereof) gives me data about engagement, understanding, and pronunciation of the new vocabulary. We pause to discuss the terms as we encounter them in the text (when necessary). Before a second reading of a text, we might revisit the vocabulary words via a cloze task[4] with a word bank. Or we might complete a matching task to place the correct definition and image with each term. Lastly, I have students use their new vocabulary in a spoken or written output task in order to demonstrate mastery and*

---

[3]See Figure 5.10 for an example of a Frayer Model.

[4]A cloze task is an activity in which students have to fill in the blanks in a passage of text.

understanding. In all stages of vocabulary development, I encourage students to share explanations or ideas in their home language, both orally and in writing, to make connections between their funds of knowledge and new learning. Strategically moving between the home language and English is essential for all proficiency levels but especially newcomer ML students and emergent MLs. Utilizing students' linguistic assets is essential in vocabulary and concept development (personal communication, May 3, 2023).

<u>Cell City Writing Task</u>

Write to describe your cell city. Explain how each city part relates to the part of the cell it represents. You can write your sentences using the models below:

Example	Response Frame
I chose the landfill to represent the lysosomes because both break things down. Lysosomes break down sugars and a landfill breaks down boxes and trash.	I chose the (<u>city part</u>) to represent the (<u>cell part</u>) because (<u>reason/explanation</u>).
The lysosome is represented by the landfill because both the landfill and the lysosomes break things down.	The (<u>cell part</u>) is represented by the (<u>city part</u>) because (<u>reason/explanation</u>).

1. lysosome:	
2. Endoplasmic reticulum:	
3. Cytoplasm:	
4. Cell membrane:	
5. Cell wall:	

ML students in Mrs. Saunders's ELD classroom demonstrate their understanding of technical science vocabulary in a writing task.

Source: Jennifer Saunders

REFLECTION QUESTIONS

1. What do you notice about how Mrs. Saunders approaches identifying vocabulary to teach and the strategies she uses to introduce and practice that vocabulary?

2. What takeaways do you have about the ways in which Mrs. Saunders addresses academic vocabulary development with her MLs?

3. What are some strategies that you use to teach and practice academic vocabulary with MLs?

 Available for download at **resources.corwin.com/FennerUnlocking2E**

If we want MLs to acquire the academic vocabulary that they need to successfully engage with content-based material, we, like Mrs. Saunders, must be purposeful about how we approach vocabulary instruction as well as academic-language instruction more broadly. This chapter will begin with an introduction to what academic language is and why it is critical for MLs to acquire academic language in order to access challenging content standards and be fully integrated into content classrooms. It will then focus in on a discussion of why teaching academic vocabulary is an essential element to MLs' academic achievement. It will also include guidelines on selecting what vocabulary to teach, strategies for teaching and reinforcing new words, and strategies for supporting MLs with independent word-learning skills. You will have an opportunity to practice these strategies throughout the chapter. This chapter is focused on academic language at the word/phrase level, and then in Chapter 6 we will take a deep dive into academic language at the sentence and discourse levels.

What Is Academic Language?

REFLECTION QUESTIONS

1. How do you define academic language?

2. What are your beliefs about teaching academic vocabulary?

3. What questions do you have about teaching academic vocabulary to MLs?

online resources Available for download at **resources.corwin.com/FennerUnlocking2E**

Academic language is one key to MLs being able to access challenging grade-level content and fully engage with their classroom context and peers. Not only MLs but all students need to have proficiency in academic language to function in their classroom, college, or career. Before you can begin to teach academic language to your students, you will need to have a working definition of what the construct is.

There is not one single definition of academic language. Definitions of academic language range from those that draw a direct contrast between everyday social language and the language of school (Bailey, 2007) to those that reject this distinction and instead call for a focus on "how students use language to engage in academic tasks" rather than on the characteristics of academic language itself (Bunch, 2014; Bunch & Martin, 2021). We acknowledge these varying definitions, and for the purposes of this book, define **academic language as the language used in classroom settings to acquire new knowledge and skills, interact with a topic, and share information with others** (August, 2018; National Academies of Sciences, Engineering, & Medicine [NASEM], 2017). This definition shifts away from the contrast between social and formal language and acknowledges that academic language encompasses both disciplinary language and everyday language (Bunch, 2014; Bunch & Martin, 2021; Molle et al., 2021; WIDA, 2020a).

In their 2020 standards framework, WIDA (2020a) repositioned their English language development standard for social and instructional language[5] to be embedded throughout the four other standards (language arts, mathematics, science, and social studies). In WIDA's previous standards frameworks, social and instructional language was a separate standard, but it now is integrated throughout their other standards. They explain that "this repositioning moves beyond the binary view of social language as a precursor to academic language" (p. 361). Instead, academic language and social language support one another, as students cannot develop academic language without using everyday, social language to grapple with academic concepts (Bunch & Martin, 2021; Molle et al., 2021). For example, when discussing information on a graph, students may first describe something as "getting bigger" or "going up" before replacing that language with more academic language such as "increasing" or "having a positive slope."

APPLICATION ACTIVITY 5.1: HOW STUDENTS USE ACADEMIC LANGUAGE

Consider academic language in your context. Brainstorm three ways students use academic language in your context. An example has been provided for you.

> **Example:** In my social studies class, students have to justify their arguments with claims and evidence.
>
> 1. _____
>
>   _____
>
> 2. _____
>
>   _____
>
> 3. _____
>
>   _____

What Is the Purpose of Academic Language, and How Is it Structured?

Academic language is used for a wide variety of purposes within classrooms. These purposes are often referred to as functions, and they identify the intent

---

[5]Social and instructional language refers to language students use to convey personal needs and wants, as well as general language functions they use to interact with content across disciplines (e.g., asking and answering questions, summarizing information from a text, explaining an argument) (WIDA, 2020a).

of a text (e.g., describe, define, explain, compare and contrast, and summarize information). Note that **text does not only refer to something that is written but also to oral language (e.g., a speech), a visual (e.g., a painting), and multimedia.** Students need to be able to use these actionable language functions on a daily basis in the classroom across multiple content areas. As mentioned in Chapter 1, through an analysis of academic content standards, research literature, and disciplinary practices, WIDA identified the top four high-leverage language uses across academic content standards, or Key Language Uses. The Key Language Uses are narrate, inform, explain, and argue (WIDA, 2020a, pp. 26–27). You can reference these Key Uses as a starting place when making decisions about which academic-language structures to teach.

When we ask educators their definition of academic language, many of them only mention vocabulary. While vocabulary is indeed one facet of academic language, vocabulary is found within the context of sentence structure, discourse, and the sociocultural context (which we will explain shortly). The WIDA ELD Standards Framework (WIDA, 2020a) conceptualizes academic language into three dimensions: the word/phrase dimension, the sentence dimension, and the discourse dimension. While WIDA uses the term "dimension," we will be referring to these as "levels." **The word/phrase level refers to precision of vocabulary use. The sentence level refers to how sentences are structured (grammar and syntax) in texts. The discourse level includes how language is organized, how it holds together, and how much language is used within a text** (WIDA, 2020a). We are going to be exploring what is meant by each of these levels in Application Activity 5.2. Although it is important for MLs to learn vocabulary to access challenging content, they also need to master the sentence- and discourse-level features of academic language in order to be positioned for academic success. While crucial, words alone will not allow MLs to access content and fully engage in classroom contexts. MLs need to know how to combine words to form sentences and how to combine sentences to create effective discourse in speaking and writing. They also need to be able to comprehend words within complex sentence and discourse structures when listening and reading.

Further, teachers of MLs need to recognize the sociocultural context in which the acquisition of the different features of academic language takes place. MLs' sociocultural context plays a distinct role in the way in which MLs acquire academic language. **The sociocultural context in reference to language use in schools refers to "the interaction among students and the classroom environment, along with the influences that dynamically shape the environment, including purpose, topic, situation, participants' identities and social roles, and audience"** (WIDA, 2020a, p. 362). The sociocultural context honors the participants who are acquiring language, as well as their experiences, in a holistic way. We also argue that the sociocultural aspect encompasses MLs' background knowledge that they can leverage when learning academic language in English.

APPLICATION ACTIVITY 5.2: LEVELS OF ACADEMIC LANGUAGE

Review Figures 5.1 and 5.2 and consider how the levels of academic language apply to your context. Brainstorm three strategies you could use to teach academic language at the word/phrase level. Note that you will be exploring strategies for the sentence and discourse levels in Chapter 6. Figure 5.1 illustrates the features of academic language, how they are nested within each other, and also framed within a unique sociocultural context. Figure 5.2 includes more information on the three levels of academic language (word/phrase, sentence, and discourse level) from the 2020 WIDA ELD Standards Framework.

Word-Level Teaching Strategies	
Strategy 1	
Strategy 2	
Strategy 3	

FIGURE 5.1   LEVELS OF ACADEMIC LANGUAGE WITHIN A SOCIOCULTURAL CONTEXT

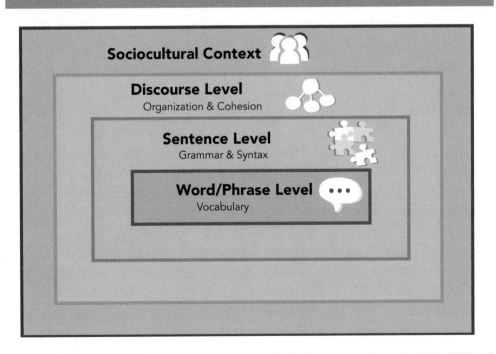

Source: Adapted from WIDA English Language Development Standards Framework, 2020 edition, https://wida.wisc.edu/teach/standards/eld/2020, © 2020 Board of Regents of the University of Wisconsin System wida.wisc.edu

FIGURE 5.2   LEVELS OF ACADEMIC LANGUAGE: DEFINITIONS AND INSTRUCTIONAL FOCUS

LEVEL	DEFINITION	DURING INSTRUCTION FOCUS ON . . .
Word/Phrase	Precision of language (vocabulary use)	How everyday, cross-disciplinary, and technical language more effectively conveys precise meaning
Sentence	Grammatical complexity of language (sentence structure)	How relationships are expressed with clauses through simple, compound, and complex sentences
Discourse	Organization of language	How ideas are coherently organized to meet a purpose through organizational patterns characteristic of the genre
	Cohesion of language (the way language holds together)	How language connects ideas within and across sentences and discourse using a range of cohesive devices
	Density of language (amount of language used)	How information in noun groups is expanded or consolidated; a noun group is a noun or pronoun and the words that modify it (e.g., the five blue shirts that Sally owns)

Source: Adapted from WIDA English Language Development Standards Framework, 2020 edition, https://wida.wisc.edu/teach/standards/eld/2020, © 2020 Board of Regents of the University of Wisconsin System wida.wisc.edu

Why Is Academic Language Important?

Content standards call for all teachers to be teachers of academic language as academic language influences how well MLs are able to engage with grade-level content along with how they tend to perform on content and English language proficiency assessments. Therefore, educators should work to bridge MLs' use of more informal language with more formalized, academic uses. Academic language provides MLs with the tools they need to interpret and express their understanding of rigorous, grade-level content. The WIDA Standards Framework (WIDA, 2020a) points out that

> the explicit teaching of how language works can help multilingual learners expand what they can do with language, thereby growing their language toolbox. The result is that students become increasingly aware and strategic in their use of language to negotiate meaning and achieve their purposes in various contexts. (p. 20)

The National Academies of Science, Engineering, and Medicine consensus study report (2017) synthesis of research identifies content-area academic-language development as a promising practice for MLs at all grade bands K–12.

Specifically, this report notes that academic-language development supports learning across content areas for MLs. Therefore, in order to provide MLs equitable access to grade-level content, educators need to dedicate time and planning to supporting MLs' academic-language development.

In doing this work, keep in mind that it is expected that MLs will produce errors in their written and spoken use of academic language at the word/phrase, sentence, and discourse levels. Emergent MLs at the beginning level of proficiency will produce the greatest number of errors in their academic language and therefore require the most scaffolds. However, as emergent MLs gain proficiency, they require fewer scaffolds, produce fewer errors, and their academic language builds at the word/phrase, sentence, and discourse levels. Even after MLs are considered English proficient, they may still face challenges with academic language. Walqui and Heritage (2018) share that teachers should be "selective in addressing errors and intentional in providing feedback." MacDonald et al. (2015) suggest focusing on providing feedback related to the language you have been working on and language errors that interfere with a student's intended meaning, rather than all errors in language production. The feedback you give on errors should be brief, clear, and actionable (Brookhart, 2020). This will ensure that your feedback helps students make sense of the content while at the same time adding precision to their language production.

Now that we have defined academic language and explained why it is a critical element of ML education, we will focus on how to support MLs at the word/phrase level of academic language.

What Is the Word/Phrase Level?

As we defined earlier, **the word/phrase level refers to the words or phrases[6] used to add precision to language.** Within the word/phrase level of academic language, there are three categories of words and phrases, which include everyday language, cross-disciplinary language, and technical language (WIDA, 2020a). You may be familiar with these categories as "tiers" of different kinds of words (Beck et al., 2002). **Everyday language, or Tier 1 vocabulary, refers to nontechnical words and phrases** (e.g., *hot* instead of *boiling*) that students usually learn through social, informal conversations. Everyday language tends to be the easiest for students to learn. Cross-disciplinary language (or Tier 2 words) and technical language (or Tier 3 words) tend to be more abstract, which makes them more difficult for students to learn, but without them, students will have a significant challenge learning and demonstrating their understanding of new content. **Cross-disciplinary words and phrases include vocabulary that shows up across content areas**, such as *solve*, *establish*, and *verify*. These cross-disciplinary words require explicit instruction

---

[6]A phrase refers to a group of two or more words that work together as a unit (e.g., branches of government).

and attention. **Technical language is specialized vocabulary words and phrases related to a topic within a given content area.** For example, when discussing metamorphosis in science, the word *chrysalis* would be a content-specific technical vocabulary word. Figure 5.3 summarizes this information and provides additional examples.

FIGURE 5.3	CATEGORY OF ACADEMIC VOCABULARY, DEFINITIONS, AND EXAMPLES	
CATEGORY	**DEFINITION**	**EXAMPLES**
Everyday (Tier 1)	Words and phrases usually acquired through everyday speech	boy house run fall asleep
Cross-disciplinary (Tier 2)	Academic words and phrases that appear across all types of text. These are often more complex, tend to be used across disciplines, and may have more than one meaning, depending on their use and context.	compare and contrast obvious omit prediction
Technical (Tier 3)	Domain-specific words and phrases that are tied to content. These are typically the types of vocabulary words that are included in glossaries, highlighted in textbooks, and addressed by teachers. They are considered difficult, precise words that are important to understanding content.	aristocracy hyperbole kinetic energy radius

Many cross-disciplinary (Tier 2) words hold multiple meanings that depend on the context (e.g., lunch *table*, data *table*, Periodic *table*). We have developed Application Activity 5.3 for you to consider cross-disciplinary words with multiple meanings and how you would address them with students.

APPLICATION ACTIVITY 5.3: WORDS WITH MULTIPLE MEANINGS

Identify at least one cross-disciplinary vocabulary word with multiple meanings, and define the meanings for each content area. Share how you would teach, explain, or practice its different meanings with your students. An example using the word *column* has been completed for you in the first row of Figure 5.4.

FIGURE 5.4   MULTIPLE MEANING WORDS ACROSS CONTENT AREAS

CROSS-CONTENT VOCABULARY WORD	MEANING IN ENGLISH LANGUAGE ARTS	MEANING IN MATHEMATICS	MEANING IN SOCIAL STUDIES	MEANING IN SCIENCE	HOW I WOULD TEACH ITS MEANINGS
Column	regularly appearing newspaper article	vertical division of a table	upright pillar	a form or shape (a column of smoke)	I would have students participate in a small group activity in which they work collaboratively to match the various definitions with images.

Why Teach Academic Vocabulary to MLs?

MLs learn new vocabulary gradually over time through repeated exposures to the words in different and multiple contexts (Nation, 2021; Webb, 2019). To give students these learning opportunities, teachers can intentionally plan for multiple and varied exposures to academic vocabulary over the course of a unit. Additionally, learning new vocabulary happens through both explicit, intentional instruction and incidental learning (Molle et al., 2021; Nation, 2021; Webb, 2019). **Intentional vocabulary instruction refers to when teachers explicitly plan for and teach vocabulary. Incidental vocabulary learning refers to when students learn new vocabulary as a result of engaging in other activities, such as reading or listening.** For instance, a science teacher may plan for intentional vocabulary instruction at the beginning of a unit on states of matter. Then, during an experiment, students may also experience incidental vocabulary learning when reading directions and discussing ideas with a classmate.

When planning for academic vocabulary instruction, it is important to note that knowledge of academic vocabulary in English is linked to proficiency in reading and writing (August & Shanahan, 2006). Similarly, Escamilla et al. (2022) emphasize that vocabulary development is part of a comprehensive approach to literacy development for all students. If MLs are to be able to effectively engage with complex, grade-level texts and complete standards-based content tasks, they need to develop understanding of the academic—and frequently abstract— vocabulary necessary for these tasks. However, many MLs do not have the opportunities to learn and practice academic vocabulary (August & Shanahan, 2006). All students—but MLs, in particular—need many and varied opportunities to practice their skills with assistance from the teacher, as well as independently (Grabe, 1991; McLaughlin, 1987; Molle et al., 2021).

We recommend a multifaceted approach to vocabulary instruction that includes teaching new vocabulary, practicing new vocabulary, and supporting independent word-learning strategies (Figure 5.5). While this approach focuses primarily on intentional vocabulary instruction, it also includes strategies to support MLs with incidental vocabulary learning as they work with text independently. Additionally, this approach uses recommendations from Baker et al.'s (2014) synthesis of research of effective instructional practices for teaching content and literacy to MLs, which advises teaching a set of academic vocabulary words intensively over the course of several days using a variety of instructional activities. Strategically teaching academic vocabulary and providing opportunities for students to use this new vocabulary in varied academic activities will provide MLs the support they need in order to fully understand the meaning of these words and to use them in standards-based tasks.

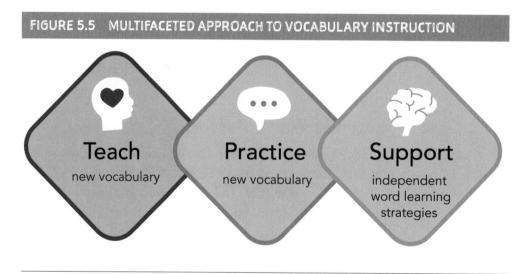

FIGURE 5.5   MULTIFACETED APPROACH TO VOCABULARY INSTRUCTION

Teach
new vocabulary

Practice
new vocabulary

Support
independent
word learning
strategies

How Should I Select Vocabulary for Intentional Instruction?

Our multifaceted approach to vocabulary instruction begins with intentionally teaching new vocabulary. You can start by selecting vocabulary for in-depth focus. We recommend you select a text that is connected to the content being addressed in class. The use of these texts can serve as a basis for MLs' acquisition of discipline-specific vocabulary and academic language related to the unit of study. The texts should be engaging, contain a variety of target cross-disciplinary and technical language, and include ideas that can be discussed from multiple viewpoints. We recommend using a variety of grade-level texts and also supplementing with texts at students' language proficiency and reading level as needed. Although all MLs may not yet be able to independently read grade-level texts, instruction can be scaffolded so as to support MLs of all levels of proficiency in understanding and discussing the grade-level text. Information on how to effectively scaffold instruction of a grade-level text is outlined in Chapters 3 and 8.

Once you have chosen the text that you will use, select five to eight words or phrases that you will focus on over the course of several lessons (Baker et al., 2014). When too many new vocabulary words are taught to MLs, it can be challenging for them to gain a deep understanding of these words and have sufficient practice with the new words. You can address other vocabulary from the text that may be challenging for MLs during the work with the text, but you should not focus on it in the same intentional way as the selected set of words. For example, when reading a text aloud if students encounter an unfamiliar word, a teacher might stop and provide a short definition or show a visual to support understanding.

In selecting which words to focus on, Baker et al. (2014) recommend choosing words that meet the following criteria:

1. Are central to understanding the text

2. Appear frequently in the text

3. May appear in other content areas

4. Have multiple meanings

5. Have affixes (prefixes and suffixes)

In other words, it is important to select vocabulary that will both help MLs in accessing the content of a particular text and support them in their learning across disciplines. For example, learning words with multiple meanings is an effective tool to help students recognize that the meaning of a word may vary depending on the content being studied. Similarly, studying words with affixes (i.e., prefixes and suffixes) affords students with opportunities to understand the way in which affixes can change a word's meaning or grammatical form (e.g., adding *dis-* to *like*; *exhibit* and *exhibition*). Figure 5.6 is an example of a type of activity that you could use with students to help them build knowledge of how word parts change the grammatical function of a word. It is important to note that not all verbs have noun, adjective, and adverb forms.

FIGURE 5.6   USING WORD PARTS TO UNDERSTAND WORD MEANING

VERBS (ACTION)	NOUNS (PERSON, PLACE, THING, OR IDEA)	ADJECTIVES (WORDS TO DESCRIBE NOUNS)	ADVERBS (WORDS TO DESCRIBE ACTIONS)
Investigate	Investigation Investigator	Investigative	Investigatively
Create	Creation	Creative Uncreative	Creatively
Pursue	Pursuit	Pursuant	Pursuantly
Opt	Option	Optional	Optionally

Source: Adapted from Baker, S. et al. (2014). Teaching academic content and literacy to English learners in elementary and middle school (NCEE 2014-4012). Washington, DC: National Center for Education Evaluation and Regional Assistance (NCEE), Institute of Education Sciences, U.S. Department of Education. Retrieved from the NCEE website: http://ies.ed.gov/ncee/wwc/publications_reviews.aspx

APPLICATION ACTIVITY 5.4: SELECTING WORDS FOR INTENTIONAL FOCUS

Read the following Grade 2–3 text excerpt from Thomson's (2010) *Where Do Polar Bears Live?* Then, decide which five to eight words you would choose for in-depth focus during a unit on animals of the Arctic. Include a short explanation of why you chose each word, citing Criteria 1–5 from Baker et al. (2014). Complete Figure 5.7.

A mother polar bear heaves herself out of her den. A cub scrambles after her. When the cub was born four months ago, he was no bigger than a guinea pig. Blind and helpless, he snuggled in his mother's fur. He drank her milk and grew, safe from the long Arctic winter. Outside the den, on some days, it was fifty degrees below zero. From October to February, the sun never rose. Now it is spring—even though snow still covers the land. The cub is about the size of a cocker spaniel. He's ready to leave the den. For the first time, he sees bright sunlight and feels the wind ruffle his fur. The cub tumbles and slides down icy hills. His play makes him strong and teaches him to walk and run in snow. Like his mother, the cub is built to survive in the Arctic. His white fur will grow to be six inches thick—longer than your hand. The skin beneath the cub's fur is black. It soaks up the heat of the sun. Under the skin is a layer of fat. Like a snug blanket, this blubber keeps in the heat of the bear's body.

FIGURE 5.7   VOCABULARY WORD, WHY CHOSEN, AND RECOMMENDATION CITED

VOCABULARY WORD	WHY CHOSEN	RECOMMENDATION CITED (1–5)
Survive	may appear in other content areas	#3

Recommendations Key:

1. Are central to understanding the text

2. Appear frequently in the text

3. May appear in other content areas

4. Have multiple meanings

5. Have affixes (prefixes and suffixes)

It is also important to consider what additional words you might teach in context as you and your students are working on a particular text. For example, a concrete word such as *cocker spaniel* (from the *Where Do Polar Bears Live?* text) would be helpful for students to understand, but you would not need to spend a lot of time having students study the word. You could provide a simple definition such as, "A cocker spaniel is a type of dog," and show a picture. Modeling how to address unfamiliar words in context reinforces independent word-learning strategies, which supports incidental vocabulary learning.

Source: iStock.com/adogslifephoto

APPLICATION ACTIVITY 5.5: ADDITIONAL WORDS TO TEACH

Review the *Where Do Polar Bears Live?* text again, and decide on five additional words that you might quickly teach to students directly as you are working together on the text. These are concrete words that you would spend less than a minute teaching to the class and would most likely not include in further instruction.

1. _____

2. _____

3. _____

4. _____

5. _____

How Can I Assess Students' Initial Understanding of These New Words?

In the opening scenario, Mrs. Saunders described several strategies she uses to assess MLs' initial understanding of key vocabulary, such as anticipation guides and selected response activities. Before beginning intentional instruction on new vocabulary, we recommend assessing student familiarity with and understanding of the new words. In performing this initial assessment, you don't want to set students up to fail or to feel that they should already know these words. Instead, you can work with students to help them self-assess their knowledge, explaining that the whole class is going to be learning the meaning of some new words, and you want to know which words they might already know. For example, you might ask students to sort words into three categories: (1) words that they don't know or have never heard before, (2) words that they have heard of but can't define or use in a sentence, and (3) words that they can accurately use in writing and speaking. You could also have them do a similar activity as a checklist. See Figure 5.8 for an example. In both cases, you should model how to do the self-assessment and walk students through your thought process (e.g., "Hmm, this is a word that I have heard before, but I can't really define it or use it in a sentence. I am going to check the middle column.")

FIGURE 5.8   STUDENT VOCABULARY SELF-ASSESSMENT EXAMPLE

Vocabulary Self-Assessment ☑

Directions:

1. Read each word.

2. Decide if . . .

   • You don't know the word

   • You have heard of the word but can't use it

   • You know and feel comfortable using the new word

3. Check the appropriate column.

Vocabulary word	I don't know this word.	I have heard this word, but I can't use it in a sentence.	I know this word and feel comfortable using it.
1. adaptation			
2. carnivore			
3. food			
4. herbivore			

Another self-assessment option would be to have students do a thumbs up (I know the word and can use it), thumbs to the side (I've heard of the word, but I don't feel comfortable using it), or thumbs down (I don't know the word). This strategy is helpful as it allows for you to quickly get a sense of which words the majority of your students already know or need more support with. You have to be careful that some MLs might not be entirely truthful in front of other students due to possible stigma associated with not knowing the word. To help with this, instruct students to hold their hand close to their chest rather than holding their hand in the air for the entire class to see.

After you have taught and practiced the new vocabulary, you may wish to have students complete another self-assessment, so they recognize the progress they have made and also identify any words that they still need more practice with.

You can also use other formative strategies (e.g., having students match pictures with words) to assess student learning as you are teaching and practicing the new words. For recommendations on more formative-assessment strategies, see Chapter 9.

REFLECTION QUESTION

What strategies do you use to assess your students' familiarity with content vocabulary?

 Available for download at **resources.corwin.com/FennerUnlocking2E**

What Strategies Should I Use for Teaching Academic Vocabulary?

When teaching academic vocabulary, Baker et al. (2014) recommend using student-friendly definitions, examples and nonexamples, and concrete representations to support students in gaining an in-depth understanding of the new words.

1. *Provide student-friendly definitions.*

It is important when learning new vocabulary that MLs have a clear and concrete definition of each new vocabulary word you've chosen that aligns with the meaning of the word as it is used in the text or within the unit. Student-friendly definitions will most likely need to be adapted from traditional dictionary definitions. For example, *Merriam-Webster* online gives the following definitions for the word *survive:* "(1) to remain alive: to continue to live; (2) to continue to exist; (3) to remain alive after the death of (someone)." If you were teaching the meaning of the word *survive* using the earlier *Where Do Polar Bears Live?* text, you would want to focus on definitions one and two. However, words such as *remain, alive,* and *exist* may present obstacles to MLs being able to understand the meaning. So, the most ML student-friendly definition for the word *survive* would be "to continue to live." Student-friendly definitions should be accompanied by visuals, examples, and translations of the word in students' home languages (as appropriate).

Figure 5.9 shares an example of how a teacher might introduce a new vocabulary word. In this example, taken from a curricular unit focused on the book *Dreaming in Cuban* (C. García, 1992), the teacher can present a new vocabulary word by showing two pictures, providing the Spanish translation and an explanation of the word, and making a connection to the story. Notice that the teacher presents a student-friendly definition of the word in her explanation: "Profits are the money that a business earns after paying expenses." In addition, students have an opportunity to practice the word through the "Partner Talk" activity.

FIGURE 5.9   INTRODUCING A NEW VOCABULARY WORD

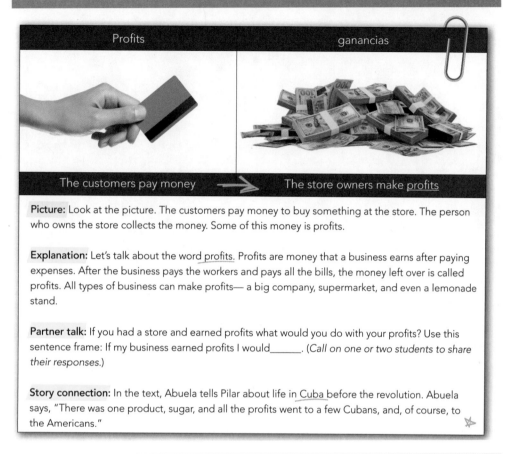

Picture: Look at the picture. The customers pay money to buy something at the store. The person who owns the store collects the money. Some of this money is profits.

Explanation: Let's talk about the word profits. Profits are money that a business earns after paying expenses. After the business pays the workers and pays all the bills, the money left over is called profits. All types of business can make profits— a big company, supermarket, and even a lemonade stand.

Partner talk: If you had a store and earned profits what would you do with your profits? Use this sentence frame: If my business earned profits I would_____. (*Call on one or two students to share their responses.*)

Story connection: In the text, Abuela tells Pilar about life in Cuba before the revolution. Abuela says, "There was one product, sugar, and all the profits went to a few Cubans, and, of course, to the Americans."

Source: August, D., Golden, L., & Pook, D. (2015). *Secondary curricular units for New York City Department of Education*, p. 18. Reprinted with permission of American Institutes for Research.

APPLICATION ACTIVITY 5.6: WRITING STUDENT-FRIENDLY DEFINITIONS

Return to the work that you did in Application Activity 5.4. Write ML student-friendly definitions for five of the words that you selected.

WORD	STUDENT-FRIENDLY DEFINITION

(Continued)

(Continued)

WORD	STUDENT-FRIENDLY DEFINITION

2. *Use examples, nonexamples, and concrete representations.*

In addition to sharing student-friendly definitions during explicit instruction of vocabulary it is also important to provide MLs with examples, nonexamples, and concrete representations of the word. For example, in the Frayer Model in Figure 5.10 you can see both examples and nonexamples of the word *equation*. Similarly, in the word map in Figure 5.11, students have created examples, nonexamples, synonyms, and antonyms of the word *enormous*. Concrete representations, such as pictures, gestures, and actions, can also help reinforce the meaning of a word.

FIGURE 5.10   EXAMPLE OF A FRAYER MODEL

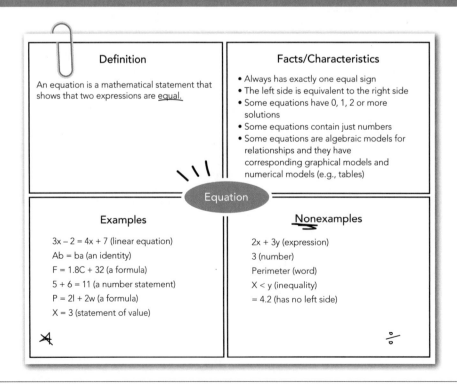

Definition

An equation is a mathematical statement that shows that two expressions are <u>equal.</u>

Facts/Characteristics

- Always has exactly one equal sign
- The left side is equivalent to the right side
- Some equations have 0, 1, 2 or more solutions
- Some equations contain just numbers
- Some equations are algebraic models for relationships and they have corresponding graphical models and numerical models (e.g., tables)

Equation

Examples

3x – 2 = 4x + 7 (linear equation)
Ab = ba (an identity)
F = 1.8C + 32 (a formula)
5 + 6 = 11 (a number statement)
P = 2l + 2w (a formula)
X = 3 (statement of value)

Nonexamples

2x + 3y (expression)
3 (number)
Perimeter (word)
X < y (inequality)
= 4.2 (has no left side)

FIGURE 5.11 EXAMPLE OF A WORD MAP

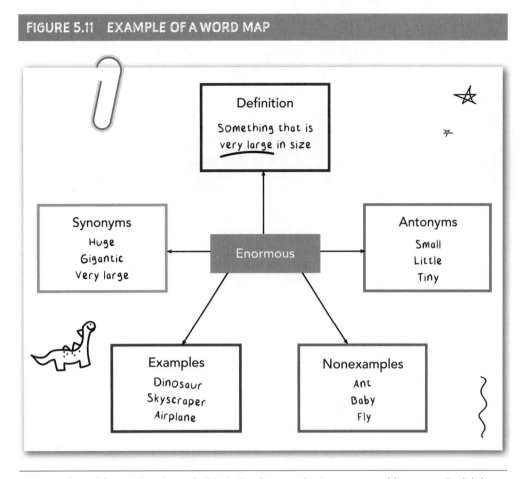

Source: Adapted from Baker, S. et al. (2014). Teaching academic content and literacy to English learners in elementary and middle school (NCEE 2014-4012). Washington, DC: National Center for Education Evaluation and Regional Assistance (NCEE), Institute of Education Sciences, U.S. Department of Education. Retrieved from the NCEE website: http://ies.ed.gov/ncee/wwc/publications_reviews.aspx

Abstract words are frequently more challenging to explain and teach to MLs than concrete objects that can be easily exemplified by pictures. Let's take another example from the *Where Do Polar Bears Live?* text used earlier in the chapter to complete Application Activity 5.7.

APPLICATION ACTIVITY 5.7: VOCABULARY PRACTICE

Reread this excerpt from the text: *A mother polar bear heaves herself out of her den. A cub scrambles after her.* What does *heaves* mean in this sentence? Using context clues, a dictionary, and a bilingual dictionary, complete the word map shown in Figure 5.12.

(Continued)

(Continued)

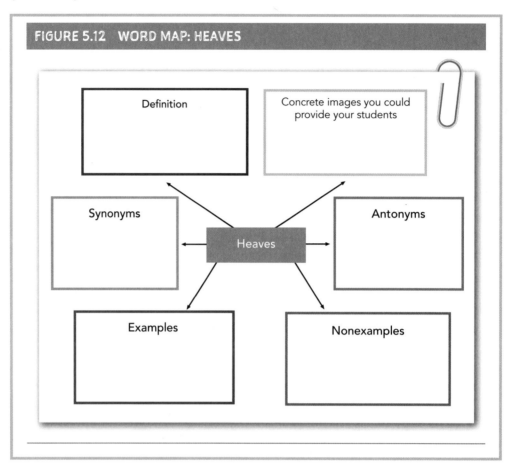

FIGURE 5.12   WORD MAP: HEAVES

What Activities Can I Use to Help MLs Practice New Vocabulary?

It is important that MLs have opportunities to practice and engage with the new vocabulary that they have been taught through a variety of listening, speaking, reading, and writing activities (Baker et al., 2014; Molle et al., 2021). In other words, once new vocabulary has been introduced through an engaging, content-specific text, students will need to test their understanding of the words over the course of several days in order to really cement their knowledge of the word. It is important to create a classroom culture in which trying out new academic words in speech and writing is encouraged and students are not expected to use words correctly the first time. There are many different activities that teachers can use to practice new vocabulary, but we have included descriptions of a few of our favorites grouped under the categories of listening and speaking, reading and writing, and games and activities (Figure 5.13). Some of these activities may be more appropriate for students in certain grade levels than others, and we encourage you to adapt these activities according to your students' grade level.

FIGURE 5.13 VOCABULARY DEVELOPMENT ACTIVITIES	
CATEGORY	**ACTIVITIES**
Listening and Speaking	• Dramatic Representations • Information Gap • Interactive Word Wall • Three Image Discussion • Video Clips • Word Experts
Reading and Writing	• Gallery Walk • Glossary • Key Word, Important Information, Memory Cue (KIM) • Text-Dependent Questions • Word Banks
Games and Activities	• Heads Up • Memory • Pictionary • Vocabulary Bingo • Vocab Jigsaw

Listening and Speaking Activities to Develop MLs' Vocabulary

- **Dramatic Representations:** Students work individually, in pairs, or in groups to act out new words. For example, if the new word is *revolve*, the person acting as the Earth would revolve around the person acting as the sun. Emergent MLs may benefit from having this activity modeled and may also benefit from working with a partner that speaks their same home language.

- **Information Gap:** Students are paired and given information involving new vocabulary words, but within the pair, Student A has information that Student B doesn't have and vice versa. They need to use new vocabulary words and exchange information in order to complete the information gap activity. Emergent MLs may benefit from the use of sentence stems or sentence frames during this activity.

- **Interactive Word Wall:** For this activity, students are placed in groups of three or four. Each group is given a piece of poster paper, some tape, markers, and vocabulary words on index cards. Students take turns choosing a vocabulary word and making a connection to another word (e.g., a *predator* hunts for its *prey*). As they make the connection, they tape both words to the poster paper and draw an arrow between them. The next student then must make a connection between one of those words and a new word (e.g., a *predator* is *carnivore*). Connections can be made to more than one word.

- **Three Image Discussion:** The teacher presents three related images to the class. After the teacher models a think-aloud, students work in pairs or small groups to discuss what the images have in common to determine which vocabulary word they represent. Depending on the activity, grade level, and ML proficiency level, students may be given a list of vocabulary words to select from during this activity. (This strategy was adapted from Amanda Angstadt.)

- **Video Clips:** Students watch short video clips that include the new vocabulary and discuss what they saw. Teachers should preview the video discussion questions with their MLs prior to watching the video. Emergent MLs may also benefit from the use of closed captions during the video and sentence stems, sentence frames, and a word bank to support their discussion.

- **Word Experts:** Students (or pairs of students) are assigned to present on a new vocabulary word that the teacher assigns them or that they select themselves. Students should share a student-friendly definition, the part of speech, an image to help remember the word, any suffixes or prefixes that can help in understanding the word, and the use of the new word in context. If you only have a small number of words, you could have students present in small groups. Emergent MLs will need to have this activity modeled for them and could also benefit from the use of bilingual dictionaries, if appropriate.

Reading and Writing Activities to Develop MLs' Vocabulary

- **Gallery Walk:** Students or pairs of students can be assigned, or they can select, one aspect of the content that they are studying. They should create a poster that explains their topic. Students are tasked to use a certain number of vocabulary words from a word bank on their poster as well as images that help explain both the topic and the vocabulary. When students are finished, they can move around the room, looking at others' posters. They can write comments or questions on sticky notes, and these can be discussed with the large group. Emergent MLs may benefit from such scaffolds as a word bank, sentence stems, and working with students who speak their home language.

- **Glossary:** Students can be asked to create a glossary to support their understanding of new content. The glossary can include a student-friendly definition, the use of the word in the text, an image to represent the word, and whether or not the word is a cognate in their home language.

- **KIM:** KIM is an acronym for <u>K</u>ey word, <u>I</u>mportant information, and <u>M</u>emory clue. In a vocabulary notebook, students create a table with the headings, K, I, and M. Under "K" they write the key word. Under "I" they write important information related to the word, and under "M" they sketch an image or write a sentence that will help them remember the meaning of the word.

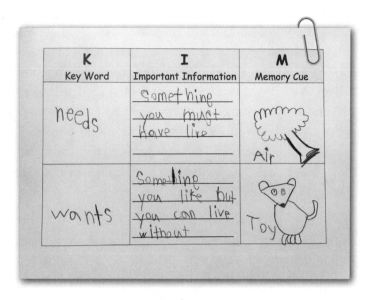

Here you see an example of the KIM strategy.

- **Text-Dependent Questions:** Text-dependent questions are an excellent way for MLs to practice their understanding of new words using a text. A teacher might develop a question such as the following: Sentence 2 says, "Like a snug blanket, this blubber keeps in the heat of the bear's body." What do you think *blubber* means in this sentence? Students can be given sentence frames, sentence stems, and word banks to support their work.

- **Word Banks:** Students can be given a prompt connected to the content they are studying and be asked to write a response using the vocabulary words in the word bank. Emergent MLs may need sentence frames or paragraph frames as additional support. They could also discuss with a partner before writing or do this activity in pairs.

Games and Activities to Develop MLs' Vocabulary

- **Heads Up:** Students are paired or put into small groups and given a set of unit vocabulary words on index cards. One student in each group is assigned as the guesser, and the remaining members of the group are clue givers. The guesser places a card on their head (without looking), and the clue givers share clues about the meaning of the word. Group members take turns being the guesser until the teacher calls time.

- **Memory:** For this game, vocabulary words can be written on one card, and a definition, picture, or example can be written on another. Students play memory to match the vocabulary word with its pair. As students play the game, they should say the vocabulary word aloud for the pictures and definitions to reinforce their understanding and practice with the words.

- **Pictionary:** In a modified version of the game Pictionary, students take turns drawing sketches of images and guessing the vocabulary word. Students are placed into small groups of four to six students. Each group is split into two teams and provided with a set of cards with key unit vocabulary written on them. A student from each team is identified as the drawer. The drawers have one to two minutes to draw a sketch of their word while their team members guess the word. Whichever team is able to guess the word first earns a point. Team members take turns being the drawer and guesser. Emergent MLs may benefit from having a word bank of key vocabulary to reference during this game.

- **Vocabulary Bingo:** Students write or glue their vocabulary words on bingo cards. The teacher or a student reads a definition or shares an example of the word, and students put a marker on their bingo card if they have that word. A student wins when they have marked five vocabulary words in a row.

- **Vocab Jigsaw:** For this activity, students are placed in groups of four. Each person on the team gets one clue about the word (e.g., what letter the word starts with, the number of syllables in the word, an antonym, or definition). Students take turns reading their clues, and as a group, they try to figure out the mystery vocabulary word.

REFLECTION QUESTIONS

1. Which activity for practicing key vocabulary would you like to try out in your context? Why?

2. How can you include opportunities for students to use the new vocabulary when speaking, reading, writing, and listening in your instruction?

 Available for download at **resources.corwin.com/FennerUnlocking2E**

How Can I Support MLs in Becoming Independent Learners of New Vocabulary?

In addition to intentionally teaching and practicing new academic vocabulary, it is also important to give students opportunities to practice skills that will help them figure out the meaning of unfamiliar words and acquire new vocabulary independently (Baker et al., 2014; Molle et al., 2021). Teaching these skills supports incidental vocabulary learning as students become better equipped to make logical inferences about unfamiliar words as they encounter them. Such skills include the following:

- Using context clues

- Understanding word parts

- Understanding cognates and false cognates

We describe each skill in more depth in the following sections.

Using Context Clues

One strategy to support MLs' independent learning of new words is to plan for opportunities for them to practice determining the meaning of unfamiliar words using clues from the sentence that include the unfamiliar word or using clues from surrounding sentences. The teacher can use a think-aloud to model how they use context clues to determine the meaning of an unfamiliar word and develop mini lessons, such as the one in Figure 5.14, to give students opportunities to practice this skill. As you can see in Figure 5.14, the students are presented with a short list of words that may be unfamiliar, the location of the word, and the location of the clues. Working in pairs, the students read the sentences that contain the word and the clues, select clues that help them determine the meaning, and write a definition for the word. This activity is designed to support secondary students' work with excerpts from a text called *The Great Fire* (Murphy, 1995).

FIGURE 5.14   MINI LESSON ON USING CONTEXT CLUES

Mystery Word	Location	Clues
1. jerrybuilt	Line 5	Lines 5–6
Clues: looked solid, but stone or brick exteriors hid wooden frames and floors Definition: structures built in a cheap way		
2. stately	Line 19	Lines 19–20
Clues: Definition:		
3. lined	Line 21	Lines 21–22
Clues: Definition:		
4. soggy	Line 25	Lines 24–25
Clues: Definition:		
5. showers	Line 35	Lines 35–36
Clues: Definition:		
6. drooped	Line 36	Lines 36–37
Clues: Definition:		

Source: August, D., Golden, L., Staehr Fenner, D., & Snyder, S. (2015). *Secondary curricular units for New York City Department of Education*, p. 128. Washington, DC: American Institutes of Research. Reprinted with permission of American Institutes for Research.

Understanding Word Parts

In addition to practicing how to discern the meaning of new words using context, MLs (as well as non-MLs) will also benefit from explicit instruction of word parts including prefixes, suffixes, and root words[7] as a tool to make predictions about the meaning of unknown words. Again, the teacher should model their thought process aloud to students in order to demonstrate how to make such predictions. Students can also practice using different forms of words that they are learning. In the following vignette from Mr. Clark's class, the teacher incorporates understanding of word parts into his teaching on a regular basis. Students add to a list of the meaning of word parts throughout the year, and the teacher gives them opportunities to practice their understanding through short in-class exercises.

Mr. Clark's Class: Understanding Word Parts

Mr. Clark's ninth-grade history class is studying different forms of government. Seven out of 23 students in the class are emergent MLs. They are all at an intermediate or advanced level of language proficiency. The students have learned the definition for the term *democracy*. Mr. Clark writes the following terms on the board: *democratic*, *democratically*, and *undemocratic*. He asks his students to work in pairs and use their knowledge of word parts that he has already taught to determine a meaning for each of the words. They should write an example of how the word might be used based on the content that they are studying. Students have practiced using word parts previously and have a list in their notebooks of the meanings of different affixes that they have studied. The students know that the suffixes *-ic* and *-ly* indicate the part of speech. They also know that the prefix *un-* is used to indicate what something is not. They discuss the words in pairs. While they are working, Mr. Clark checks in with pairs that are struggling.

The strategy used in this vignette will support MLs in recognizing and understanding the meaning of words that come from the same word families (e.g., *patience*, *patiently*, and *impatient*). Teachers who speak MLs' home languages can also point out similar types of affixes if they occur in the home language. For example, the prefix *ante-* means *before* in Spanish. In addition, MLs can also benefit from explicit instruction in determining the meaning of compound words, two words joined together to make a new word (e.g., firefly and softball). Note that this strategy will also benefit non-MLs.

Understanding Cognates and False Cognates

Cognates are words in different languages that are derived from the same original word or root. In addition to having the same meaning, the words look and sound similar. For example, *conclusion* in English is *conclusión* in Spanish. While it might seem like the use of cognates is a tool that MLs will use naturally and without prompting, it is beneficial for them to be given

---

[7]A root word is the base word to which prefixes and suffixes can be added. It can also stand on its own. For example, in the word *lovely*, *love* is the root word and *-ly* is the suffix.

explicit instruction in recognizing and using cognates in their work. Students also need to be aware of false cognates, or "false friends" as they are sometimes called. These are words that look and sound similar in two languages but actually have very different meanings. For example, the word *assist* in English means to help, but the phrase *assister à* in French means to attend an event. Additionally, students who have had interrupted schooling or who have not had the benefit of extensive formal education in their home language may be familiar with an academic word that is a cognate but may not understand the meaning of the word (e.g., *electrode* in English and *électrode* in French and *eletrodo* in Portuguese). Teachers can't assume this knowledge, which underscores the importance of all teachers of MLs knowing their students' background experiences.

How Do I Put All of the ML Vocabulary Strategies Together?

In this chapter, we have outlined several recommendations for teaching and practicing academic vocabulary as well as supporting independent word-learning strategies. It may be helpful to begin by using one or two strategies so as to not get overwhelmed by all of the possible strategies that you might use. In order to help you remember and use the strategies, we have developed a "Vocabulary Instruction Checklist" (Figure 5.15) that you may find helpful when teaching vocabulary. You could use a checklist such as this to keep track of vocabulary that you have taught, as well as to take notes on specific activities that worked well or did not work well to refine your instruction. You could also use the checklist to keep track of word-learning strategies that you have practiced with students and any challenges that they had. Using the Vocabulary Instruction Checklist will support you as you continue to bolster students' understanding and use of academic vocabulary.

FIGURE 5.15 VOCABULARY INSTRUCTION CHECKLIST

UNIT VOCABULARY		
STEPS	**COMPLETED**	**NOTES**
1. I have selected a short, engaging, content-related text to use for vocabulary selection.		
2. I have selected five to eight words that are central to understanding the text, appear frequently in the text, may appear in other content areas, have multiple meanings, or have affixes.		
3. I have assessed students' initial understanding of these words.		
4. I have taught the words using student-friendly definitions, visuals or actions, synonyms, antonyms, examples, and nonexamples.		

(Continued)

(Continued)

UNIT VOCABULARY		
STEPS	COMPLETED	NOTES
5. I have given students opportunities to practice the words in varied ways using multiple domains (i.e., speaking, reading, writing, and listening).		
6. I have given students opportunities to practice word-learning strategies (e.g., context clues, word parts, and cognates).		
7. I have reassessed student understanding of the new words.		

 Available for download at **resources.corwin.com/FennerUnlocking2E**

Let's now explore specific considerations for teaching academic vocabulary to ML newcomer students and students with limited or interrupted formal education (SLIFE) and the role that collaboration, equity, advocacy, and leadership can play in the instruction of academic language at the word/phrase level.

ML NEWCOMER STUDENTS AND SLIFE CONSIDERATIONS

What Are Key Considerations for Supporting ML Newcomer Students and SLIFE With Academic Language at the Word/Phrase Level?

We offer three important considerations when teaching academic language at the word/phrase level to ML newcomer students and SLIFE.

Considerations:

- ML newcomer students and SLIFE can create their own individual vocabulary books that include the definition in English and their home language, an illustration, and an example of how the word is used in a sentence. When students create their own books, rather than simply referring to a dictionary, they are more likely to take ownership of the words. (DeCapua et al., 2020). These vocabulary books can be used across content areas and travel with students throughout the school day for students to reference and add to as needed.

- Focusing on key affixes can support ML newcomer students and SLIFE's vocabulary development across content areas. When students are taught the meaning of key affixes (e.g., *un-*, *re-*, *-able*), it can help them in unlocking the meaning of many other words they encounter throughout their school day (DeCapua et al., 2020). For example, once they understand that the meaning of *un-* is *not*, they can apply that understanding to words that will encounter throughout their school day (e.g., *unfair, unhealthy, uncover*).

- When developing ML newcomer students and SLIFE's academic language at the word/phrase level, it is important to model how to use vocabulary words in context. Students need explicit instruction on how to use new words and phrases in complete sentences. Using sentence frames can be very helpful for this as they provide students with the grammatical structures needed to produce a complete sentence. Teachers can also have students work collaboratively to put together a mixed-up sentence. For this activity, the teacher gives students a sentence cut up into pieces (words and/or phrases) and then the students work together to put the sentence together.

Example: Joseph, the seventh-grade student from the Democratic Republic of Congo who was introduced in Chapter 2, encounters new vocabulary words daily in his classes. His ELD teacher, Ms. Frank, worked with him to set up a vocabulary book that travels with him throughout the school day. Joseph created the vocabulary book in a three-ring binder, alphabetically, so that he can easily add to it when he encounters new, important words during the school day. For each word, he includes the English definition and a translation in French or Swahili, an illustration, and an example of the word used in context. In collaboration with her administrator, Ms. Frank set up time to meet with all of Joseph's teachers to share with them about Joseph's vocabulary notebook and suggest strategies for using it to support Joseph's academic-language development at the word/phrase level in their classes. The teachers agreed that this approach would be helpful in supporting Joseph and developed various ways to incorporate it into their classroom. For instance, the physical education and health teacher, Mr. Engel, created a list of key unit vocabulary words for Joseph to add into the notebook. During independent work time, he worked individually with Joseph to add these key words into his vocabulary notebook and was intentional about encouraging Joseph to refer to his notebook throughout the unit.

What Is the Role of Collaboration in Teaching Academic Vocabulary to MLs?

When ELD teachers and content teachers collaborate, it can be highly beneficial to both MLs and the teachers of MLs (Honigsfeld & Dove, 2019). Sharing responsibility of planning for and teaching academic vocabulary is an excellent opportunity to build such collaboration. Content teachers and ELD teachers can share their expertise as they work together to select a small set of vocabulary words that is both essential to the content being covered and that may present challenges to MLs. Content teachers can lend their expertise in determining content-specific texts that will allow students to see the new vocabulary embedded in rich content material. They can also share information with the ELD teacher on the key vocabulary that students need to know in the unit. ELD teachers can suggest concrete ways of teaching and practicing the new vocabulary. ELD teachers can also give explicit instruction on the pronunciation, morphology (word parts), syntax (how words are put together to form phrases and sentences), and function of the new word, as well as address its word family members or root of the word. Both teachers can work together to develop activities and materials that will support MLs of varying proficiency levels in gaining deeper understanding of the new vocabulary and practicing using the new words in multiple modalities.

What Is the Role of Equity, Advocacy, and Leadership in Teaching Academic Vocabulary to MLs?

In order to comprehend instruction and access challenging grade-level texts, MLs need a solid grasp of the academic vocabulary connected to the content and the texts. Non-MLs may already have a working knowledge of this vocabulary, so it is each teacher's responsibility to intentionally teach MLs the vocabulary they need to fully engage in instruction and set up opportunities for incidental vocabulary learning. Teaching MLs vocabulary the same ways you teach non-MLs vocabulary may not be effective, so you will need to try out and adopt new strategies that are effective with the MLs in your classroom. It is also essential that you give MLs multiple opportunities to practice this new vocabulary in the four domains (i.e., reading, writing, listening, and speaking). In addition, you can leverage your leadership skills to ensure that all teachers you work with are aware of MLs' strengths and needs in terms of academic vocabulary and collaborate with other teachers in your grade level or content area. Administrators must demonstrate they value the importance of collaboratively teaching MLs vocabulary by allocating time and creating a structure for content and ELD teachers to collaboratively plan for supporting MLs' academic vocabulary development.

Next Steps

In order to practice and adopt the word/phrase level academic-language strategies outlined in this chapter, please complete the following application activity.

APPLICATION ACTIVITY 5.8: PLANNING TO TEACH ACADEMIC VOCABULARY

Think about the key vocabulary in the unit you are planning. Use the Academic-Vocabulary Planning Template (Figure 5.16) to select the vocabulary you will teach explicitly within the unit sequence. Note that the Academic Vocabulary Planning Template can also be used as a standalone tool or as a supporting tool to accompany the Unlocking MLs' Potential Unit Planning Template (Appendix A).

FIGURE 5.16 ACADEMIC VOCABULARY PLANNING TEMPLATE

Unit or lesson topic:

Text:

A. Select **five to eight words that you will teach. For each word, write a student-friendly** definition.

WORD	STUDENT-FRIENDLY DEFINITION
1.	
2.	
3.	
4.	
5.	
6.	
7.	
8.	

(Continued)

(Continued)

B. **Explain how you will assess the students' understanding and use of the vocabulary (prior to instruction).**

_____

_____

_____

_____

C. **Explain how you will introduce or teach this set of vocabulary words.**

_____

_____

_____

_____

D. **Explain what activities you will use to help students learn and practice these new words (e.g., word map, use of visuals, vocabulary bingo, or information gap).**

_____

_____

_____

_____

E. **Determine what, if any, word-learning skills (e.g., understanding cognates, determining meaning from context, or understanding word parts) you will have students practice. What will the activity include?**

_____

_____

_____

Now, add your plans to the *Unit Preparation* section of the Unlocking MLs' Potential Unit Planning Template (Appendix A). Appendix A can be found on the online companion website. To access the companion website, please visit resources.corwin.com/FennerUnlocking2E.

UNLOCKING RESOURCES

resources.corwin
.com/FennerUnlocking2E

FIGURE 5.17	PORTION OF THE UNLOCKING MLs' POTENTIAL UNIT PLANNING TEMPLATE (APPENDIX A)

UNIT PREPARATION

Analyze the Language Demands of the Unit

Figure 5.15 Vocabulary Instruction Checklist

Figure 5.16 Academic Vocabulary Planning Template

Figure 6.6 Checklist for Increasing Academic-Language Awareness

Appendix F Checklist for Supporting MLs' Academic-Language Development in Speaking and Writing

Word/Phrase Level. Which key vocabulary (5-8 words) will be unfamiliar and is essential to teach in order for MLs to meet the unit objectives?

Conclusion

In this chapter, we highlighted what the concept of academic language entails with a focus on developing MLs' academic language at the word/phrase level. We have explained why the explicit and strategic instruction of academic vocabulary is so important to MLs' acquisition of language and learning of content. We have also shared some recommendations for how to select the vocabulary you will teach, outlined several strategies for teaching and practicing new vocabulary, as well as given you ideas for supporting MLs' independent word-learning skills. In the next chapter, we will be including information on how to teach and support MLs at the sentence and discourse levels of academic language.

SupportEd TOOLBOX

For ready-to-use, practical tools to support academic-language development at the word/phrase level, please see SupportEd .com/unlocking-toolbox.

CHAPTER 5 REFLECTION QUESTIONS

1. How do you plan to adapt your current strategies for teaching new vocabulary to MLs?

2. What is one new activity for practicing vocabulary with MLs that you would like to use? How will you adapt it for your context?

3. What is one skill for supporting MLs with learning new vocabulary independently that you would like to try out in your classroom? Why?

 Available for download at **resources.corwin.com/FennerUnlocking2E**

TEACHING ACADEMIC LANGUAGE TO MLs AT THE SENTENCE AND DISCOURSE LEVEL

6

Ms. Zavala-Aguilera teaches kindergarten in an urban school district at Oakwood Elementary.[1] Thirty-eight percent of the students at the school qualify for English language development (ELD) services, and the vast majority are from families in which Spanish is spoken in the home. Ms. Zavala-Aguilera seeks out opportunities for her students to practice academic language throughout the school day. One systematic way that she has made time for academic-language practice is during her daily calendar routine. In addition to the familiar topics that are often included during calendar or morning meeting time in kindergarten classrooms, Ms. Zavala-Aguilera has added in some unique features to her calendar routine. To start the routine, students sing the days of the week and the months of the year in both English and Spanish. Ms. Zavala-Aguilera explains, "I like showing pride in my culture with Spanish, and it gives some of the students pride to sing [these songs] in their language." She also asks students to answer how many syllables are in the current month, bringing in literacy practice. When talking about the days of the week, students speak in full sentences to explain "Yesterday was . . . , Today is . . . , Tomorrow will be . . .".

Students in Ms. Zavala-Aguilera's kindergarten classroom talk about tally marks, ten-frames, and graphing during a daily meeting.

Source: Ana Zavala-Aguilera

---

[1]*Source:* The description of this calendar routine was shared with us by Ana Zavala-Aguilera, a kindergarten teacher who we collaborated with during the 2022–2023 school year. The name of the school is a pseudonym.

During the calendar routine, students also track how many days that they have been in school. They note this amount using numbers, tally marks, and ten-frames. Students repeat specific language and gestures to support their understanding of the use of tally marks and ten-frames. For example, students chant together, "When we tally we go 1, 2, 3, 4, diagonal" and use gestures to support their understanding. Ms. Zavala-Aguilera feels that this language and action help the students visualize a group of five. After students count by 5s, the calendar helper crosses out the number of the days of school in the 180 chart (the number of days in the school year), and then moves on to the ten-frame. Ms. Zavala asks students why it is called a ten-frame, and they respond that it is called a ten-frame because it has ten spaces (answering in a complete sentence). She reminds students (and soon students are able to say it with her) that when the ten-frame is full, they count by 10s, and when it is not full, they "count on." The calendar helper adds a circle to the ten-frame to represent the day in the school year, and then the class practices identifying how many more circles are needed to make 10. Students use the sentence frame to chorally say "___ and ___ make 10," and then they convert it into an equation, "___ + ___ = ___ ." The last step in the calendar routine incorporates graphing while talking about the weather. Ms. Zavala-Aguilera asks what the weather is like, and the calendar helper colors in a block in the graph (personal communication, March 31, 2023).

REFLECTION QUESTIONS

1. What takeaways do you have about the way in which Ms. Zavala-Aguilera embeds academic-language practice into her calendar routine?

2. What do you notice about how she supports students in practicing academic language at the sentence level?

3. What are some ways that you or your colleagues include academic-language practice outside of specific content instruction time (e.g., practicing language for explaining reasoning during a warm-up activity)?

online resources   Available for download at **resources.corwin.com/FennerUnlocking2E**

In the previous chapter, we explored the levels of academic language and the importance of academic-language development for multilingual learners (MLs). We also explored strategies for selecting, introducing, and practicing academic vocabulary. In this chapter, we'll discuss how to analyze a text's academic language in order to determine what academic language to teach. We'll also explore strategies for teaching academic language at the sentence and discourse levels. Over the course of this chapter, we hope that you'll be able to apply your understanding of academic language across grade levels and content areas. The chapter also provides guidance on how to leverage different types of teachers' strengths in order to effectively collaborate on weaving together academic language and content instruction.

Why Don't MLs Just Need Assistance With Vocabulary?

In order for MLs to comprehend complex content instruction, teachers need to expand their repertoire to move beyond focusing on academic language only at the word/phrase level. However, you don't need to spend a long time on the grammatical rules and terms. It's more important to help students understand the function, meaning, and organization of the language they're encountering so that they are able to deconstruct complex texts, engage in academic discourse, and produce cohesive pieces of writing. The added bonus is that exploring academic language at the sentence and discourse levels will likely benefit your non-MLs as well. Before moving on to discussing strategies, let's take a closer look at the components of academic language at the sentence and discourse levels.

What Is the Sentence Level?

As we described in Chapter 5, academic language at the **sentence level is the grammar and syntax MLs need to acquire in order to access complex concepts and texts and engage with their peers and teachers.** The WIDA ELD Standards Framework (WIDA, 2020a) describe academic language at the sentence level as the "grammatical complexity of language," and note that it includes such features as simple, compound, and complex sentences, coordinating and subordinating conjunctions, and dependent and independent clauses (pp. 32–33). Knowing grammatical features can help MLs to understand how relationships are expressed through clauses (a group of words that includes both a subject and a predicate). Depending on your background and expertise, the use of these grammatical terms may give you flashbacks to high school English classes or even have you asking, "Why does this matter to me?". Having an understanding of the different types of grammatical features that MLs need to be able to understand and produce will be very helpful in supporting MLs' language development. Complete Application Activity 6.1 to explore some of the grammatical features you'll want to be familiar with to strengthen MLs' academic-language development at the sentence level.

APPLICATION ACTIVITY 6.1: EXPLORING SENTENCE STRUCTURES

Look at the four sentences that follow. We selected these sentences because they represent the variety of sentence types related to one topic that might be found in a science textbook. Determine which one you think might be most challenging for MLs. Focus only on sentence structure, not vocabulary. Then, complete the sentence stems. Use Figure 6.1 as a resource. Please note that specific grammatical terms and examples in Figure 6.1 have been color-coded or underlined to support your understanding. We

(Continued)

(Continued)

have used color-coding to match specific grammatical constructs with their examples (e.g., *subject* and *the boy*). We have used underlining to identify the conjunctions. Using color-coding to highlight similarities and differences in content or language can be a great way for MLs to visually make connections.

Sentences

1. The water table can rise or fall depending on the amount of water in the aquifer.

2. Groundwater is either stored or it flows underground.

3. Water from precipitation may seep below the surface and become groundwater.

4. The storage space in an aquifer is measured by porosity, the percentage of the rock that is composed of pore space.

Text source: Holt McDougal Science Fusion (2012, p. 36).

Focusing only on the sentence structure and not evaluating the vocabulary, which sentence do you think might be most difficult for MLs? Why?

1. I think the most difficult sentence is _____ because _____

   _____ .

2. Something that might help MLs understand this sentence is _____

   _____ .

FIGURE 6.1   GRAMMATICAL FEATURES

GRAMMATICAL FEATURE	DEFINITION	EXAMPLES
Clauses		
Clause	A group of words containing a subject and a predicate (part of the clause with the verb); not every clause is a sentence	The boy walks. If I see her
Independent clause	Clauses that can stand independently as a complete sentence	I see a house.
Dependent clauses (also known as subordinate clauses)	Clauses that cannot stand independently as a complete sentence	Before I go to school

GRAMMATICAL FEATURE	DEFINITION	EXAMPLES
Sentences		
Simple sentence	Consists of at least one subject and one predicate and can stand alone (the same as an independent clause)	She bought a car.
Compound sentence	Consists of two or more independent clauses of equal grammatical importance	I went to the park, <u>but</u> my sister stayed home.
Complex sentence	Consists of a main independent clause and one or more dependent clauses; the clause can be embedded	I didn't go to the game <u>because</u> it was raining. The child who was responsible for the broken window ran away.
Conjunctions		
Coordinating <u>conjunction</u>	Words that join elements that are grammatically equal Examples: and, but, or	Jorge <u>and</u> Rebecca are teachers. Jorge lives in Virginia, <u>but</u> Rebecca lives in Oregon.
Subordinating <u>conjunction</u>	Words that join a dependent clause to a main independent clause Examples: because, although, while, whenever, before	<u>Although</u> we were hungry, we didn't stop to eat.

Source: Adapted from Celce-Murcia, M., & Larsen-Freeman, D. (1999).

As you probably identified in this activity, sentences one and four are the most complex. In order to support students in being able to deconstruct complex sentences, it can be helpful to provide an opportunity for them to think about the relationships of clauses within sentences. Figure 6.2 identifies each sentence type from our four sample sentences and possible challenges for MLs. Please note the independent and dependent clauses are color-coded, and the conjunctions are underlined.

FIGURE 6.2   SENTENCE TYPES AND POSSIBLE CHALLENGES

SENTENCE	SENTENCE TYPE	POSSIBLE CHALLENGES FOR MLs
1. The water table can rise or fall <u>depending on</u> the amount of water in the aquifer.	Complex sentence	This sentence includes a dependent clause. If MLs are not familiar with the use of "depending on," they may find it challenging to identify the relationship between the independent and dependent clauses.
2. Groundwater is <u>either</u> stored <u>or</u> it flows underground.	Compound sentence	This sentence is fairly straightforward if students understand the vocabulary. MLs may need support in understanding the use of "either" / "or." Another challenge MLs may have is understanding what the pronoun "it" refers to.
3. Water from precipitation may seep below the surface <u>and</u> become groundwater.	Simple sentence	This sentence is fairly straightforward if students understand the vocabulary. This sentence includes a compound predicate as there are two verb phrases ("may seep" and "become").
4. The storage space in an aquifer is measured by porosity, the percentage of the rock that is composed of pore space.	Complex sentence	This sentence includes a dependent clause that provides the definition for the word "porosity." It's important that MLs recognize the way in which academic texts may provide embedded definitions of academic terms within a sentence without a conjunction to support understanding of the term.

What Is the Discourse Level?

In our work with teachers, we have found that the concept of the discourse level can be the most abstract and, by default, the most challenging to grasp, as compared with the word/phrase and sentence levels. The word *discourse* also has multiple meanings, and sometimes people think about the word *discourse* in terms of having a conversation with someone. However, **when referring to academic language, the discourse level features include the organization, structure, and purpose of text or talk as a whole.** Zwiers (2008) describes discourse as the "message level" of communication, including voice and register; clarity and coherence; and purpose, functions, and audience. These nuances at the discourse level such as register (e.g., the level of formality used in language when speaking with an adult versus a peer) can make the discourse level especially challenging for MLs who may still be acquiring a level of English needed to be aware of such components of discourse and to use them consistently.

REFLECTION QUESTIONS

Consider how a lab report is different from a poem.

1. What is different about the purpose of each?

2. What are the features that make each unique?

 Available for download at **resources.corwin.com/FennerUnlocking2E**

As we described in Chapter 5, the WIDA ELD Standards Framework (WIDA, 2020a) describes discourse as the organization, cohesion, and density of language. Figure 6.3 provides a short explanation of each.

FIGURE 6.3   DISCOURSE FEATURES

Organization	How ideas are organized in order to support the text purpose
Cohesion	How language is used to connect ideas within and across sentences
Density	How loosely or tightly language is packed throughout a text

Source: Adapted from WIDA English Language Development Standards Framework, 2020 Edition: https://wida.wisc.edu/teach/standards/eld/2020, © 2020 Board of Regents of the University of Wisconsin System wida.wisc.edu.

In terms of what MLs need to be able to do with language at the discourse level, they will need to navigate academic text to understand the gist, summarize or explain the meaning of a text, and also extract key information from text. They also need to be able to understand the distinct structures of a variety of texts used in different content areas. For example, they will need to know how texts that are intended to persuade are organized differently from texts that are intended to inform. The WIDA ELD Standards Framework (WIDA, 2020a) describes these different text types as "**genre families—categories of texts that share specific characteristics, such as purpose, organization, or other similar patterns of language use**" (p. 26). For example, if you are discussing a genre of texts that intend to persuade, students might watch a persuasive speech and read a letter to the editor in order to discuss similarities across these texts.

In addition to understanding discourse-level features of texts, students will also need to be able to produce academic language at the discourse level, orally, in writing, and through multimodal texts. **Multimodal texts are texts that use a combination of different modes of communication such as images, sounds, and words** (Gee, 2007; Jewitt, 2014). An example is a PowerPoint slide with a written text, an embedded audio recording, and a visual. Based on the academic task, students will need to be able to create coherent texts, connect ideas across the texts, and elaborate or condense their ideas (WIDA, 2020a).

In order to provide an opportunity to further explore the three levels of academic language in greater depth, we have created an activity framed around WIDA's (2020a) explanation of the levels of academic language, the definition of each, and possible areas to focus on during instruction. We introduced these in Chapter 5 (see Application Activity 5.2). In Application Activity 6.2, we are going to give you an opportunity to apply these concepts to classroom examples.

APPLICATION ACTIVITY 6.2: ACADEMIC-LANGUAGE CLASSROOM EXAMPLES

1. Review Figure 6.4 including the classroom examples provided in the final column. The examples represent what MLs might do at a range of English language proficiency levels or with different types of scaffolded support.

2. Next, choose two of the classroom examples to focus on, and complete Figure 6.5. Decide what you might do to assist the ML in the example in continuing to develop academic language at that academic-language level. The word/phrase level is filled in for you as an example.

FIGURE 6.4   ACADEMIC-LANGUAGE LEVELS, DEFINITION, FOCUS, AND CLASSROOM EXAMPLES

LEVEL	DEFINITION	DURING INSTRUCTION FOCUS ON . . .	CLASSROOM EXAMPLES
Word/phrase	Precision of language (vocabulary use)	How everyday, cross-disciplinary, and technical language more effectively conveys precise meaning	When writing about the life cycle of a butterfly, an emergent ML uses the word *cocoon* instead of *chrysalis*.
Sentence	Grammatical complexity of language (sentence structure)	How relationships are expressed with clauses through simple, compound, and complex sentences	When describing how they solved a math problem, an emergent ML uses simple sentences to explain each step (*I subtract.*).
Discourse	Organization of language	How ideas are coherently organized to meet a purpose through organizational patterns characteristic of the genre	An emergent ML retells a story using two common signal words (*first, next*).

LEVEL	DEFINITION	DURING INSTRUCTION FOCUS ON . . .	CLASSROOM EXAMPLES
Discourse (continued)	Cohesion of language (the way language holds together)	How language connects ideas within and across sentences and discourse using a range of cohesive devices	An emergent ML explains what they learned about Maya civilization and repeats the phrase *The Maya made . . .* at the beginning of several sentences during the explanation.
	Density of language (amount of language used)	How information in noun groups is expanded or consolidated; a noun group is a noun or pronoun and the words that modify it (e.g., the five black shirts that Sally owns)	An emergent ML writes a short narrative of an event that happened in their life. They include some descriptive language in two- or three-word noun groups (*a small cat, warm milk*).

Source: Adapted from WIDA English Language Development Standards Framework, 2020 Edition, https://wida.wisc.edu/teach/standards/eld/2020, © 2020 Board of Regents of the University of Wisconsin System wida.wisc.edu.

FIGURE 6.5 WHAT I MIGHT DO TO SUPPORT MLs' ACADEMIC-LANGUAGE DEVELOPMENT

CLASSROOM EXAMPLE FROM FIGURE 6.4	WHAT I MIGHT DO TO SUPPORT MLs' ACADEMIC-LANGUAGE DEVELOPMENT AT THIS ACADEMIC-LANGUAGE LEVEL
When writing about the life cycle of a butterfly, a student uses the word cocoon instead of chrysalis.	I might reinforce understanding of the unit's technical language by reviewing the vocabulary using images, by having students match pictures with vocabulary words, and by having students write captions for pictures using a word bank of key terms.

(Continued)

(Continued)

CLASSROOM EXAMPLE FROM FIGURE 6.4	WHAT I MIGHT DO TO SUPPORT MLs' ACADEMIC-LANGUAGE DEVELOPMENT AT THIS ACADEMIC-LANGUAGE LEVEL

How Do I Increase My Awareness of the Academic Language MLs Need to Access Challenging Content?

Teachers must be aware of the academic language that is essential for their students' access of content before they can teach it. However, it's not always obvious that certain elements of academic language may pose challenges to MLs. This is because, without training, many teachers may simply not be attuned to vocabulary, sentence structures, and discourse features that may inhibit MLs' access to academic content. It takes practice to learn to be able to identify challenges that MLs might have, and this type of training is generally not included in preservice education programs. One way to become more aware of the vast quantity of academic language MLs encounter in their content classes is to analyze the academic language you find in a text that students use during instruction.

We recommend that content teachers collaborate with ELD teachers to analyze texts in order to discover which elements of academic language may present barriers to MLs comprehending and working with these texts. When direct collaboration with an ELD teacher is not possible, we recommend content teachers collaborate with other content teachers, reading specialists, instructional coaches, or special education teachers to unlock the academic language necessary for instruction. Academic language is aligned and intertwined with content, ELD standards, objectives, texts, and assessments.

REFLECTION QUESTIONS

1. How prepared do you feel to analyze the academic-language demands of the content you teach or to support colleagues in analyzing the language demands of their content?

2. Who might you collaborate with to do this work?

online resources ▶ Available for download at **resources.corwin.com/FennerUnlocking2E**

How Can I Figure Out What Academic Language Might Be Challenging for MLs?

One way you can develop a general sense of which aspects of language might make MLs' access to content challenging is by collaborating with a teacher to determine which areas of content and language might present the most barriers. For Application Activity 6.3, consider the following math problem adapted from the New York State Testing Program (2016) and answer the reflection questions. If possible, discuss this problem with a colleague.

APPLICATION ACTIVITY 6.3: ANALYZING THE ACADEMIC-LANGUAGE DEMANDS

Addison wants to ride her scooter more than 100 miles this month. She has already ridden her scooter 12 miles. Which inequality could be used to determine the mean number of miles, m, she would need to ride her scooter each day for 20 more days to achieve her goal?

A. $20m + 12 < 100$

B. $20m - 12 < 100$

C. $20m + 12 > 100$

D. $20m - 12 = 100$

Source: Adapted from New York State Testing Program (2016).

APPLICATION ACTIVITY 6.3: REFLECTION QUESTIONS

1. What might be difficult for MLs in terms of the content?

_____

_____

(Continued)

(Continued)

2. What might be difficult for MLs in terms of the language expectations?

_____

_____

3. How can you scaffold this problem so that MLs can access its meaning and answer it?

_____

_____

4. What could you explicitly teach MLs in order to support them in independently tackling a similarly structured or worded problem in the future?

_____

_____

online resources   Available for download at **resources.corwin.com/FennerUnlocking2E**

Collaboratively analyzing a question like this can be very helpful in understanding the content and language demands of a particular question or task. This series of questions could be adapted and used with any content area material. And if you were wondering about the correct answer to the math problem, it's C.

Checklist for Increasing Academic-Language Awareness

Another way educators can increase their awareness of academic language is by completing Figure 6.6, the "Checklist for Increasing Academic-Language Awareness." We suggest you collaborate with an ELD teacher or content teacher to do a deep dive and analyze the academic language found in a text that you will use during your instruction. Begin by noting the purpose for using the text, and then identify the different levels of academic language found in the text. By working through this checklist, you can develop a deeper understanding of the levels of academic language in authentic texts and prioritize which features of academic language are important for lessons based on a particular text and purpose for using the text. You can prioritize which features of academic language to teach in mini lessons or point out to students during instruction. We provide a modified version of this checklist to support MLs' language development for speaking and writing in Appendix F in the online companion website. To access the companion website, please visit resources.corwin.com/FennerUnlocking2E.

Following the checklist in Figure 6.6, you can read about the takeaways Mr. Marhamati and Ms. Peake, an ELD teacher and a third-grade teacher, had when using this checklist with the text *Moonshot: The Flight of Apollo 11*.

UNLOCKING RESOURCES

resources.corwin .com/FennerUnlocking2E

FIGURE 6.6   CHECKLIST FOR INCREASING ACADEMIC-LANGUAGE AWARENESS

Lesson Objectives:	Text:
Text type (e.g., biography, poem, lab report, word problem):	Text purpose (e.g., to inform, to persuade)
Academic tasks students will complete (e.g., summarize a text excerpt, discuss the main idea):	

AWARENESS-BUILDING QUESTIONS	EXAMPLE(S) FOUND IN TEXT (IF PRESENT)	PRIORITY FOR INSTRUCTION
WORD/PHRASE LEVEL		
Are there **everyday words** (e.g., ruler) that may be unfamiliar to MLs?		☐
Are there **cross-disciplinary academic words** (e.g., analyze or describe) that may be unfamiliar to MLs?		☐
Are there **content or technical words** specific to the topic you're teaching that may be unfamiliar to MLs?		☐
Does the vocabulary in the text lend itself to any **mini lessons on word-learning strategies** (e.g., words with multiple meanings, determining meaning of words in context, cognates, or affixes)?		☐
SENTENCE LEVEL		
Are there aspects of **grammar** (e.g., clauses, verb tense, or interrogatives) that may be challenging for MLs?		☐

(Continued)

(Continued)

	AWARENESS-BUILDING QUESTIONS	EXAMPLE(S) FOUND IN TEXT (IF PRESENT)	PRIORITY FOR INSTRUCTION
SENTENCE LEVEL			
	Are there any **complex sentences** that might be confusing to MLs? (Consider these for a language dive or mentor sentence)		☐
	Are there any **conventions** that may be new or confusing (e.g., punctuation, spelling)?		☐
DISCOURSE LEVEL			
	How is the text **organized or structured to support the text purpose**? What challenges might MLs have in identifying organizational features or text purpose?		☐
	What **cohesive devices** (use of synonyms, pronoun substitution, connecting words or phrases) may be challenging for MLs?		☐
	Are there any challenges for MLs related to **language density** (e.g., use of adjectives, modifiers, prepositional phrases)?		☐
SOCIOCULTURAL CONTEXT			
	Does the text assume any **experience**, **background knowledge**, and/or **awareness** for students to understand it?		☐
	Could students' first **language and/or home culture** impact their understanding of the text?		☐

Source: Adapted from WIDA English Language Development Standards Framework, 2020 Edition, https://wida.wisc.edu/teach/standards/eld/2020, © 2020 Board of Regents of the University of Wisconsin System wida.wisc.edu. Icons by iStock.com/Tiyas and iStock.com/MaksimAnkuda.

Based on your analysis of the text, what is a mini lesson you might want to add to your lesson to support MLs' engagement with the text and academic-language development?

_____

_____

_____

Moonshot: The Flight of Apollo 11 **by Brian Floca (2009)**

High above there is the Moon, cold and quiet, no air, no life, but glowing in the sky.

Here below there are three men who close themselves in special clothes, who—click—lock hands in heavy gloves, who—click—lock heads in large round helmets.

It is summer here in Florida, hot, and near the sea. But now these men are dressed for colder, stranger places. They walk with stiff and awkward steps in suits not made for Earth.

They have studied and practiced and trained, and said good-bye to family and friends. If all goes well, they will be gone for one week, gone where no one has been.

Their two small spaceships are Columbia *and* Eagle. *They sit atop the rocket that will raise them into space, a monster of a machine: It stands thirty stories, it weighs six million pounds, a tower full of fuel and fire and valves and pipes and engines, too big to believe, but built to fly—the mighty, massive Saturn V.*

The astronauts squeeze in to Columbia's *sideways seats, lying on their backs, facing toward the sky—Neil Armstrong on the left, Michael Collins in the right, Buzz Aldrin in the middle.*

Click and they fasten straps.

Click and the hatch is sealed.

There they wait, while the Saturn hums beneath them.

Near the rocket, in Launch Control, and far away in Houston, in Mission Control, there are numbers, screens, and charts, ways of watching and checking every piece of the rocket and ships, the fuel, the valves, the pipes, the engines, the beats of the astronauts' hearts.

As the countdown closes, each man watching is asked the question: GO/NO GO? And each man answers back: "GO." "GO." "GO." Apollo 11 is GO for launch.

Teacher Takeaways

Background and Purpose for Using the Text: Mr. Marhamati and Ms. Peake coteach a third-grade English language arts class that has a total of 25 students, 10 of whom are emergent MLs who speak Farsi, Vietnamese, Spanish, and Ukrainian at the beginning and intermediate levels. The teacher team referred to their content and English language development (ELD) standards and decided the purpose for which their students would read this text would be to demonstrate their understanding of it. They would also focus on having the students determine the meaning of some key words and phrases in the text that help unlock the meaning for students.

Word Level: Mr. Marhamati and Ms. Peake decided to focus on cross-disciplinary vocabulary words and also make sure their students grasped key words that would help them unlock the meaning of the text. Based on that approach, they chose the six words *practiced, trained, weighs, tower, launch,* and *mission.* In addition, they chose the word *click,* which is not a cross-disciplinary word but is key for understanding the text.

Sentence Level: At the sentence level, they noted the use of the present perfect verb tense (*have studied* and *has been*) and decided to highlight this structure for students, realizing that their emergent MLs, as well as their fluent English speakers, would benefit from knowing more about this verb tense. They also noted some complex sentences ("If all goes well, they will be gone for one week, gone where no one has been"). They decided to have students break this complex sentence into more manageable pieces to dig deeper into its meaning. Mr. Marhamati also pointed out that there were participle phrases ("lying on their backs," "facing toward the sky"), but the team decided not to focus on participle phrases at this point in time.

Discourse Level: At the discourse level, Ms. Peake pointed out that the text is organized as a narrative, nonfiction text. Mr. Marhamati noticed its use of stanzas, similar to a poem. The team also recognized how the word *click* is used to signify the sequence of events, which underscores the importance of students knowing the meaning of the word *click* in this context. They decided to focus on eliciting students' observations on how the text uses language to form a cohesive message.

Sociocultural Context: The teacher team recognized that their MLs will need to bring some background knowledge to their approach to this text, including some knowledge of space exploration and who the astronauts are. In addition, they will need to be as familiar as non-MLs with NASA (e.g., Mission Control and Houston). The teachers recognized that Mr. Marhamati, the ELD teacher, can concisely preteach some essential background the MLs will need to fully access the text. In addition, the teachers noted how their MLs are encouraged to use their home languages in summarizing and accessing complex texts, which they plan to intentionally build into their instruction using this text.

How Do I Teach Academic Language to MLs at the Sentence Level?

Once you have completed the checklist and determined an area of priority in teaching sentence-level academic language, it's time to add some tools to your toolbox so your MLs can focus on unlocking academic language. There are many ways to teach sentence-level academic language to MLs, and we'll share three ways to do so in this chapter: unpacking juicy sentences, structured sentence books, and picture scene descriptions. All three of these activities can be linked to mini lessons focusing on a specific aspect of language that connect to your language objectives and content.

Unpacking Juicy Sentences

One sentence-level strategy is Wong Fillmore and Fillmore's (2012) *juicy sentences* approach in which students analyze sentences from grade-level texts that may be particularly challenging in order to unlock these sentences' meanings. A similar activity is known as Sentence Detectives (California Department of Education, 2015). There are a variety of approaches to take when using this strategy, but one approach is as follows:

1. Teachers select a sentence that comes from texts that relate to classroom content as a way to build on students' prior knowledge and vocabulary (Student Achievement Partners, 2022). The sentence should be one that can be easily divided into chunks of text and contain multiple pieces of information in one sentence.

2. Write the sentence on a poster paper or display it on an interactive whiteboard, and work with students to break the sentence into smaller chunks.

3. Ask students to "unpack" the meaning of each sentence chunk, summarizing each chunk in their own words (in either their home language, English, or a combination of the two). Teachers can ask questions to help students focus on particular grammatical structures, vocabulary, themes, or figurative language (Student Achievement Partners, 2022). A variation on having students summarize the chunk is to have them sketch the meaning of the chunk or act out the chunk.

4. Finally, have students summarize the entire sentence as a whole, discussing how they were able to unpack its meaning.

5. Once a sentence has been unpacked or deconstructed, teachers can also ask students to create their own sentences using key language structures found in the juicy sentence.

While it isn't possible to unpack every juicy sentence students come across in their encounters with texts, teachers can teach students how to do this on their own. Students' skills in deconstructing and unpacking dense sentences will serve them well across multiple content areas.

Our colleague, Kent Buckley-Ess, shared with us how first-grade teacher Ms. Hoover used juicy sentences to help students with their understanding of the essential question for a unit. The essential question was "How do animals survive in nature?" Ms. Hoover showed the class the focus sentence chosen from the text: "They sniff, search, for foods that . . . REEK!" (Sayre, 2017). While gestures, actions, and synonyms had been used during the read aloud, Ms. Hoover's goal

In this picture you can see how Ms. Hoover's class explained the juicy sentence chunks.

Source: Becky Hoover

with the juicy sentence activity was to help students make sense of the main idea of the story.

Students were placed in pairs and asked to think about the first part of the sentence: "They sniff." Student pairs were asked to think of words that meant the same as "sniff." Groups were asked to share their thinking, and "They smell things" was selected for their understanding of the phrase. A similar approach was conducted for each section of the chosen sentence.

When the pairs discussed how to summarize "REEK!," there were many synonyms considered and a lot of enthusiasm for the discussions. Student pairs talked with other pairs as the discussion focused on which word was the most appropriate to describe the bones and carcasses in the story. One group also suggested "asqueroso" which is Spanish for "disgusting." There was a lot of oral language engagement and academic content being discussed as students justified their reasoning for the grossest word!

Once each chunk had been summarized, the class read the original sentence and then read student-generated sentences, using different combinations of summarized language. Although time ran out, additional language development activity possibilities include the following:

- students writing their own sentences using the juicy sentence chart as a support,

- students creating artwork with labels to show their understanding of the main idea, and

- partner groups working independently on creating a juicy sentence chart for another chosen sentence. (Kent Buckley-Ess, personal communication, March 29, 2023).

Two other activities for supporting MLs' language development at the sentence level were shared by elementary ELD teacher and author Dr. Katie Toppel. Structured sentence books can be used to support MLs' writing at the sentence level, and picture scene descriptions connected to content can be used to support MLs' oral production. Both of these activities could be used following a mini lesson focusing on a particular aspect of grammar (e.g., past tense, conditional tense, pronoun use). We will describe these activities next.

Structured Sentence Books

In Chapter 3, we discussed using sentence stems and frames as a scaffold to support MLs' writing and oral language use. Additionally, writing stems can be intentionally planned to foster more complex language use as a way to facilitate MLs' language development. As you think about providing stems or frames consider the following questions:

1. What is the academic language or language structure that you want students to use?

2. How will the stem or frame support students in being able to produce that language?

3. How will you model the use of the stem or frame for MLs?

4. What is your plan for having students transition to producing this same language without the use of the stem, frame, or word bank?

In describing this activity, Dr. Toppel explained,

> I use sentence stems and frames with vocabulary words that intentionally incorporate compound, complex, and cause/effect sentences. Rather than eliciting the target vocabulary word in the blank, the sentences are open-ended in ways that bring forth more nuanced connections to the target vocabulary based on students' perspectives, background knowledge, and proficiency in writing. The quantity of writing students do is minimized, but they are constructing more complex ideas which requires attention to grammar and syntax in order to successfully complete the missing part of the sentence. This also provides a great way to evaluate where students may need more instruction or support in grammar such as subject verb agreement, use of pronouns, use of plurals, and verb tenses. (personal communication, April 9, 2023)

Dr. Toppel gives students the sentence stems on separate pieces of paper with space for students to complete the sentence. She compiles the sentences into a booklet for students. If time permits, students can also draw a supporting visual to accompany their sentences. While Dr. Toppel uses this activity with students at the elementary level, the activity could also be adapted for secondary students in higher grades to work on specific language structures related to the content being discussed (e.g., cause-and-effect language).

I heard a squeak, so I _used echo location to catch food._

When the bat hears the echo, _they find food._

The bat swoops down, so _it can catch food._

In this image, you can see sentence stems and sample responses from students as they discussed bats and their behaviors. Dr. Toppel intentionally gave students sentence stems to support more complex sentence structures. This academic writing task integrated students' understanding of the content and also fostered students' academic-language development.

Source: Student samples were provided by Katie Toppel with students' permission.

REFLECTION QUESTION

What do you notice about the sentence stems that Dr. Toppel provided her students?

online resources →   Available for download at **resources.corwin.com/FennerUnlocking2E**

Picture Scene Description

Another activity that Dr. Toppel uses to support language development at the sentence level is picture scene descriptions. Dr. Toppel explained,

> We use picture scenes and pictures of images from puzzles to engage students in orally producing descriptive sentences. We find picture scenes that connect to the content being studied and/or align with a set of vocabulary words. We ask students to use the vocabulary words in context based on what they see in the images. We can also use picture scenes to focus on a variety of different parts of speech, with flexibility in what we are asking students to produce based on their language level and grade level. For students who are very new to English, we may ask them to point to specific nouns that we name. For emerging students, we can ask them to take turns sharing simple sentences that name a noun and the verb that corresponds to what the noun is doing. For more advanced students, we might ask for sentences that include a subject, verb, adjective, and detail (such as a prepositional phrase) or ask for a particular type of sentence such as a compound sentence or a sentence that expresses a cause-and-effect relationship. (personal communication, April 9, 2023).

While Dr. Toppel has used this activity for students in grades K–3, she explained that it could be used across grade levels and content areas. For students in older grade levels, you would want to make sure that the images were engaging and appropriate for their age, as well as connected to content being studied.

In this image, you can see an example image of a picture scene that Dr. Toppel asked students to discuss. The captions are student-generated language. Students used if . . . then sentence stems to share their responses.

Source: Sentence stems and student language: Katie Toppel; Illustration: *Kids CAN Make A Difference Philanthro-Peas 48-Piece Children's Floor Puzzle,* by Our Little Treehouse

As you can see, all three of these sentence-level activities provide an opportunity for students to acquire understanding of different aspects of language at the sentence level and can be structured in order to support students in progressing to the next level of language proficiency. Next, let's turn our attention to discourse-level strategies.

How Do I Teach Academic Language to MLs at the Discourse Level?

When teaching academic language to MLs, it is essential to remember that language and content should be taught in tandem. However, in order to be able to connect teaching language and teaching content, it is important to consider what types of functions and features of language are frequently present in a particular content area or a specific genre within that content. As you think about integrating discourse-level strategies, ask yourself these key questions:

- What can I teach my students about this text type to support how they approach a text in this genre?

- What scaffolds can I provide my students to facilitate their production (oral, written, or multimodal) of this type of text?

In this section, we'll be exploring three strategies for teaching academic language at the discourse level. These strategies are analyzing mentor texts, analyzing sequencing, and using visual scaffolds. As you read about these strategies, consider how you might adapt them for use in your context.

Analyzing Mentor Texts

One way to support students in understanding texts at the discourse level is by having students deconstruct or analyze mentor texts. **Mentor texts are pieces of texts that model essential aspects of a particular genre of text for students that you would like students to be able to understand or produce.** For example, if you would like students to write a narrative text, you might have them analyze a short narrative that contains a way to hook the reader in, descriptive language, dialogue, and a sense of closure. While it is best if the mentor texts are authentic texts, teacher-created mentor texts can also be valuable for teaching specific aspects of a text genre to emergent MLs at lower levels of language proficiency so that they are able to focus on the aspects of language specific to that genre without being sidelined by unfamiliar vocabulary or complex grammar structures (Huynh, 2016). There are a variety of different questions that you can ask students during the analysis phase, but the questions should align with those genre-specific features that you would like students to understand. Let's give this a try in Application Activity 6.4.

APPLICATION ACTIVITY 6.4

1. Select a short text or text excerpt from your content area.

2. Read the text and jot down answers to the following questions:

    •   What do you notice about how the text is organized?

    •   What kinds of organizational words or connectors are used in the text?

    •   What types of sentences are used in the text (i.e., simple, compound, complex)?

    •   What do you notice about the language that is used in the text? For example, which types of verbs are used?

    •   What kind of descriptive language did the author use?

    •   What choices do you think the author made when writing this text? Why did the author make those choices?

    •   What do you notice about the punctuation used?

    •   How is this text different from a text in a different content area?

APPLICATION ACTIVITY 6.4: REFLECTION QUESTIONS

1. What did you notice about the language of the text that you analyzed?

_____

_____

2. What other types of questions might you ask students that would help students identify key features of texts in your content area?

_____

_____

online resources   Available for download at **resources.corwin.com/FennerUnlocking2E**

Once you have modeled how to analyze a text in this way, you can ask students to read and discuss the selected text in pairs to share what they notice. Following the pair work, ask students to tell the whole group what they noticed. The large group share out is a great opportunity to create an anchor chart on key aspects of the text type or genre.

Once students have analyzed a mentor text, you can give them an opportunity to create their own example using the features of the genre. This work can either be done in pairs or independently, depending on the level of support that you feel students may need. Huynh (2016) assists students with this work by either providing a list of key ideas that he would like students to include in their writing and specific language features that students should use as they co-construct their paragraph or by having them work in pairs to identify these pieces before beginning to write.

The process of analyzing and then creating a text while focusing on specific aspects of language is a powerful tool to foster language development at the discourse level. Another strategy to build discourse-level academic language is having students focus specifically on sequencing in a text.

Analyzing Sequencing in Texts

As we noted earlier, one aspect of discourse is the cohesion of a text and how ideas are connected across sentences and paragraphs. MLs will need to build their awareness of cohesive devices used in different types of texts, and they can apply this knowledge across content areas to help them unlock the meaning of challenging academic texts. One way you can help MLs learn about cohesive devices in a text is by doing a sentence strip sorting activity to determine the proper order of a text. For this activity, each sentence strip contains one sentence, and students put the text in order based on clues that they find within the text. You can provide extra scaffolding by giving students the first and last sentences and by working with a shorter text. As students work to put the text in order, ask them to think about the clues that they are using in the text to determine the correct order. This activity can also be adapted to analyze the sequencing of paragraphs in an essay or speech as a way to provide students an opportunity to think about how paragraphs are organized to support a specific essay or speech type (e.g., compare and contrast, problem solution, persuasive). Application Activity 6.5 is an opportunity for you to try out the activity.

APPLICATION ACTIVITY 6.5: SEQUENCING IN PARAGRAPHS

Carefully read the six sentences. Determine the correct order for the paragraph, and number the sentences from 1 to 6. Circle any words that provided you clues to the correct order.

_____ Many of the remaining buildings (even the ones proclaimed to be "fireproof") looked solid, but were actually jerry-built affairs; the stone or brick exteriors hid wooden frames and floors, all topped with highly flammable tar or shingle roofs.

_____ The city boasted having 59,500 buildings, many of them—such as the Courthouse and the Tribune Building—large and ornately decorated.

_____ It was also a common practice to disguise wood as another kind of building material.

_____ The trouble was that about two-thirds of all these structures were made entirely of wood.

_____ Chicago in 1871 was a city ready to burn.

_____ The fancy exterior decorations on just about every building were carved from wood, then painted to look like stone or marble.

Text Source: The Great Fire by Jim Murphy, 2006, p. 18

APPLICATION ACTIVITY 6.5: REFLECTION QUESTIONS

1. How might an activity like this support MLs in building their understanding of academic language at the discourse level?

_____

_____

2. How might you scaffold an activity like this for MLs of varying proficiency levels?

_____

_____

3. How might you adapt this activity for your teaching context?

_____

_____

online resources ↘ Available for download at **resources.corwin.com/FennerUnlocking2E**

As you probably noted during the activity, this paragraph did not have many of the usual sequencing words (e.g., first, next, then) that we might teach when we are talking with students about text organization, but it is also important for students to learn other cohesive devices that writers use to connect ideas across sentences and paragraphs. For example, in this text, the pronouns and the language used to refer to the buildings provide clues to the order. For the correct answer to this activity and identified clues, please see Figure 6.9 at the end of the chapter.

Using Visual Scaffolds to Support Understanding

In addition to practice with sequencing, another way to highlight different aspects of discourse features is to use visual clues. Secondary teacher Matt Clements uses a color-coding system to support MLs in his class in building their ideas within a paragraph using a claim, evidence, and reason format (Teaching Channel, n.d.). Students write the claim in one color, provide evidence in another color, and give the reason why the evidence supports the claim in a third color. He tells students that the claim should be the shortest amount of text with the evidence being a little longer, and the reason being the longest of the three. Mr. Clements also uses a color-coded anchor chart as a scaffold for students when writing their paragraphs.

Mr. Clements uses this same format to support students in preparing for a debate on a particular topic. Once they have written their claim, evidence, and reason, they post their idea in one of two places in the room depending on whether they are in favor or against the debate prompt. This strategy of physically separating arguments and counterarguments is another visual way to support students in thinking about the connection of ideas and the specific language that might

Claim
I believe...
They are...
In my opinion...

Evidence
According to the text...
The text states...
For example...

Reason
This is important because...
This is significant because...
Therefore...

This color-coded anchor chart is adapted from the one that Mr. Clements uses in his classroom to support students in writing their claim, evidence, and reason paragraphs.

Source: Adapted from Teaching Channel (n.d.), *Scaffolding Text Structure for ELLs.*

be used when presenting arguments (e.g., in favor of, in support of, in opposition to, counter to).

Former ELD teacher Dorina Sackman also advocates for using a visual approach to assist students in learning about text structure through a strategy that she calls the writing recipe (Sackman, 2018). When writing an essay, students begin by creating a manipulative made out of large index cards. The introduction and conclusion index cards are placed above and below the body paragraph index cards. These cards are outlined in the same color to represent that the three reasons or ideas to support the thesis statement will be presented first in the introduction and summarized in the conclusion. Each one of the body paragraphs is outlined in a different color. This use of color to connect the key reasons to the thesis could also be included in the text that students write. For example, if a student is arguing that one reason social media can be detrimental to mental health is the online bullying that can occur, the idea in the thesis statement and the body paragraph that explains that idea could be highlighted in the same color. Figure 6.7 provides a visual of what this manipulative looks like.

FIGURE 6.7   THE WRITING RECIPE MANIPULATIVE

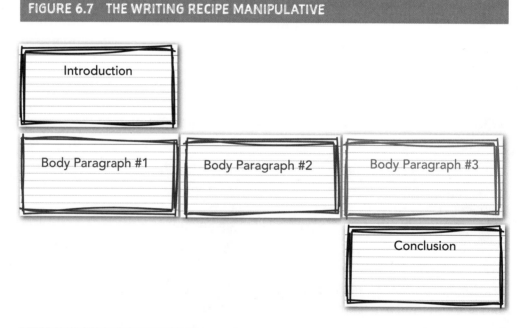

Source: Adapted from Sackman, D. (2018).

REFLECTION QUESTIONS

1. As you think about the sentence- and discourse-level strategies that we have shared in this chapter, what is the strategy that you would most like to try in your context or share with colleagues?

2. How might you collaborate with other educators to support the integration of academic language at the sentence and discourse level?

Now that we've explored strategies to support academic-language development for MLs, let's take a look at some considerations for ML newcomer students and students with limited or interrupted formal education (SLIFE) and the role of collaboration, equity, advocacy, and leadership when teaching academic language to MLs at the sentence and discourse levels.

ML NEWCOMER STUDENTS AND SLIFE CONSIDERATIONS

What Are Key Considerations for Teaching Academic Language at the Sentence and Discourse Levels to ML Newcomer Students and SLIFE?

We offer two important considerations when teaching academic language to ML newcomer students and SLIFE.

Considerations:

- In order to support ML newcomer students and SLIFE's use of academic language, it is important for students to understand why academic language is important to them and their educational and career goals (DeCapua & Marshall, 2023; DeCapua et al., 2020; DeCapua, 2023). You can share with students the important role that academic language plays in learning new content and on assessments. You can also tell them how practice with academic language can also assist them in acquiring language that may help them get a job in the future.

- Because academic language may feel abstract or awkward to students, it can be helpful to discuss the ways that our language use changes across contexts and with different audiences. You can provide opportunities for students to think about their language use and how they can increase their use of academic language. Zwiers and Soto (2016) developed an activity they call Fortify a Conversation in which students take an informal dialogue on a topic and turn it into a more academic one. You can ask students to integrate more academic vocabulary and phrases into the discussion and use evidence to support their ideas.

Scenario: Mx.[2] Martin is Joseph's seventh-grade math teacher in a foundational skills math class for newcomers. To support Joseph and other students in the class in using academic language to describe the steps that they took to solve a problem, Mx. Martin asks the class to first practice using sequencing language to describe the steps that they take to get ready for school in the morning. Students use a word bank of words and phrases such as "first," "next," "then," and "finally." Then Mx. Martin asks the students to use this same language to record themselves explaining how they solved a problem. As additional scaffolds, students are given a word bank of key terms and sentence stems that they can use. They also practice in pairs before doing the recording. Mx. Martin has found that giving ML newcomer students and students with interrupted schooling ample opportunities to use the academic language in structured practice leads to students using this language more authentically during classroom conversations and also supports their understanding of math.

---

[2]Mx. is a gender-neutral honorific used by people who don't want to be identified by gender. It is pronounced as "mix."

What Is the Role of Collaboration When Planning Lessons That Integrate Academic-Language Instruction and Content Instruction?

As more schools, districts, and states move toward a collaborative teaching model, content teachers will have a greater role in teaching MLs features of academic language at the sentence as well as discourse level. Content teachers can leverage their ELD teachers' expertise to consult with them on which features of academic language at the sentence and discourse levels they may wish to focus on during instruction. ELD teachers can provide guidance around mini lessons content teachers could teach to focus on developing MLs' academic language at the sentence and discourse levels. Once students learn academic language in one content area, they can transfer this knowledge to other content areas. Developing and implementing lessons that integrate academic-language instruction with content instruction is a multistep process that benefits from close collaboration between ELD and content teachers. This collaboration recognizes both types of teachers' strengths, builds upon them, and is shown in Figure 6.8.

FIGURE 6.8	STEPS TO COLLABORATIVELY PLAN AND TEACH CONTENT THAT INTEGRATES INSTRUCTION OF ACADEMIC LANGUAGE AND CONTENT	
	STEP	**POSSIBLE LEAD TEACHER**
1.	Identify content standards that guide the lesson, and create content objectives.	Content teacher
2.	Identify ELD standards that support the linguistic demands of the content standards and lesson, and create language objectives where appropriate.	ELD teacher
3.	Analyze the text(s) you'll use during instruction and the expectations for students' language use in academic tasks. Identify features of academic language MLs at different levels of English language proficiency will need to access the text(s) and engage with the academic task in order to meet content and ELD standards.	Content and ELD teacher
4.	Design (a) mini lesson(s) to teach challenging academic language from a text or to support language production during academic tasks.	ELD and content teacher
5.	Integrate scaffolds to support instruction for MLs at different levels of English language proficiency.	ELD teacher
6.	Teach the lesson.	Content and ELD teacher
7.	Reflect on what was effective and what needs improvement in terms of MLs learning academic language and content simultaneously.	Content and ELD teacher
8.	Revise the lesson based on reflection. Repeat Steps 1 through 8 as needed.	Content and ELD teacher

REFLECTION QUESTIONS

1. What are your takeaways from Figure 6.8?

2. What changes might you want to make to how you currently collaborate with other educators to support MLs or to how teacher expertise is leveraged in your context?

 Available for download at **resources.corwin.com/FennerUnlocking2E**

What is the Role of Equity, Advocacy, and Leadership to Promote Academic-Language Development?

As many researchers point out (e.g., August, 2018; Bailey, 2012; Wong Fillmore & Fillmore, 2012; Shanahan, 2013), educators must expose MLs to the discourse as well as content of the content areas. Providing MLs limited access to the content that their grade-level peers receive puts them on a remedial track that may deny them access to the coursework they will need to graduate and experience success after Grade 12. Further, only providing MLs texts at their reading level also does them a disservice. While academic standards focus on grade-level reading and content, educators must strike a balance between providing MLs access only to grade-level texts, which may frustrate MLs if sufficient scaffolding is not provided, and only giving them texts at their reading level, which may deny them access to the complex academic language and content that their grade-level English-fluent peers are exposed to.

We suggest that educators supplement grade-level texts with texts at MLs' reading levels to preview and reinforce content, academic language, and concepts they encounter in grade-appropriate content instruction. In this way, MLs gain confidence in content through working with texts at their reading level (or in their home language) and also benefit from exposure to challenging grade-level content and texts with appropriate scaffolding.

We also caution educators to keep in mind that a focus on the academic language that MLs lack falls into the deficit perspective. It is always important to recognize the language MLs bring with them, whether in the home language or in English. Sometimes, MLs may not be literate in their home language, but they may bring with them rich oral traditions that can be leveraged in their acquisition of academic language in English.

REFLECTION QUESTION

Reflect on your approach to academic-language instruction for your MLs. How have you identified your students' strengths?

 Available for download at **resources.corwin.com/FennerUnlocking2E**

Next Steps

Complete the Checklist for Increasing Academic-Language Awareness (Figure 6.6) for the unit plan that you have been developing. Then, add your ideas to the *Unit Delivery: ML Strategies* and *Sequence and Activities* sections of the Unlocking MLs' Potential Unit Planning Template (Appendix A). Consider what activities you will teach to support academic-language development at the sentence and discourse level dimension based on your unit objectives. For additional considerations, use Appendix F, Checklist for Supporting MLs' Academic-LanguageDevelopment in Speaking and Writing. Appendix A and Appendix F can be found on the online companion website. To access the companion website, please visit resources.corwin.com/FennerUnlocking2E.

UNLOCKING RESOURCES

resourcescorwin .com/FennerUnlocking2E

APPLICATION ACTIVITY 6.6: UNIT PLANNING FOR ACADEMIC LANGUAGE AT THE SENTENCE AND DISCOURSE LEVEL

UNIT PREPARATION
Analyze the Language Demands of the Unit *Figure 5.15 Vocabulary Instruction Checklist* *Figure 5.16 Academic Vocabulary Planning Template* *Figure 6.6 Checklist for Increasing Academic-Language Awareness* *Appendix F Checklist for Supporting MLs' Academic-Language Development in Speaking and Writing* **Sentence Level.** Which sentence structures might be challenging for MLs? What support might MLs need at the sentence level to meet the unit objectives?

Discourse Level. Which discourse level structures might be challenging for MLs? What support might MLs need at the discourse level to meet the unit objectives?

Conclusion

This chapter took a deeper dive into what academic language entails at the sentence and discourse level. The chapter also provided example activities that exemplify how teachers can integrate academic-language instruction at the sentence and discourse levels into their instruction. As we described in Chapter 5, the framework for academic language is embedded within a sociocultural lens, which includes MLs' background knowledge. In the next chapter, we will share information on how to select what background knowledge to teach and strategies for tapping into prior knowledge and building new background knowledge.

SupportEd TOOLBOX

For ready-to-use, practical tools to support academic-language instruction, please see SupportEd.com/unlocking-toolbox.

CHAPTER 6 REFLECTION QUESTIONS

1. What types of academic language from your content area at the word/phrase, sentence, and discourse levels might be challenging for MLs?

2. How can you embed opportunities for academic-language development at the sentence and discourse level into content instruction?

3. How might you collaborate with ELD or content teachers to strengthen your teaching of academic language?

online resources Available for download at **resources.corwin.com/FennerUnlocking2E**

Figure 6.9 provides the answers to Application Activity 6.5: Sequencing in Paragraphs.

FIGURE 6.9   TEXT SEQUENCING ANSWER KEY

1. Chicago in 1871 was a city ready to burn.

2. The city boasted having 59,500 buildings, many of them—such as the Courthouse and the Tribune Building—large and ornately decorated.

3. The trouble was that about two-thirds of all these structures were made entirely of wood.

4. Many of the remaining buildings (even the ones proclaimed to be "fire-proof") looked solid, but were actually jerrybuilt affairs; the stone or brick exteriors hid wooden frames and floors, all topped with highly flammable tar or shingle roofs.

5. It was also a common practice to disguise wood as another kind of building material.

6. The fancy exterior decorations on just about every building were carved from wood, then painted to look like stone or marble.

ACTIVATING AND TEACHING MLs BACKGROUND KNOWLEDGE

7

Viktor is a Ukrainian middle school emergent multilingual learner (ML) at a high beginning level of English proficiency. He has been in the United States for six months. His social studies class is beginning a unit on the Great Depression in the United States. To prepare him for the unit, Ms. Moussa and Mr. Lopez, his social studies and ELD teachers, devote several class periods building his and his emergent ML classmates' background knowledge on the consumer economy of the 1920s, what the stock market is, "Black Tuesday," and President Hoover. However, Ms. Moussa is beginning to grow frustrated with the amount of time they are spending on building background knowledge since she has a district social studies pacing guide she needs to follow and is falling behind. She is also concerned that her native English speakers are getting bored with all the background knowledge instruction since they already know much of this material. Both teachers wonder if there is a better way to help Viktor gain enough background knowledge so he can be an active participant in the content unit while developing his academic-language skills in English.

Ms. Moussa and Mr. Lopez are not alone in wondering how to choose and teach background knowledge to MLs when more is asked of all students, including MLs, yet teachers' time constraints are so pressing. This chapter will help you take a deeper look at how you select and teach background knowledge to MLs. It explores the time investment and potential benefit to MLs when background knowledge is chosen carefully and taught succinctly. The chapter will address the need to either develop a new approach to or reconceptualize teaching background knowledge to MLs. It will highlight a four-step framework for deciding which types of background knowledge to teach MLs and ways to activate and teach background knowledge concisely. The chapter includes a flowchart, tables, and models for educators to use in deciding which background knowledge to teach and how to teach it. It also includes and models several activities that you can use in your own planning and instruction to help you put the framework into practice. Since background knowledge is especially crucial for MLs to access mathematics instruction, we include a special section on the unique areas of background knowledge and mathematics for MLs.

REFLECTION QUESTIONS

Think of one lesson in which you teach some background knowledge to MLs.

1. What background do you see as essential?

2. Why do you choose to teach it?

3. How do you teach it?

4. How long do you spend on instruction of background knowledge as part of this lesson?

---

 online resources   Available for download at **resources.corwin.com/FennerUnlocking2E**

Reflection: How Do I Feel About Teaching Background Knowledge to MLs?

Part of effectively choosing and teaching background knowledge to MLs involves first getting a sense of where you fall along the continuum of beliefs about teaching background knowledge. Consider the points on this continuum (Figure 7.1), and mark where you see yourself:

FIGURE 7.1 CONTINUUM OF BELIEFS ABOUT TEACHING BACKGROUND KNOWLEDGE		
←		→
1. *I believe MLs should not be taught background knowledge. They will gain that knowledge through engaging with the academic content.*	2. *I believe MLs should be taught some background knowledge prior to engaging with academic content unfamiliar to them.*	3. *I believe MLs should be taught ample background knowledge so that they are completely familiar with the nuances of the academic content before engaging with it.*

REFLECTION QUESTIONS

Now, think about a rationale for your answer.

1. Why did you choose your answer?

2. Has this approach worked for you and your MLs? Why or why not?

 Available for download at **resources.corwin.com/FennerUnlocking2E**

We've heard opinions that span both ends of the continuum when it comes to deciding how much background knowledge instruction is appropriate for MLs—from no background knowledge instruction whatsoever (and exclusive attention on the text) all the way to extensive preparation about the subject of the text, the author, or other topics that might or might not directly relate to the academic content. In our experience, ELD teachers' responses typically tend to gravitate more toward Point 3 on the continuum of beliefs about teaching background knowledge (Figure 7.1), whereas content teachers' responses usually tend to align somewhere between Point 1 and Point 2. Naturally, there are outliers in both groups of teachers. While we know that providing more experiential-type background knowledge instruction usually results in greater language development for MLs, it may take more class time to provide such experiences. With rigorous content standards and texts being used by teachers of MLs, we need to find a happy medium. Background knowledge is an issue that many teachers, district leaders, policy makers, and curriculum writers seem to continue to struggle with when considering how to equitably teach MLs within a standards-based framework.

How Can I Raise My Awareness About the Importance of MLs' Background Knowledge?

Now that you have considered your own stance on teaching background knowledge to MLs, you can continue raising awareness about the importance of background knowledge for MLs by putting yourself in the shoes of a student who has not yet developed background knowledge on a topic. One way to do this is to first take a look at how background knowledge influences your own understanding of a text by reading a math word problem that's written in English. Unlike most MLs' experiences learning language and content simultaneously, in theory, your knowledge of the English language should not affect your comprehension of the following short text in Application Activity 7.1.

APPLICATION ACTIVITY 7.1: MATH WORD PROBLEM

First, read this word problem, and then, discuss or think about your responses to the three reflection questions that follow.

Word Problem: *A cricketer whose bowling average is 12.4 runs per wicket takes 5 wickets for 26 runs and thereby decreases his average by 0.4. How many wickets were taken by him before the final match?*[1]

APPLICATION ACTIVITY 7.1: REFLECTION QUESTIONS

1. What would you need to know in order to solve this problem?

   _____

   _____

2. How does background knowledge play a part in your understanding of this problem?

   _____

   _____

3. How would you approach trying to solve this problem? What resources would you use?[2]

   _____

   _____

online resources   Available for download at **resources.corwin.com/FennerUnlocking2E**

Maybe you were able to solve the problem without linguistic or mathematical supports, but consider how much the answer "85 wickets taken before final match" actually means to you if you're not familiar with cricket and the amount of information it provides. Now, suppose you're in a mathematics class in England where wickets and cricket vocabulary might be part of regular conversation. Would you ask the teacher what cricket is and what the rules are in front of the class? Would you interrupt instruction and also immediately draw the whole class's attention to yourself as a speaker of U.S. American English? What if you also did not have the

---

[1] See https://www.quora.com/A-cricketer-whose-bowling-average-is-12-4-runs-per-wicket-takes-5-wickets-for-26-runs-thereby-decreases-his-average-by-0-4.

[2] Please see the end of the chapter for the solution.

math skills to solve this problem, let alone the understanding of the terms? This experience also underscores that you should not rely on MLs' responses to teachers' questions about context such as, "You know what a baseball field is, right?" or, "Have you ever heard of NASA?" Students may be self-conscious about sharing the range and depth of information that is unfamiliar, and they may not be entirely candid in publicly identifying cultural or linguistic information they do not yet know (August, Staehr Fenner, & Bright, 2014).

What Does the Research Say About Background Knowledge?

Now that you've had the opportunity to see how your own background knowledge plays out in solving an algebra problem, let's take a look at some of the relevant research on the concept of background knowledge. According to Marzano (2004), "What students already know about the content is one of the strongest indicators of how well they will learn new information relative to the content" (p. 1). In addition, the research synthesis *Reaping the Rewards of the Reading for Understanding Initiative* (Pearson et al., 2020) cites multiple studies that suggest background knowledge has a direct influence on reading comprehension and that the influence of background knowledge on reading comprehension is particularly important for adolescents as grade levels increase. Further, Billings and Walqui (2017) share that "When a teacher assigns either a text or a task that does little to draw on MLs' prior experiences and understandings, they are likely to struggle with comprehension of the text and with successful engagement in the task" (p. 3).

It is generally true that what we know and are already familiar with can influence new learning and the comprehension of what we read (McNamara & Kintsch, 1996; Pearson et al., 2020). Background knowledge does not have to be knowledge gained from a text. It can also be built through a piece of art, a diagram, a cartoon, a picture, or a video. Further, peer learning activities that foster intellectual engagement with a topic also support building the wide array of background knowledge that students need for success from one content class and text to the next (Fisher et al., 2012).

MLs bring great diversity to classrooms in terms of their language proficiency, background knowledge, and experiences. It is critical that teachers take an assets-based perspective to the knowledge and experience MLs bring to the classroom. Teachers should provide targeted support by building on MLs' prior knowledge and addressing gaps that may exist in their background knowledge for them to acquire new language and content (National Academies of Sciences, Engineering, and Medicine [NASEM], 2018). Taking a few minutes to "jump-start" students' schema, finding out what they know or have experienced about a topic, and linking their knowledge directly to a lesson's objective will result in greater understanding for MLs (Echevarria et al., 2004). Additionally, connecting to students' prior knowledge and experiences will foster ML engagement as it provides an opportunity for students to see themselves in the curriculum (Snyder & Staehr Fenner, 2021). Research supports that the relationship between students' background knowledge and comprehension increases with age (Pearson et al., 2020). Also, vocabulary and background knowledge have the potential to be two of the more powerful means of improving learning and comprehension, particularly for adolescent readers (Ahmed et al., 2016; Cromley & Azevedo, 2007). For these reasons, it is critical to learn what background knowledge MLs already have and also to find the gaps in MLs' background knowledge to provide concise explicit instruction in order to facilitate learning new content.

What Is a Framework I Can Use for Building MLs' Background Knowledge?

Through our review of the research, as well as work with MLs and their teachers, we have developed a framework for building MLs' background knowledge when working with complex texts or topics. The framework consists of four sequential steps, each of which we outline in more detail in this chapter, and it takes place within a context of collaboration among teachers. It is important to remember that not all background knowledge is created equal in terms of relevance when it comes to lesson planning and instruction, and this framework will provide a tool for you to determine what is most relevant for MLs and worth your precious time. Figure 7.2 provides a visual representation of the framework.

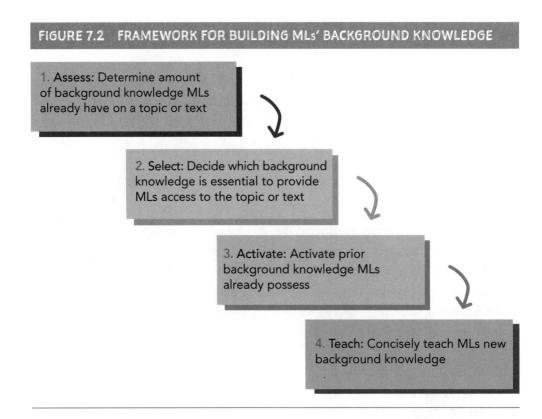

FIGURE 7.2   FRAMEWORK FOR BUILDING MLs' BACKGROUND KNOWLEDGE

1. **Assess:** Determine amount of background knowledge MLs already have on a topic or text

2. **Select:** Decide which background knowledge is essential to provide MLs access to the topic or text

3. **Activate:** Activate prior background knowledge MLs already possess

4. **Teach:** Concisely teach MLs new background knowledge

Step 1: How Do I Find Out MLs' Prior Knowledge on a Particular Topic or Text?

In order to maximize your instructional time on new content, assessing your MLs' background knowledge to gauge their level of familiarity on a certain topic can provide valuable insight for lesson planning. You will need to figure out how much MLs already know about a topic or text prior to teaching it so you can determine whether to activate prior knowledge, build new background, or do a combination of both. This kind of informal assessment can be accomplished through many means that do not require much time and can be seamlessly woven into instruction. In addition, you should concentrate this informal assessment on background you already feel may be essential for MLs to fully engage with the topic or comprehend the text you're planning to base your instruction on. For example, teachers can have MLs participate in oral discussions or use anticipation guides, checklists, and self-rating activities to inform them of MLs' background knowledge and adjust instruction accordingly. In addition, Fisher et al. (2012) suggest cloze assessments, word sorts, opinionnaires, and caption writing to find out what students already know on a given topic. Let's look at one type of informal assessment in a little more depth.

Anticipation Guides are a series of statements students can complete that demonstrate students' background knowledge on a particular topic. Teachers can use them before instruction on a topic and then again after instruction to see what students knew prior to instruction and what they learned. Figure 7.3 provides a sample anticipation guide that teachers could use to determine the level of students' background knowledge on a health lesson about nutrition before reading a text or discussing the topic. Students would answer the before reading questions individually, then discuss their answers in pairs, and finally discuss with the entire class. This exercise, which can be used with all students, would allow teachers to determine how much background individual MLs have on the topic without singling them out. After students read a text on nutrition or discuss the topic as a class, they revisit the anticipation guide and complete the after reading section. To ensure MLs of varying English proficiency levels can respond to the anticipation guide, you will need to write statements in a way so that they will be linguistically accessible to emergent MLs. In addition, you may need to add scaffolds, such as glossaries in English or the home language and visuals, so that emergent MLs can fully engage with anticipation guides.

FIGURE 7.3   HEALTH LESSON ANTICIPATION GUIDE EXAMPLE

Before Reading	Why?	Statement	After Reading	Why?
Yes No		1. I am active, so the kinds of food I eat do <u>not</u> matter.	Yes No	
Yes No		2. Taste is <u>more</u> important than nutrition.	Yes No	
Yes No		3. The government <u>should limit</u> the size of junk food and soda containers.	Yes No	
Yes No		4. It's reasonable to exercise for <u>thirty</u> minutes a day.	Yes No	

Step 2: How Do I Decide How Much Background Knowledge to Provide to MLs?

Research suggests that there is a minimum amount of background knowledge students need on a topic in order to comprehend a text about that topic (O'Reilly et al., 2019). When trying to decide how much background knowledge to teach MLs, it's important to first figure out how critical the background knowledge is to MLs' understanding of the topic or text. This is the area that is the biggest departure from traditional thinking on MLs' background knowledge and can be the most challenging for teachers to change their practice. Fisher et al. (2012) note that *core background knowledge* is what students need to understand in order for the new information to be learned. They contrast *core background knowledge* with *incidental knowledge*, which is knowledge that is merely interesting and not likely to be used or recalled in the future. We refer to the background knowledge that is needed as *essential*. When you're considering preteaching some background about a text your MLs will be working with or a topic they will be discussing, use the following flowchart to help you decide whether knowledge fits into the *essential* category. Figure 7.4 provides considerations within a flowchart for determining which background knowledge to teach.

FIGURE 7.4   FLOWCHART FOR DETERMINING BACKGROUND KNOWLEDGE TO TEACH MLs

1. **Do non-MLs have background knowledge on the topic?**

    Teachers must ensure that MLs approach the lesson or text with comparable levels of background knowledge that non-MLs already have. If non-MLs already approach the text with certain background knowledge, teachers should make sure MLs have the same information as a matter of equity.

    NO →

    YES ↓

2. **Does the background provide different information from what the author provides in the text?**

    The background information provided can't give away the text. (No spoilers!) Students must gather information from the text itself instead of learning it from background knowledge the teacher provides. MLs will still need support and scaffolding to gather information from the text itself.

    NO →

    YES ↓

3. **Is the background knowledge about big issues that will help students make sense of the text?**

    Teachers must focus instruction only on the background knowledge that is critical to MLs comprehending the lesson or text. MLs don't need to know everything possible related to the topic in order to access it. As part of the decision-making process, consider what background knowledge is critical to understanding and the topic and where there are opportunities to make connections to students' prior knowledge.

    NO →

    YES ↓

    Teach background knowledge.

    Do not teach background knowledge.

    ↓

    Now that you've decided what background knowledge to teach, how will you teach it concisely?

    It is important to be concise when teaching background knowledge in order to maximize instructional time for addressing the content area standards. To do so, you could provide some background knowledge via a small group lesson or homework that students complete prior to class time. Then, students can briefly discuss the background during class.

Source: Adapted from Staehr Fenner, D. (2013b).

 Available for download at **resources.corwin.com/FennerUnlocking2E**

Step 3: How Do I Activate MLs' Background Knowledge That They Already Possess?

After taking part in Step 2, you may have a few areas of background knowledge you'd like to teach. However, some MLs may actually already have some related background knowledge you can tap into instead of teaching outright. Shanahan (2013) outlines two essential areas of background knowledge that teachers can effectively use with students. One area is providing background knowledge where none previously exists. A second area is activating existing prior knowledge. Existing prior knowledge is also a form of background knowledge, and teachers can efficiently draw upon what students already know. For example, teachers can use the title of a text as a springboard to help the students make a connection between the title and their existing knowledge of a topic without giving away what students will learn in the text. Figure 7.5 provides further explanation and examples of the differences between providing background knowledge and activating existing prior knowledge.

FIGURE 7.5 DIFFERENCES BETWEEN PROVIDING BACKGROUND KNOWLEDGE AND ACTIVATING EXISTING PRIOR KNOWLEDGE

TEACHER ACTIONS RELATED TO BACKGROUND KNOWLEDGE	DEFINITION	EXAMPLES
Providing background knowledge	Giving students background knowledge that they do not already have on a particular topic or text	• Showing students a visual of Inuit art prior to them engaging in a lesson on the topic • Showing students a video clip on Betsy Ross
Activating existing prior knowledge	Finding out and leveraging pre-existing knowledge on a topic or text	• Having students discuss what they think the title of a text titled "Hurricane Katrina" means in pairs • Having students write a paragraph in their journals about what they previously learned about the Revolutionary War

REFLECTION QUESTION

What ways do you activate your MLs' existing prior knowledge?

 Available for download at **resources.corwin.com/FennerUnlocking2E**

Three ways to activate MLs', as well as non-MLs', prior knowledge are through carousel brainstorming, sentence starters, and categorized sticky notes. There are many other ways as well.

- **Carousel brainstorming:** The teacher posts a series of questions or statements on chart paper around the room. Students are split up into small groups to respond to the question or statement posed at the top of the paper. These questions or statements should be written at a linguistic level that MLs can use to access the questions' meaning and should represent components of students' upcoming texts. After a short period of time, student groups move on to another piece of chart paper, read what has been written about that topic, and add to or respond to it. You can use these charts and responses as ungraded baseline formative assessments because they represent the prior knowledge and current understandings of the group.

- **Sentence starters:** Provide a sentence starter or prompt for students that requires them to complete a sentence or phrase on the topic or text you will be working on. You can use this for example: One thing I already know about _____ is _____. You could post these starters around the room and have students view and discuss each other's sentence starters.

- **Categorized sticky notes:** Give students sticky notes and a question or topic related to the upcoming lesson. For example, when beginning a unit on bees, you can ask students, "What is one thing bees do?" Students respond to the question or topic on their sticky notes and then post their notes on the board, door, wall, or a chart. The space they post their notes to can be divided into positives and negatives, for example, so students will have to categorize their responses. See Figure 7.6. (For example, the sticky note with "Bees give us honey" written on it would go in the "positive" section while the sticky note with "Bees sting" would go in the "negative" section). Students will return to those responses at the end of the lesson to confirm, revise, or add to their thinking and may need to move their sticky notes.

FIGURE 7.6   CATEGORIZED STICKY NOTES

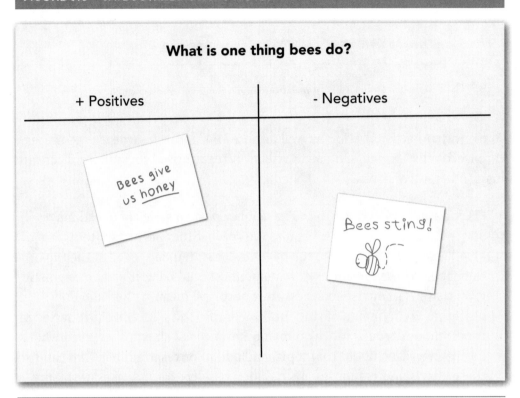

FIGURE 7.6   CATEGORIZED STICKY NOTES

Step 4: What Are Some Strategies for Concisely Teaching MLs Background Knowledge?

After you have determined which background knowledge MLs already have on a topic or text (Step 1), decided which background knowledge is essential (Step 2), and activated MLs' prior background knowledge (Step 3), it is now time to focus on concisely teaching any new background knowledge that is necessary for MLs (Step 4). There are several strategies for teaching new background knowledge (August, Staehr Fenner, & Snyder, 2014), which include the following:

1. Short, teacher-developed text, with guiding and supplementary questions

2. Online resources (in English or home language)

3. Brief video clips or visuals

4. Text-based instruction

5. Home language support (e.g., text, website, or video)

Background knowledge instruction can be pretaught, or it can be embedded into instruction. How much background knowledge you teach depends on the amount of instruction that is needed, students' English language proficiency levels, and your lesson objectives. It's important to consider how to make the most out of limited instructional time and how to teach background knowledge concisely. Some ways to teach background knowledge to MLs that do not interrupt class time are for ELD teachers to teach it during a small-group ELD lesson or to assign it for homework prior to all students working with the content. This approach will require collaboration between content and ELD teachers. Content teachers could also address background knowledge in small groups such as during a station rotation time or at a differentiated center. Another option that we've seen work well with MLs is to hold an after-school homework club for MLs to meet with their ELD or content teacher, socialize a bit, and also work on a background knowledge lesson. This provides a setting in which MLs can feel safe to ask questions about the background as well as take risks with the language.

Osprey

Maryland Blue Crabs

In a third-grade classroom in Maryland, students are preparing to read a text about environmental issues facing the Chesapeake Bay. The emergent MLs in the class who recently moved to the area are not as familiar with the Chesapeake Bay as the other students in the class who grew up in the area. To prepare the emergent MLs to access the text, the teacher used images and a brief video to introduce key concepts prior to having the students engage with the text. Concisely preteaching emergent MLs about these key concepts prior to reading increased their ability to comprehend the text when reading independently.

Source: Photographs by iStock.com/OKRAD and iStock.com/Iris_Savoy

To see how educator Megan Brown helps build her students' background knowledge before beginning a lesson on the Trail of Tears, watch the video titled *Activating and Building Background Knowledge* (Snyder & Staehr Fenner, 2021). The video can be found on the online companion website. To access the companion website, please visit resources.corwin.com/ FennerUnlocking2E

What Are Some Examples of Teaching Background Knowledge?

In what follows, we present two different examples of how teachers of MLs determined what background knowledge to teach and concisely taught that background knowledge to support MLs in accessing the content of challenging, grade-level texts and topics. The first example is at the first-grade text level, and the second example is at the ninth-grade text level.

Grade 1 Text Example

First-grade teacher Ms. Young and ELD teacher Mr. Goodman taught background knowledge to their first-grade ML students related to the following sample text. The teachers read the text aloud to students.

A Father and His Son in Mesopotamia

Almost four thousand years ago, a father and a son were walking together on the banks of a great river, close to what was then possibly the biggest city in the world: Babylon. The father, whose name was Warad, said to his son Iddin, "See, my son, the great Euphrates River. If this river did not flow, there would be no wonderful city of Babylon, no palaces, no gardens, not even any houses . . . They dug ditches cut into the earth, which we call canals. The water flowed out of the river and through the canals to the areas of the city farther from the river. Then farmers could grow crops even where the rivers didn't flow." "Our great king, Hammurabi, did the same thing. He had canals dug to move water all over our country from the two great rivers, the Tigris and the Euphrates. And King Hammurabi and his helpers used an ancient way to collect rainwater. When the winter rains come, the water doesn't just wash away downstream. They made the waters run into a reservoir so that after the rains stopped, there would be water for drinking or for watering crops."

Source: Core Knowledge Foundation (2013). *Early World Civilizations: Tell It Again!™ Read-Aloud Anthology: Listening & Learning™ Strand: Grade 1: Core Knowledge Language Arts®* New York Edition (p. 16). Charlottesville, VA

Figure 7.7 shows how, in deciding which background knowledge to teach to MLs, Ms. Young and Mr. Goodman planned for teaching the meaning of the word *ancient*. Figure 7.7 outlines their thinking using Step 2 of the framework. All students learned about similarities and differences between people today and people in ancient Mesopotamia.

Figure 7.8 shows how Ms. Young and Mr. Goodman concisely taught two meanings of the word *ancient* to MLs in an engaging way. They used two images, partner talk, and questions that are accessible to MLs as scaffolds for this activity.

FIGURE 7.7 BACKGROUND KNOWLEDGE CONSIDERATIONS AND COMMENTS ON THE WORD *ANCIENT*

BACKGROUND KNOWLEDGE CONSIDERATIONS	COMMENTS
1. Do non-MLs have background knowledge on the topic?	Yes, non-MLs know what the word *ancient* means.
2. Does the background provide different information from what the author provides in the text?	Yes, it does.
3. Is the background knowledge about big issues that will help students make sense of the text?	Yes, knowing what *ancient* means will help students make sense of the text.
4. If you've decided to teach background knowledge, how will you teach it concisely?	We will provide this background knowledge concisely by showing two visuals and having MLs discuss them.

FIGURE 7.8 TEACHING BACKGROUND KNOWLEDGE OF THE WORD *ANCIENT*

Instructions for Teachers

- Show students the first picture.

- The picture shows a village, or town, in Mesopotamia from a long time ago.

Partner Talk: How can you tell this village is from a very long time ago?

- Show students the second picture.

- Tell students that the word ancient can also mean very, very old. This picture shows a very old tree.

Partner Talk: How can you tell this tree is very old?

Source: Adapted from August, D., Staehr Fenner, D., & Snyder, S. (2014). Scaffolding instruction for English language learners: A resource guide for ELA. (p.25). Reprinted with permission of American Institutes for Research. Retrieved from https://SupportEd.com/wp-content/uploads/Scaffolding_Instruction_for_ELLs-Resource_Guide_for_ELA.pdf. Images by iStock.com/LuisaFumi and iStock.com/Michael_VerSprill

Grade 9 Text Example

Mrs. Luu, a ninth-grade English teacher, used the following text in the first lesson of a unit centered on an excerpt of the first chapter of the book *Animals in Translation* (Grandin, 2005). Here is the text excerpt:

> *People who aren't autistic always ask me about the moment I realized I could understand the way animals think. They think I must have had an epiphany. But it wasn't like that. It took me a long time to figure out that I see things about animals other people don't. And it wasn't until I was in my forties that I finally realized I had one big advantage over the feedlot owners who were hiring me to manage their animals: being autistic. Autism made school and life hard, but it made animals easy. (Grandin, 2005, p. 1)*

The book draws from the author's own experiences with autism spectrum disorder, which provides her insight into how animals think, act, and feel. However, Mrs. Luu knew that the concept of autism would be unknown to some of her MLs. Some did not know the meaning of the word *autism* in English but knew it in their home language. Also, in some cultures, disabilities may not be acknowledged due to possible stigma, and the concept of autism will not exist in the home language. Thus, Mrs. Luu worked through these considerations when deciding whether to teach background knowledge on autism spectrum disorder. Figure 7.9 outlines her thinking using Step 2 of the framework.

FIGURE 7.9   BACKGROUND KNOWLEDGE CONSIDERATIONS AND COMMENTS ON TEACHING AUTISM AS BACKGROUND TO *ANIMALS IN TRANSLATION*

BACKGROUND KNOWLEDGE CONSIDERATIONS	COMMENTS
1. Do non-MLs have background knowledge on the topic?	Yes, I believe most non-MLs would know what autism is.
2. Does the background provide different information from what the author provides in the text?	Yes, knowing what autism is will not provide information in place of what the author will provide in the text.
3. Is the background knowledge about big issues that will help students make sense of the text?	Yes, knowing what autism is in general will be critical to MLs comprehending the text.
4. If you've decided to teach background knowledge, how will you teach it concisely?	I will present this information concisely in one paragraph with some guiding questions.

Based on Mrs. Luu's responses to these questions, she recognized that her MLs were more likely to be able to successfully engage with the first chapter of *Animals in Translation* if they were provided background knowledge about the concept of autism spectrum disorder in a concise manner. Accordingly, she developed a short text (eight sentences) on autism that provided basic information about the disorder and the challenges, strengths, and behaviors of individuals with autism spectrum disorder. She also developed a glossary to support her MLs in understanding key words of the autism text that may be unfamiliar to them. In addition, Mrs. Luu created a few supporting questions to check for students' understanding. To support her emerging MLs with beginning English language proficiency, she used sentence stems and sentence frames and a word bank to scaffold the questions. Additionally, Mrs. Luu knew that the concept of autism might be perceived differently in different cultures, and the supporting questions provided an opportunity to address those different perceptions.

How Can I Apply the Four-Step Framework When Teaching Background Knowledge to MLs?

To better illustrate how to apply the four-step framework from start to finish, let's take a look at a sample social studies text. Banting's (2004) *England: The Land* is suggested to be at a Grade 4–5 reading level. Take a look at an excerpt from this informational text, and think about what kinds of background knowledge your MLs would need to fully access the meaning:

England: The Land Text Excerpt

Low fences, some of which are thousands of years old, divide much of England's countryside. These fences, called hedgerows, were first built by the Anglo-Saxons, a group of warriors from Germany and Scandinavia who arrived in England around 410 A.D.

As they gained control of sections of land, they protected their property with walls made from wooden stakes and spiny plants. Dead hedgerows, as these fences were called, were eventually replaced by fences made from live bushes and trees.

Recently, people building large farms and homes in the countryside have destroyed many live hedgerows. Other people are working to save the hedgerows, which are home to a variety of wildlife, including birds, butterflies, hedgehogs, and hares.

Source: Banting, E. (2004).

Step 1: Determine the amount of background knowledge MLs already have.

Fourth-grade teacher Ms. Linton and ELD teacher Mrs. Jarboe coteach social studies. They are using Banting's text with fourth-grade MLs at varying levels of English proficiency. First, they decided to find out their MLs' knowledge of the following:

- The history of the Anglo-Saxons
- What was happening during the time period described in the text (410 AD)
- Their knowledge of low fences or hedgerows
- The importance of protecting one's property in the time period described and today
- How large farms and homes in the English countryside look today
- The wildlife mentioned in the text

At first, Ms. Linton and Mrs. Jarboe were tempted to develop lessons on all of the aforementioned topics in order to fully prepare MLs to read this text. They recognized that their MLs may have very little background knowledge on the many topics contained in this text, let alone be familiar with all of the terms and academic-language structures used in the text. However, they decided not to spend the majority of their instruction on building their MLs' background knowledge and instead selected key topics to teach concisely based on the strengths and needs of their MLs.

REFLECTION QUESTION

Which topics from the bulleted list might you prioritize with your MLs? Why?

---

online resources   Available for download at **resources.corwin.com/FennerUnlocking2E**

One way Ms. Linton and Mrs. Jarboe determined MLs' existing knowledge on the topic was to have all students do some caption writing individually and then assess how much background knowledge MLs had on the topics pertaining to low fences. They gave students a visual of the English countryside from Anglo-Saxon times, a visual of English countryside today, and a visual of low fences and had them write a caption for each visual, first modeling their expectations for what a caption should look like. The teachers collaborated to support their emerging MLs with engaging in this task by providing sentence starters and word walls to complete the captions. The following is the image of a low fence they used:

Source: iStock.com/daseaford

After determining what MLs already knew about the topic through caption writing, Ms. Linton and Mrs. Jarboe learned that all the MLs could describe an image of the English countryside of today. They could not describe a visual of the English countryside during Anglo-Saxon times well and could only provide basic information on the low fence visual. Caption writing allowed the teachers to note how their MLs' background knowledge might differ from a personal connection to a text. For example, one student had some knowledge about what the English countryside looks like today from a documentary she had seen about England. On the other hand, another student had a personal connection to this image based on an event in the student's life that took place in the countryside. Where background knowledge from the documentary will most likely support the student's understanding of the text, the student's personal connection might not accomplish the same goal (Staehr Fenner, 2013a).

Step 2: Decide what background knowledge is needed.

Ms. Linton and Mrs. Jarboe worked together and determined that MLs might need more instruction on what low fences are. They then walked through the considerations that follow to determine whether they should teach background knowledge on low fences or not. Figure 7.10 outlines their decision-making process.

FIGURE 7.10   BACKGROUND KNOWLEDGE CONSIDERATIONS AND COMMENTS FOR LOW FENCES

BACKGROUND KNOWLEDGE CONSIDERATIONS	COMMENTS
1. Do non-MLs have background knowledge on the topic?	Through Step 1, caption writing, we determined that MLs do not have background knowledge on what low fences or hedgerows are.
2. Does the background provide different information from what the author provides in the text?	Yes, knowing what low fences or hedgerows are will not provide information in place of what students will read in the text.
3. Is the background knowledge about big issues that will help MLs make sense of the text?	Yes, knowing what low fences or hedgerows are will help students make sense of the text.
4. If you've decided to teach background knowledge, how will you teach it concisely?	We can provide this background precisely through a guided group work discussion about the same visual we used in Step 1, caption writing.

Step 3: Activate the prior background knowledge MLs already possess.

Through the caption-writing activity described in Step 1, Ms. Linton and Mrs. Jarboe learned that most MLs could write some key words about the English countryside. Some MLs wrote the word *fence* under the image of the low fence or hedgerow, and some wrote "fence" in their home language. That information told them that many MLs knew what a fence was at a surface level of knowledge, and they decided to activate that specific prior knowledge about fences. They then chose to activate MLs' prior background knowledge about fences by doing a carousel brainstorm. To do so, they created three poster papers with the statements for their MLs to respond to, answering true, false, and then stating why (Figure 7.11).

Students worked in pairs to provide answers to each poster paper, rotating through the papers. Then, they had students come together as a large group to share their answers. This gave the teachers the opportunity to listen to students as they discussed their prior background knowledge on fences and also to introduce some new vocabulary to them to discuss fences (e.g., fence, join, and land). Bringing them together in the large group also provided an opportunity to respond to any misconceptions they might have about fences—for example, that they cannot be made of wood or plants.

FIGURE 7.11   CAROUSEL BRAINSTORM

Fences are used to join two pieces of land together. I think this statement is (true/false) because _____.	Fences can be made of wood. I think this statement is (true/false) because _____.	Fences can be made of plants. I think this statement is (true/false) because _____.

Step 4: Concisely teach new background knowledge.

Next, after completing Steps 1 through 3, it was time to concisely teach some new background knowledge to prepare students to read an excerpt from *England: The Land*. The teachers looked back at what they decided to do as a team in Step 2 and referred to the same visual they used for Step 1, caption writing. This time, they used the visual as a basis for a guided discussion around what low fences or hedgerows are. The entire discussion took only 10 minutes of time and was centered on the following questions (Figure 7.12), which students discussed in small groups while viewing the image.

FIGURE 7.12   DISCUSSION QUESTIONS

What is the purpose of the low fence (or hedgerow) in this photo?

The low fence or hedgerow in the photo is used to _____.

What is the low fence (or hedgerow) in the photo made of?

The low fence or hedgerow in the photo is made of _____.

After the students discussed the answers to the questions, Ms. Linton and Mrs. Jarboe brought them together as a large group to talk about what low fences or hedgerows are and what they are used for. They also elicited their responses to what low fences are made of. This conversation "primed the pump" for them to read and comprehend an excerpt from the text *England: The Land* without spoiling the meaning of the text.

Figure 7.13 captures how Ms. Linton and Mrs. Jarboe used the four-step process to plan their instruction of background knowledge for MLs with this lesson.

FIGURE 7.13   BACKGROUND KNOWLEDGE PLANNING FRAMEWORK FOR LOW-FENCES LESSON

STEP	OUTCOME	NEXT STEP
1. Determine the amount of background knowledge MLs already have on a topic or text.	Through caption writing, they determined that MLs were already familiar with what fences are.	They wanted to determine what essential background knowledge they needed to provide to MLs.
2. Decide which essential background knowledge is needed to provide MLs access to the topic or text.	They decided that MLs needed to know about low fences or hedgerows in order to take part in this lesson.	They needed a quick way to teach this to them, so they decided they would use a visual and guided discussion.
3. Activate the prior background knowledge that MLs already possess.	Through the caption writing, they learned that their MLs already knew a little about fences, but they wanted to dig deeper and activate more detailed prior knowledge.	They activated that prior knowledge through carousel brainstorming about fences.
4. Teach the new background knowledge.	Their MLs needed new background knowledge on low fences or hedgerows.	They decided to show them a picture of a low fence and have a brief, 10-minute discussion about it using guiding questions.

How Do I Build or Activate MLs' Background Knowledge in Mathematics?

Now that we have focused on teaching MLs background knowledge in general, we'd like to narrow our focus for special considerations of MLs' background knowledge in mathematics. Many MLs will have developed mathematical concepts in their home language or in prior schooling (for information on supporting ML newcomer students and students with limited or interrupted formal education [SLIFE] with background knowledge, see the ML Newcomer Students and SLIFE Considerations section). While many MLs will be able to engage with mathematical concepts, such as addition or division, math is not a universal language, and MLs may not have the background knowledge in the language (or even culture) of math. Therefore, MLs may need additional support to comprehend the stimulus or prompt texts used in many mathematics lessons (August, Staehr Fenner & Bright, 2014). Not only might the technical vocabulary of math be new to some MLs, but the linguistic constructs and the so-called "real-life" contexts or situations used in mathematics words problems may also be unfamiliar and not relate to the MLs' lived experiences (NASEM, 2018). As with our previous examples in English language arts and social studies, there may be times when MLs will need a succinct and purposeful explanation of a scenario, illustration, or other information that is not part of the mathematical content related to the lesson (Chval et al., 2021).

Mathematical word problems, in particular, may contain contexts or situations that are culturally bound. To support MLs in accessing the concise background information necessary to understand contexts or situations used in math word problems, it can be useful to show them images or short video clips. For example, if a word problem references passing yards in American football and students are unfamiliar with the sport, it may be helpful to show a brief video clip from a football game. Think back to the cricket math problem in Application Activity 7.1 at the beginning of the chapter and how helpful a brief overview of the game may have been for your understanding. Also, keep in mind that students may think they recognize a context but may not fully understand it or may be tripped up by a word with multiple meanings. For example, when working with a math word problem about a state fair, students may recognize the word "fair" as meaning things are equal rather than a public event. It's important to clear up these misconceptions MLs may have while not singling them out or embarrassing them in front of their peers.

One step to providing background knowledge to MLs in mathematics is constructing or adapting problems so that they are grounded in MLs' context or lived experiences while maintaining the same level of mathematical rigor (Chval et al., 2021). Problems that are more grounded in students' contexts will mean less of a need to spend time providing background knowledge.

Figure 7.14 details tips, explanations, and examples to build MLs' background knowledge in mathematics.

FIGURE 7.14   ML BACKGROUND KNOWLEDGE IN MATHEMATICS TIPS, EXPLANATIONS, AND EXAMPLES

MATHEMATICS ML BACKGROUND KNOWLEDGE TIP	EXPLANATION	EXAMPLES
Build knowledge from real-world examples.	Revise unfamiliar situations in word problem scenarios to make them more familiar. Try to reinforce concepts with familiar examples that students can picture, and engage in a think-aloud to talk students through the situation.	Original word problem: *A parking garage has 3 levels. Each level has 40 parking spaces for compact cars. What is the total number of parking spaces in the garage for compact cars?* Revised word problem: *A school has 3 floors. Each floor has 40 rooms. What is the total number of rooms in the school?*
Modify the linguistic complexity of language, and rephrase math problems.	Students will understand the problem better if it is stated in shorter sentences and in language they understand.	Instead of *Alex worked for 5 hours raking leaves in the fall. How many minutes are equivalent to 5 hours?*, reword the problem to *Alex worked on a project for 5 hours. How many minutes are equivalent to 5 hours?*.
Guide students to cross out the unnecessary vocabulary in word problems and circle the necessary vocabulary.	Crossing out unnecessary words and circling necessary vocabulary allows students to focus on the math function required instead of getting bogged down with unnecessary language. This strategy is especially helpful for students on end-of-year tests that aren't teacher-created.	See the model of the unnecessary vocabulary crossed out of this word problem and then rephrased: A set of football jerseys contains only odd-numbered jerseys. Which could be 3 of the jersey numbers from this set of uniforms? A set of ~~football jerseys~~ contains only odd-numbered ~~jerseys~~. Which could be 3 of the ~~jersey~~ numbers from this set of ~~uniforms~~? A set contains only odd numbers. Which could be 3 of the numbers from this set?
Use manipulatives purposefully.	Manipulatives can be very useful in having students represent the numbers in the problems and manipulating them to get the answer.	A teacher uses cubes and the terms *hot numbers* and *cold numbers* when teaching with the concept of negative numbers. Students use the red cubes as hot, or positive, numbers and the blue cubes as cold, or negative, numbers. As students lay out the number of hot cubes and cold cubes represented, they can easily see if the answer would be a positive or negative number by which color had the most cubes.

Source: Adapted from Kristina Robertson, *Math Instruction for English Language Learners* (http://www.colorincolorado.org/article/math-instruction-english-language-learners) and the Virginia Department of Education (http://www.doe.virginia.gov/testing/sol/standards_docs/mathematics/plain_english_information.pdf).

It is important to acknowledge that students will be required to interact with unfamiliar contexts embedded in mathematical word problems in both their math curriculum and on state tests, and we recognize that MLs also need opportunities to practice with problems that are less grounded in their experiences. In order to prepare them for successfully engaging with these problems that contain unfamiliar content, we can intentionally and incrementally remove scaffolds over time, including teaching background knowledge specific to the problem. Strategies that teach students how to interpret and dissect a mathematical word problem, such as the Three Read Protocol (Kelemanik et al., 2016) or Reading and Understanding Mathematics Problems (Stanford Understanding Language, 2021), will help support students in being able to solve these problems independently. For more on the Three Read Protocol, please see Chapter 8.

Now that we've explored a framework for deciding which types of background knowledge to teach MLs and ways to activate and teach background knowledge concisely, let's take a look at some considerations for ML newcomer students and SLIFE and the role of collaboration, equity, advocacy, and leadership when activating and teaching MLs background knowledge.

ML NEWCOMER STUDENTS AND SLIFE CONSIDERATIONS

What Are Key Considerations for Supporting Background Knowledge for ML Newcomer Students and SLIFE?

While it is important to be intentional about selecting, activating, and concisely teaching background knowledge to all MLs, this concept warrants a deeper look with ML newcomer students and SLIFE.

Considerations:

- ML newcomer students and SLIFE will need more time dedicated to building background content-area knowledge than other students (DeCapua et al., 2020; DeCapua, 2023). ELD and content teachers can collaborate to support building content-area background knowledge during ML newcomer students and SLIFE-focused classes or through mini lessons during small-group instruction, homework assignments, and after-school learning opportunities.

- Getting to know ML newcomer students and SLIFE is imperative when activating and teaching background knowledge. It is important not to make generalized assumptions about students and take time to learn about their individual prior educational and life experiences. Use Figure 2.3 What I Know About My ML from Chapter 2 to gather information about your ML newcomer students and SLIFE and continue to add to it throughout the school year as you learn more about each student.

(Continued)

(Continued)

- ML newcomer students and SLIFE come to our schools with knowledge, language, and experiences that educators can use as a springboard for new learning. It is important that learning be immediately relevant to ML newcomer students and SLIFE; therefore we should intentionally make connections to their linguistic and cultural backgrounds to help bridge familiar and unfamiliar concepts (DeCapua et al., 2020). This not only supports new learning but also fosters engagement as they see themselves in the curriculum (Snyder & Staehr Fenner, 2021).

Example: Joseph, the seventh-grade student from the Democratic Republic of Congo who was introduced in Chapter 2, is beginning a unit about the Great Depression in his social studies class. His teacher, Ms. Jones, knows that Joseph does not have background knowledge on the topic that other students in the class do, so she reaches out to his ELD teacher, Ms. Frank, to collaborate. Together, they determine that they will need to build Joseph's background knowledge on banking and the stock market. They develop a plan to first make the learning relevant to Joseph by making connections to his lived experiences and then to build Joseph's background knowledge on the topic. To begin, Ms. Frank works with Joseph in a small group, and they brainstorm a list of what people need to live (e.g., food, clothing) and how they obtain those things (e.g., money, bartering) on an anchor chart. She then uses the anchor chart to make a direct connection to what they will be learning about in their social studies classroom, the Great Depression. In the subsequent lessons, Ms. Frank introduces the concept of banking and the stock market using a video (in French), visuals, and a brief teacher-created text. Throughout the lessons, Ms. Frank makes explicit connections to what Joseph is learning in his social studies class and emphasizes key academic vocabulary, such as *bank, stock market, economy, crisis, and impact*. Ms. Jones communicates with Ms. Frank regularly so that she is also able to make connections between what Joseph has learned in Ms. Frank's small group and what he is learning in her social studies classroom.

What Is the Role of Collaboration in Teaching Background Knowledge?

Our teachers Ms. Moussa and Mr. Lopez, whom we introduced at the beginning of this chapter, had already decided they would coteach background knowledge to Viktor and his other emergent ML classmates. However, there are different options that you might wish to explore to use your precious instructional and planning time, as well as your colleagues' time, when selecting and teaching background knowledge to MLs. Which option you use depends on the type of ELD program that is in place at your school, the grade level(s) you teach, your students' level of proficiency, and the content you're working on. Figure 7.15 describes different background teaching options for program models and suggests roles the content teacher and ELD teacher can take in selecting and teaching background knowledge to MLs.

FIGURE 7.15	PROGRAM MODELS AND TEACHERS' POSSIBLE ROLES IN TEACHING BACKGROUND KNOWLEDGE	
PROGRAM MODEL	CONTENT TEACHER'S ROLE	ELD TEACHER'S ROLE
Cotaught elementary or secondary class	Determine which background knowledge non-MLs already have, share essential learning from the text, lesson, or unit with ELD teachers; coteach background knowledge	Determine which background knowledge MLs need and at what point in instruction; develop activities to assess it, activate it, and teach it; coteach background knowledge
Small-group elementary-level ELD	Share relevant, grade-level content standards and classroom materials with ELD teachers who teach MLs at that grade level; reinforce background knowledge throughout content instruction	Determine which background knowledge MLs already have and need; develop activities to activate it and teach it as part of ELD instruction
Stand-alone secondary-level ELD	Share relevant content standards and classroom materials with ELD teachers who teach MLs enrolled in those content classes (e.g., algebra or world history); reinforce background knowledge throughout content instruction	Determine which background knowledge MLs already have and need in key content classes; develop activities to activate it and teach it as part of ELD instruction

What Is the Role of Equity, Advocacy, and Leadership in Teaching Background Knowledge?

Activating and concisely teaching background knowledge to MLs requires a more defined skill set and targeted training for all educators who work with MLs. Engaging MLs in the close reading of grade-level texts and rigorous topics often presents challenges that go beyond balancing the building of background knowledge with working with the actual text. Such challenges for educators of MLs include choosing appropriate grade-level texts, providing MLs with supplementary texts at different reading levels or texts in the home language, scaffolding instruction, and creating tasks that MLs can access to help them unlock the meaning of texts. We recognize that background knowledge is just one piece of the puzzle that gives MLs a greater chance at accessing equitable instruction.

In addition to learning about MLs' level of background knowledge, teachers themselves will benefit from building their own background knowledge of their students. In particular, teachers will need to learn about their students' and students' families' cultures to have a sense of what valuable background knowledge MLs bring. Teachers of MLs should also learn about the ways in which mathematics, social studies, science, and language concepts are approached in students' or their families' home countries or communities to the degree possible. When teachers of MLs employ an assets-based approach that highlights what students already know and can do, teachers may shift instruction appropriately to be more inclusive of MLs. Many opportunities exist for you to leverage your leadership skills when sharing this framework with colleagues and also if conflicts arise in terms of your colleagues' approach to assessing, selecting, activating, and teaching background knowledge. Your focus on the students and support of colleagues as they reflect on their practice will be key in approaching background knowledge in a different way.

Next Steps

The following application activity will help you synthesize your learning on activating and teaching MLs background knowledge.

APPLICATION ACTIVITY 7.2: BACKGROUND KNOWLEDGE PLANNING TOOL

Consider the topics and texts you will address in the unit you are planning. Use the Background Knowledge Planning Tool (Figure 7.16) to plan for activating and teaching MLs background knowledge needed to access the unit content. Note that the Background Knowledge Planning Tool can also be used as a standalone tool.

FIGURE 7.16   ACTIVATING AND BUILDING MLs' BACKGROUND KNOWLEDGE PLANNING TOOL

Content Topic and Objective(s)

Text and/or Tasks

STEP 1. ASSESS

What strategies will you use to assess MLs' background knowledge related to the topics described above?

STEP 2. SELECT

What is the essential background knowledge that all students need to know to engage with the content? For each item, determine if you think you will activate prior background knowledge or teach new background knowledge. You may select both if you think you will provide different instruction for different groups of students.

Topic #1:	☐ Activate prior background knowledge ☐ Teach new background knowledge ☐ Both (depends on my students)
Topic #2:	☐ Activate prior background knowledge ☐ Teach new background knowledge ☐ Both (depends on my students)
Topic # 3:	☐ Activate prior background knowledge ☐ Teach new background knowledge ☐ Both (depends on my students)

STEP 3. ACTIVATE

Describe the strategies that you will use to activate MLs' prior background knowledge.

STEP 4. TEACH

Describe the strategies that you will use to concisely teach new background knowledge.	Describe how you plan to differentiate for the strengths and needs of different MLs.

online resources

Available for download at **resources.corwin.com/FennerUnlocking2E**

(Continued)

(Continued)

UNLOCKING RESOURCES

resources.corwin
.com/FennerUnlocking2E

Now, add your plans to the *Unit Preparation: Identify Required Background Knowledge* section of the Unlocking MLs' Potential Unit Planning Template (the portion of Appendix A reproduced in Figure 7.17). Appendix A can be found on the online companion website. To access the companion website, please visit resources. corwin.com/FennerUnlocking2E.

FIGURE 7.17 PORTION OF THE UNLOCKING MLs' POTENTIAL UNIT PLANNING TEMPLATE (APPENDIX A)

UNIT PREPARATION

Identify Required Background Knowledge

Figure 7.16 Background Knowledge Planning Tool

What is the **essential background knowledge** that all students need to know to access the unit?

How will you assess MLs' **current prior knowledge** on the topic?

How will you build on MLs' **cultural and linguistic backgrounds**?

SupportEd TOOLBOX

For ready-to-use, practical tools to support activating and developing MLs' background knowledge, please see supported.com/ unlocking-toolbox.

Conclusion

This chapter has focused on the need to rethink the way we frame the selection and instruction of background knowledge for MLs within the context of time constraints and challenging texts and topics. We have provided a four-step framework to assess background knowledge, select essential background knowledge, activate MLs' existing background knowledge, and teach background knowledge concisely through modeling and examples. We have also highlighted the specific issues of teaching background knowledge in mathematics; ideas for supporting background knowledge for ML newcomer students and SLIFE; and considerations for collaboration, advocacy, equity, and leadership when teaching background knowledge to MLs. The next chapter builds on this learning around background knowledge as a vehicle to support MLs' access and understanding of lessons and texts. Chapter 8 deepens our conversation, focusing on supporting MLs' reading and writing in the content areas.

CHAPTER 7 REFLECTION QUESTIONS

1. How will you change or refine how you approach the activating and teaching of background knowledge to MLs?

2. Who will you collaborate with in activating and teaching background knowledge, and how will you collaborate?

 Available for download at **resources.corwin.com/FennerUnlocking2E**

Application Activity Responses

Solution to Mathematics Problem in Application Activity 7.1

Here's one way to solve the problem:

x = number of wickets before final match

(x wickets)(12.4 runs/wicket) = 12.4x runs

After taking another 5 wickets for 26 runs, his average is 12.4 − 0.4 = 12 runs/wicket

Total runs = 12.4x + 26

Total wickets = x + 5

(12.4x + 26)/(x + 5) = 12

x = 85

85 wickets taken before final match

ENGAGING MLs IN READING AND WRITING IN THE CONTENT AREAS

8

Chef Renaldo teaches culinary arts in a career and technical education (CTE) program for high school juniors and seniors. Students come to him for a half-day program to learn culinary arts skills. He integrates both math and English language arts instruction into his curriculum. He has noticed that in recent years, some of his students have a difficult time getting started with writing tasks and also find it challenging to keep writing over a set period of time. As a result, he has begun including regular opportunities for informal writing into his instruction by having students use a writing journal. Chef Renaldo provides prompts related to different topics that they are learning about in class, but students also have the freedom to write about whatever they would like. Students also have a choice in whether Chef Renaldo reads or doesn't read each journal entry.

In addition to journal writing, Chef Renaldo also integrates larger written assignments into his instruction. Students are currently working on a project in which they have to plan a themed dinner party for a group of 10 guests, some of whom have specific dietary needs. His goal for the project is not only to have students successfully plan the menu but also to be able to explain their choices using specific details and technical language that they have been working on throughout the year. In order to scaffold the assignment for the four emergent multilingual learners (MLs) in his class as well as three other students who need additional support with writing, Chef Renaldo has integrated a variety of scaffolds. He began the project by having all students take part in a background-activating carousel activity in which they answered questions posted around the room related to different considerations in planning a dinner party including budget, preparation time, dietary considerations, and flavors. He has broken the assignment down into a series of discrete tasks that culminate in the submission of a final report and oral presentation. He has also developed a student checklist that students can use to assess their writing with opportunities for feedback and revision throughout the project. He has strategically grouped students in pairs for the assignment and has provided specific guidelines to support equitable participation in completing the assignment. Two of the emergent MLs in the class are bilingual Arabic-speakers at an intermediate level of language proficiency in English. He has paired these students together so that they can speak Arabic in planning their project. These students also have access to a glossary of technical terms and phrases that they can refer to as needed for their writing, and Chef Renaldo has worked with a small group of students including these two on strengthening their use of details in their writing.

REFLECTION QUESTIONS

1. What strategies has Chef Renaldo used to support MLs' writing development?

2. What suggestions do you have for Chef Renaldo to further strengthen the themed dinner project?

 Available for download at **resources.corwin.com/FennerUnlocking2E**

Our Lens

Literacy instruction (which includes both reading and writing) for MLs is a complex topic. What effective literacy instruction looks like for all students is an important topic in the field of education. Because the aim of this book is to offer strategies for supporting MLs' access to and engagement with academic content, we do not focus on teaching MLs how to read and write in this chapter. Rather, we highlight research-based strategies for supporting MLs' engagement in reading and writing across content areas through scaffolded instruction and collaborative, peer learning practices. We will begin with an overview of research related to literacy instruction for MLs that we feel should inform educators' practice when engaging MLs in reading and writing about grade-level content that can support language development. We have chosen to include reading and writing together in this chapter because they are reciprocal processes; when students read, it informs their writing just as the skills that they practice as writers impact who they are as readers. We will take a closer look into the connection between reading and writing in the next section. An additional priority of ours through this book is the focus on language development, so this chapter includes strategies that not only are designed to support MLs' reading and writing but also to foster language growth.

What Does Research Say About Engaging MLs in Reading and Writing Across Content Areas?

In order to offer equitable education to MLs, we must give them with access to challenging, grade-level texts and academic writing tasks. However, as we described in Chapter 3, MLs also need support to effectively engage with these texts and academic writing tasks (August, 2018; Billings & Walqui, 2021). Unfortunately, there is insufficient research on effective instructional practices for building on MLs' cultural and linguistic assets when engaging students in reading and writing practices. In their synthesis of research on reading for understanding, Pearson et al. (2020) make a call for equitable research that examines best practices for supporting MLs in reading for understanding. They write,

> Even though [MLs] bring rich language experiences to the classroom, we seem unable to exploit their first language or interlingual (first to second language connections) linguistic resources to craft effective programs for deep reading experiences in English as a second language. (p. 7)

APPLICATION ACTIVITY 8.1: ANNOTATING THE RESEARCH

In the next few paragraphs, we will provide a brief (and by no means comprehensive) synthesis of what research has taught us about engaging MLs in reading and writing practices. We highlight this research synthesis as a way to connect what research has taught us about supporting MLs when reading and writing with the practical instructional strategies that we share in the remainder of the chapter. As you read this information, we encourage you to note themes that you see repeated throughout the research, questions that you have, and ideas that surprise or interest you. This type of text annotation is an activity that you can have students work on collaboratively in order to support their engagement and understanding of content-based texts. As you read, consider annotating the text in this way:

T–Write a T in the margin to indicate a repeated theme in the research.

?–Write a question mark in the margin to indicate where you have a question.

!–Write an exclamation point in the margin to indicate something that surprised or interested you.

While we are not taking a deep dive into early literacy instruction for MLs, we do want to highlight key ideas from Escamilla et al.'s (2022) white paper entitled *Toward Comprehensive Effective Literacy Policy and Instruction for English Learner/Emergent Bilingual Students* that can be applied more broadly to supporting ML engagement with reading and writing in all content areas. In their white paper, Escamilla et al. emphasize that literacy instruction must include both the teaching of reading and the teaching of writing, and that it should incorporate all five components highlighted by the National Reading Panel in 2000 (i.e., phonemic awareness, phonics, fluency, vocabulary, and comprehension) in an integrated way. However, these researchers

(Continued)

(Continued)

also cite findings from the *National Literacy Panel on Language Minority Children and Youth* (August & Shanahan, 2006) report which indicates that effective literacy instruction for MLs must go beyond these five components and include additional instructional practices targeted at the strengths and needs of MLs. Escamilla et al. (2022) articulate that literacy instruction cannot be a one-size-fits-all approach but must consider the specific backgrounds of the students and recognize the important role that home language has in literacy development, specifically being aware of the "uniqueness of the dual-language brain" (p. 14). Language processing in a bilingual brain is different from language processing in a monolingual brain as the acquisition of an additional language occurs on the foundation of the first with the learner making constant comparisons between key aspects of language such as vocabulary, phonological components, and grammatical structures (Escamilla et al., 2022; Pierce et al., 2015).

Additionally, Escamilla et al. (2022) state that research on second language literacy for MLs has identified some critical conclusions. Their conclusions include the following:

- Literacy and language instruction should be integrated into the learning of new content.

- Oral language development is a critical component of literacy development.

- Scaffolded literacy instruction for MLs is essential to support students' understanding, engagement, and language development.

- MLs' cultural and linguistic assets should be leveraged as foundations for learning during literacy instruction.

- A focus on reading comprehension is critical for academic literacy.

- Writing is a fundamental literacy skill.

Since we have shared research in previous chapters that addresses many of these topics, in the remainder of this section we will highlight research around reading comprehension and writing instruction for MLs.

Reading Comprehension

Reading comprehension is critical to support students' development of academic literacy. Billings and Walqui (2021) describe the importance of pedagogical scaffolding to make complex texts more accessible to MLs. Specifically, they discuss the importance of building background and supporting the development of students' metacognitive skills and metalinguistic awareness. **Metacognitive skills are the skills students need to develop an awareness and understanding of their own thinking which leads to independent learning (e.g., self-reflection, monitoring learning). Metalinguistic awareness is the ability to be able to think about and discuss language (e.g., understanding and being able to discuss grammatical rules). When MLs are given** opportunities to build metacognitive and metalinguistic skills, they will be better equipped to have a greater role in their language development.

Research highlights that one of the most successful interventions for building reading comprehension skills, particularly for older students, is having students take part in collaborative close reads of challenging texts in which they discuss and explore the text with the goal of gaining new information and insight that they can apply to their learning and to new experiences (Escamilla et al., 2022; Pearson et al., 2020). Shanahan (2013) explains that **close reading is a concept that indicates where meaning resides (in the text) and what readers must do to gain access to this meaning (read the text closely, weighing the author's words and ideas, and relying heavily on the evidence in the text).** He sees close reading as a way to place emphasis on readers grappling with a high-quality text in order to figure it out. By engaging in close reading throughout their education, Shanahan says students are poised to develop a rich body of knowledge about the world, and their reading practices will become ingrained habits of mind. Thus, if we support MLs in developing these close reading skills, they will be able to apply these skills across content areas and text types and be better positioned to have greater autonomy in their learning.

Writing for MLs

In addition to intentional instruction on reading comprehension, writing is an essential component of literacy development. Integrating writing opportunities across content areas will support MLs in applying new content that they are learning and offer opportunities for language practice and language development (Baker et al., 2014; Graham et al., 2020). Based on a synthesis of research on effective practices for supporting MLs in the content areas, Baker et al. (2014) recommend providing students with regular, structured opportunities to develop writing skills. Specifically, they state that educators of MLs should do the following:

- Link writing assignments to content learning and focus on academic-language development (in addition to writing skills).

- Provide language-based supports (e.g., graphic organizers, sentence stems, word walls) to facilitate MLs' engagement with writing and development of writing skills.

- Incorporate small group or pair work to give opportunities for students to collaborate around different aspects of writing.

- Regularly assess students' writing to identify areas of need and to give positive, constructive feedback (Baker et al., 2014).

These recommendations emphasize the need to offer MLs frequent opportunities for collaborative, scaffolded writing in the content areas. Such collaborative-writing tasks can also facilitate students becoming stronger readers.

(Continued)

(Continued)

Shanahan (2020) specifies three ways in which reading and writing are connected for all students:

1. Reading and writing make use of the same skills and knowledge. For example, if students are learning about spelling patterns or particular discourse patterns in reading, this information will also support them with their writing. Similarly, when students as writers think about their audience and how their writing will impact the readers of what they write, they are learning important skills that will strengthen who they are as a reader (e.g., understanding author's perspective, being able to evaluate an author's credibility).

2. When reading and writing are combined, students are found to have a greater understanding of the content and greater retention of it.

3. Teaching students how to read and synthesize key ideas from a text for a select purpose (e.g., comparing ideas across text) will support students in writing text syntheses.

As a result, reading and writing strategies that are integrated across content areas, that are scaffolded for MLs of varying language proficiency levels, and that include opportunities for collaborative discussions with peers will have a positive impact on MLs' understanding and participation.

APPLICATION ACTIVITY 8.1: REFLECTION QUESTIONS

1. What are the themes that you noted as you read this section? How do these themes apply to your work with MLs?

   _____

   _____

2. What questions do you have?

   _____

   _____

3. What is something that surprised or interested you from the research?

   _____

   _____

How Can I Use Peer Learning Routines and Scaffolded Instruction to Support MLs in Reading and Writing Across Content Areas?

Many of the strategies that we share in this chapter are intended to support structured peer learning routines in reading and writing tasks. **A peer learning routine is a specific instructional strategy that includes a set of steps that students follow to complete an academic task when working with one or more peers to support their learning.** A strategy becomes a routine when it is implemented regularly with students, and they know what to do without needing a lot of modeling or direction. An example of a strategy that could easily become a peer learning routine is Think-Pair-Share, during which students first are given time to think independently about a question, next share their ideas with a partner, and finally discuss their ideas with the entire class. We believe peer learning routines used across content areas can lead to greater ML engagement and understanding and also foster the development of students' metacognitive skills, which ultimately leads to increased student autonomy in their reading and writing.

When introducing a new peer learning strategy, we encourage you to explain and model the strategy with the whole class. Depending on the strategy, it can be helpful to introduce it in stages and talk about expectations for collaboration. As with any new instructional strategy, it will take practice and refinement before students are able to take part in the strategy independently, making it a routine. You'll also want to consider the additional scaffolds (beyond modeling and practice) that MLs might need to effectively take part in the routine such as sentence stems or frames, visuals, or anchor charts and consider how to strategically group students for each activity. Taking time at the beginning of the year to set up the protocols for these routines will allow you to build on and modify the peer learning routines throughout the school year. Routines should be reviewed regularly throughout the year to reinforce expectations and support MLs who are new to the class.

In addition to the discussion of peer learning routines, we'll be highlighting other scaffolds in this chapter that can be highly effective in supporting MLs' engagement in reading and writing across the curriculum. These are scaffolds that can be used both in conjunction with peer learning activities and when students are working individually. We'll explore the use of amplified texts, strategies for activating background knowledge when preparing students to read, and the use of checklists for student writing.

Why Do MLs Read, and How Can I Support Them With Their Reading?

Source: iStock.com/FrazaoStudio

Source: iStock.com/monkeybusinessimages

APPLICATION ACTIVITY 8.2: SUPPORTING MLs IN READING FOR DIFFERENT PURPOSES

In the box below, make a list of the different reasons that students are asked to read or are read to during the school day. Then, note possible scaffolds that MLs might need when they are reading for different purposes. We added one idea to get you started.

Students read . . .	Possible scaffolds that MLs need to read for different purposes are . . .
• To learn new content	• A graphic organizer to support identification of main ideas of text

As you probably realized during your brainstorming, MLs are asked to read or are read to for a variety of different reasons including (but not limited to) practicing specific skills, gaining new information, exploring different perspectives, or reading for pleasure. While the reason that you ask students to read may be very clear to you, it may not always be clear to students. As you explore the reading strategies that follow, consider what you might say to students as you introduce a new strategy in order to foster the development of the metacognitive skills that we described earlier. Our first strategy, text engineering, is a strategy that can be used when developing materials for a lesson.

Text Engineering: Chunking and Amplifying the Language of a Text

One question that educators often ask is whether they should simplify texts for multilingual learners. As we discussed in Chapter 3, we know that in order to offer equitable educational opportunities for MLs, we must give them access to grade-level texts, but at the same time, we also must give students the support to be able to engage with grade-level text in meaningful ways. When teachers take steps to simplify a text to make it seemingly more comprehensible to learners, they often remove the language and text features that help give context to students. As a result, a simplified text can often be more challenging for students to understand (Billings & Walqui, 2021). Compare these two examples:

- "Original Text: Because he had to work at night to support his family, Paco often fell asleep in class.

- Simplified Text: Paco had to make money for his family. Paco worked at night. He often went to sleep in class." (Billings & Walqui, 2021, p. 2).

REFLECTION QUESTIONS

1. What do you notice about the two texts?

2. Why might the simplified text be more confusing for MLs?

---

online resources ☞ Available for download at **resources.corwin.com/FennerUnlocking2E**

Rather than simplifying a text, Billings and Walqui (2021) recommend text engineering as one way to support ML engagement with complex texts. **Text engineering is the process of reworking a text in order to chunk the text into meaningful segments, embed text-based supports such as headers and subheaders to help orient students to the content of the text, and strategically amplify the language within a text.** Teachers can amplify the language in a text by adding linguistic clues such as embedded definitions and repetition of key terms (Billings & Walqui, 2021). Before reworking a text, Billings and Walqui (2021) recommend that educators ask themselves:

"(1) What makes a specific text difficult for my students? (2) How can I, as a teacher, make a text more accessible to my students?" (p. 2). The following are some key elements of text engineering:

- **Chunking text** into meaningful units, adding headings and subheadings to signal to students what they will read next, and including focus questions at the start of each section of text to guide students to the essential information. These focus questions also help set a purpose for the reading.

- **Including linguistic clues** such as embedded definitions or synonyms.

- **Adding visuals and captions** to support comprehension.

- **Providing an audio version** of the text (if text is online).

Let's give it a try in Application Activity 8.3.

APPLICATION ACTIVITY 8.3:
PART 1 *I AM FRIDA KAHLO.*

Read the following passage and then answer the reflection questions that follow.

I am Frida Kahlo

Of the almost 150 paintings that Frida created, over half of them were self-portraits. Frida said she painted herself more than any other subject because she knew herself so well. She never smiled in her self-portraits. (It is said this is because she had bad teeth.) Her serious face gives the paintings a certain solemn feeling. It is perhaps a message from Frida that although she loved having fun and enjoying herself, much of her life had been spent in pain and overcoming hardship. (Fabiny, 2013, p. 88)

APPLICATION ACTIVITY 8.3:
REFLECTION QUESTIONS, PART 1

1. What might make the text difficult for MLs at lower levels of language proficiency?

2. How might you amplify rather than simplify this text to make it more accessible to MLs?

APPLICATION ACTIVITY 8.3: PART 2

Review the engineered text below. Is there anything else you would change or add to make it more accessible to MLs of varying levels of proficiency?

_____

_____

What did Frida Kahlo show about herself in her self-portraits?

Of the almost 150 paintings that Frida created, over half of them were self-portraits (pictures she painted of herself). Frida said she painted herself more than any other subject because she knew herself so well. She never smiled in her self-portraits. (It is said this is because she had bad teeth.) Her serious face gives the paintings a certain solemn (serious) feeling. It is perhaps a message from Frida that although she loved having fun and enjoying herself, much of her life had been spent in pain and overcoming hardship (getting past difficult things). (adapted from Fabiny, 2013, p. 88)

Source: Frida Kahlo, *Self-Portrait With Hummingbird and Thorn Necklace,* Martin Shields/Alamy.

We know that teachers have very full plates, and the practice of text engineering takes time. This isn't a strategy to use for all texts, but it is one that, when used strategically, can support MLs in developing skills to approach complex texts. They can begin to apply these skills (e.g., reading with a purpose in mind, using text structures to chunk ideas and support understanding) on their own even when texts are not intentionally engineered (Billings & Walqui, 2021). Next, let's explore some specific peer learning strategies for reading.

Peer Learning Strategies for Reading

In the remainder of this section, we will share four peer learning strategies that can support students as they prepare to read, during reading, and after reading. Figure 8.1 lists each strategy and when it might be used. These strategies, when effectively modeled, practiced, and implemented regularly, will become routines that your students will be familiar with.

FIGURE 8.1   READING STRATEGIES AND WHEN TO USE THEM

READING STRATEGY	PREPARING TO READ	DURING READING	AFTER READING
Activating Background Knowledge: Gallery walk of text images	x		
Activating Background Knowledge: Writing questions based on text features	x		
Three Read Protocol (for math)		x	
Collaborative close reads	x	x	x

Activating Background Knowledge

As we described in Chapter 7, when MLs' background knowledge is activated prior to reading and the purpose for reading is made explicit, the text will be more meaningful to students. Using images and text features from a text can be used to activate students' background knowledge and boost understanding of the purpose for reading the text. ELD educator Erica Daniels shared two activities with us—gallery walk of text images and writing questions based on text features—to activate students' background knowledge and prepare them for reading.

Gallery Walk of Text Images (Preparing to Read). For this activity, students take part in a picture gallery walk. As they walk around the room looking at different images, students discuss the images in pairs or small groups and make predictions about what they will read (Kester & Daniels, 2019). The images can be taken directly from the text you will read, or additional images can be used if the ones in the text aren't sufficient. Students add sticky notes to the posters about what they see and predict. Sentence stems can be given to MLs who may need additional support. The gallery walk can be followed by a whole class debrief and restating the purpose for the reading. In Figure 8.2, students discuss images of the women's suffrage movement in the United States prior to reading a text about the movement. In partners, they move around the room describing what they see. Students predict what the reading will be about based on what they see in the pictures and what they read in the picture captions.

Writing Questions Based on Text Features (Preparing to Read). Another way to support MLs in activating background knowledge and preparing to read is to have them work in pairs or small groups to write questions that they will answer during the reading (Kester & Daniels, 2019). For this activity, students look at a piece of text and develop questions based on text features such as headings, subheadings, figures, and images. In order to introduce this activity to students, begin by modeling the process with the whole class. You could also develop an

FIGURE 8.2   WOMEN'S SUFFRAGE MOVEMENT GALLERY WALK

I see _____.   I predict _____.

I read _____.   I predict _____.

Based on _____, I predict _____.

Sources: (1914) *Help US to Win the Vote.*, 1914. [Photograph] Retrieved from the Library of Congress, https://www.loc.gov/item/97500240/; (1915) *Suffragists marching, probably in New York City in.* New York, 1915. [Photograph] Retrieved from the Library of Congress, https://www.loc.gov/item/97500064/.

anchor chart of the types of questions you might want to ask about a piece of text and the language needed for that question. In Figure 8.3 you can see examples of student questions added to this science text.

Next, let's explore a math strategy that can be used to support comprehension when reading mathematical word problems.

The Three Read Protocol for Math Word Problems (During Reading)

The Three Read Protocol is a peer learning strategy that students can use to approach word problems in math (Kelemanik et al., 2016). As we discussed in Chapter 7, MLs might find word problems challenging not only because of the technical vocabulary in the word problem but also the situations that are presented in the problem (National Academies of Sciences, Engineering, and Medicine [NASEM], 2018). The goal of the Three Read Protocol is to support students in developing a process for breaking down complex word problems. While there are different ways to approach the Three Read Protocol, the essential strategy is that students read the problem three times looking for different pieces

FIGURE 8.3   WRITING QUESTIONS BASED ON TEXT FEATURES

The oceans

What chemicals are found in the ocean?

Chemical composition

Earth's oceans are its most stable habitats. Their salt content has been stable for 600 million years. The salt itself is composed of several chemicals, including sodium, calcium, chloride, magnesium, potassium, and sulfate (see **Figure 1**). The combined concentration of salts is 35 parts per thousand (ppt). This means there are 35 grams of salt in every liter of ocean water.

What are the different zones in the ocean?

The ocean's zones

Scientists group different parts of the ocean into different layers or zones depending on what they study (see **Figure 2 below**). These zones begin at the surface and go to the deepest parts of the ocean. The deeper you go, the greater the pressure becomes, while both temperature and light decrease.

How deep are the different zones?

Chemical	Concentration (ppt)
Chloride	19.3
Sodium	10.8
Sulfate	2.7
Magnesium	1.3
Calcium	0.4
Potassium	0.4
Bicarbonate	0.1

Figure 1: The main chemicals found dissolved in ocean water

How much light reaches the different zones?

Zone	Depth	Pressure	Temperature	Sunlight
Sunlight zone	0 - 200 meters	Low	0 to 25° C	Visible
Twilight zone	200 -1,000 meters		4 to 5° C	Low to very low light
Dark zone	1,000 - 10,000 meters	High	0 to 4° C	No light

Figure 2: Ocean zones with depth, pressure, temperature, and sunlight facts

Is there life in all parts of the ocean?

Ocean life

Most ocean life subsists where there is the most sunlight. Because light does not reach deeper than 200 meters below the surface, plant life cannot grow in the deepest parts of the ocean. This makes life difficult for anything that lives in the deepest zones. There, life has adapted to overcome lack of light, freezing temperatures, and high pressure. Some organisms even produce their own light to find food, deter predators, and attract mates .

Figure 3: Crystal jellies (*Aequorea victoria*) are commonly found off the west coast of North America

Source: Text adapted from CPO Focus on Life Science (2007). Photograph of crystal jellies by istock.com/GaryKavanagh

of information each time. During the first read, students read to understand the story of the problem. During the second read, they read to understand the math. During the third read, students read in order to make a plan to solve the problem. During each of the three steps, students discuss their responses in pairs or small groups. We will first present the Three Read Protocol and then in Figure 8.5 share suggested scaffolds for MLs for each step of the process.

One way to first introduce the Three Read Protocol is to share the problem without numbers or without the question that needs to be solved. In this way, students can focus on what the problem is about. Next, the numbers can be added to the problem, and students can brainstorm what questions could be answered by the problem. There could be multiple questions that might be asked. Finally, the question can be shared, and students can collaboratively make a plan to solve the problem. In Application Activity 8.4, we give you an opportunity to try out the process. Figure 8.4 is a model of this activity.

FIGURE 8.4 THREE READ PROTOCOL EXAMPLE

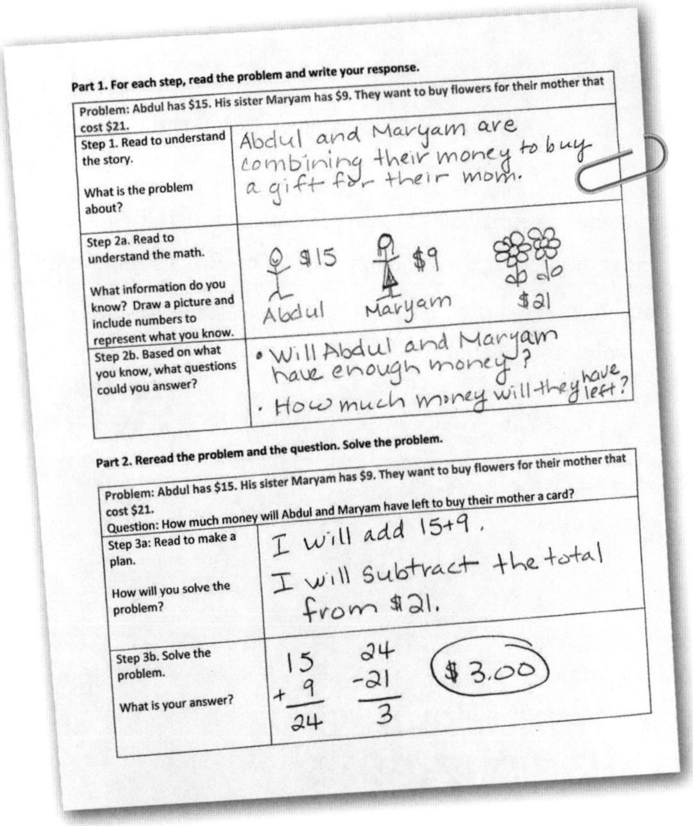

APPLICATION ACTIVITY 8.4: THREE READ PROTOCOL

Part 1. For each step, read the problem, and write your response.

Problem: Rosa is a fisherwoman. She works on a team with five other women. Rosa and her team caught 550 fish. They sold each fish for $3.	
Step 1. Read to understand the story. What is the problem about?	
Step 2a. Read to understand the math. What information do you know? Draw a picture and include numbers to represent what you know.	
Step 2b. Based on what you know, what questions could you answer?	

Part 2. Reread the problem and the question. Solve the problem.

Problem: Rosa is a fisherwoman. She works on a team with five other women. Rosa and her team caught 550 fish. They sold each fish for $3. **Question:** How much money will each person on Rosa's team earn?	
Step 3a: Read to make a plan. How will you solve the problem?	
Step 3b. Solve the problem. What is your answer?	

APPLICATION ACTIVITY 8.4: REFLECTION QUESTIONS

1. How does this strategy support MLs in understanding both the language and the math needed to solve a word problem?

_____

_____

2. What additional scaffolds might some MLs need to engage in this activity?

_____

_____

 Available for download at **resources.corwin.com/FennerUnlocking2E**

In Figure 8.5, we share the key questions and possible scaffolds for MLs that can support each of the three read steps.

FIGURE 8.5   THREE READ PROTOCOL: STEPS, KEY QUESTIONS, AND POSSIBLE SCAFFOLDS FOR MLs

STEPS	KEY QUESTION(S)	POSSIBLE SCAFFOLDS FOR MLs (ALIGNED TO LANGUAGE PROFICIENCY LEVELS)
1st read: Read to understand the story.	What is the problem about?	• Teacher reads the problem aloud. • Teacher shows visuals to support understanding of unfamiliar vocabulary. • Students use a graphic organizer to assist them during each step of the three reads activity. • Students discuss what the problem is about in pairs or small groups using sentence stems (e.g., I think the problem is about . . . ; The problem says . . .).
2nd read: Read to understand the math.	What are the quantities (or numbers) in the problem? How do the quantities (or numbers) relate to each other?	• Students choral read the problem with the teacher. • Students draw a picture on the graphic organizer to represent the problem and the connection between the numbers. • Students discuss their understanding of the numbers in pairs or small groups using sentence stems (e.g., One number in the problem is . . . It represents. . . .).
3rd read: Read to make a plan.	How can we solve the problem?	• Students complete the graphic organizer to write an equation and solve the problem. • Students discuss the steps for solving the problem in pairs or small groups using sentence stems (e.g., First, we need to . . . Next we should . . .)

Source: Adapted from San Francisco Unified School District, Mathematics Department. https://www.sfusdmath.org/3-read-protocol.html

 Available for download at **resources.corwin.com/FennerUnlocking2E**

Collaborative Close Reads (Preparing to Read, During Reading, and After Reading)

As we described in the research section of this chapter, having students engage in close reads in which they read a complex text multiple times for different purposes is beneficial to support student understanding of the text and can also help with the development of metacognitive skills that students can use when they read independently. Using a collaborative routine to approach close reads is helpful for MLs because students have an opportunity to hear and use academic language related to the topic, and they can practice both reading for understanding as well as reading to analyze and infer. Close reads can also serve as a jumping-off point for student writing. Figure 8.6 Collaborative Conversations for Close Reading is a four-step strategy with key questions that was adapted from Ward Singer's (2018) book *EL Excellence Every Day*. These questions could be further adapted based on grade level and content area. As you review Figure 8.6, consider how you could use this strategy in your classroom.

FIGURE 8.6   COLLABORATIVE CONVERSATIONS FOR CLOSE READING

STEPS	QUESTIONS FOR DISCUSSION
1. Anticipate	• Based on the title, what do we predict the text will be about? • After looking at the headings and the images, what do we predict the text will be about? • What questions do we think the text might answer?
2. Read to understand	• What is the gist (the main point) of what we read? • What don't we understand? • How do our predictions about the text compare to what we read?
3. Reread to analyze and infer	• What inferences can we make about what we read? • What conclusions can we make about what we read? • What connections can we make between this text, and what we have read about or discussed in the past?
4. Collaborate to write with text evidence	• What is our claim? • What evidence from the text best supports our claim? • How can we explain the connection between our evidence and the claim?

Source: Snyder and Staehr Fenner (2021), p. 127; Adapted from Ward Singer (2018), p. 175.

REFLECTION QUESTIONS

Consider the reading strategies that we shared in this section:

• Text engineering

• Gallery walk of images

• Writing questions based on text features

• Three Read Protocol for math

• Collaborative close reads

Which is a strategy that you would like to try next in your context or that you would like to discuss with a colleague?

  Available for download at **resources.corwin.com/FennerUnlocking2E**

Now that we have explored strategies for supporting MLs with reading, let's turn our attention to writing.

Why Do MLs Write, and How Can I Support Them With Their Writing?

APPLICATION ACTIVITY 8.5: SUPPORTING MLS IN WRITING

In the following boxes, make a list of the different ways that students are asked to write (both formally and informally) across content areas. Then, note possible scaffolds that MLs might need when they are completing these writing activities. We added one idea to get you started.

Students write . . . • Answers to comprehension questions	Possible scaffolds that MLs need to write for different purposes are . . . • A graphic organizer to support organization of ideas

---

In this section, we will share five strategies that you can use as you assist MLs in preparing to write, during the writing process, and after writing. Figure 8.7 gives an overview of the strategies and when each might be used. These strategies will become routines that your students will be familiar with when they are effectively modeled, practiced, and implemented regularly.

FIGURE 8.7 WRITING STRATEGIES

STRATEGY	PREPARING TO WRITE	DURING WRITING	AFTER WRITING
Talk first: Rally Robin	x		
Talk first: Dining partners	x		
Mentor sentences	x	x	x
Color-coded writing		x	
Student-friendly checklists		x	x

Talk First

Giving students an opportunity to share their ideas orally before writing will help many MLs by providing an opportunity for them to hear and practice the language they can use in their writing. Talking first can also assist students in generating ideas for writing and thinking about how they can connect and support their ideas. Rally Robin and Dining Partners are two strategies that you can use to give MLs a chance to talk before they write.

Rally Robin (Preparing to Write). Rally Robin is a Kagan Cooperative Learning Strategy in which students work in pairs to take turns generating ideas on a particular topic (Kagan & Kagan, 2009). The goal is for students to come up with as many ideas as they can in a short period of time. This can be an effective strategy if you are still in the brainstorming stage of the writing process. For example, imagine if you wanted students to write a paragraph on an important way that people can help their community. You might ask students to do a Rally Robin to think of as many ideas as they can in a minute for how people help in their community. With the Rally Robin protocol, students take turns giving responses. When we introduce this strategy in a class, we begin by modeling the activity as a whole class with a familiar topic such as delicious foods or animals that live in the water. Your practice topics can match the interests of your students. Once students are familiar with the strategy, you can have students take part in the activity to generate ideas around a particular writing topic.

Dining Partners (Preparing to Write). Dining partners is a peer learning activity that offers students an opportunity to share their ideas with different students and hear varied perspectives (adapted from Ward Singer, 2018). This strategy is a great one to use as students are preparing to write because they get a chance to share their ideas multiple times, which will support them as they begin to write. To use the dining partners activity, have students choose three different classmates that they will partner with. You can give guidelines for each partnership (e.g., someone wearing the same color as you, someone who doesn't sit at your table group), or you can let students choose partners freely. You can also assign partners if you are looking to group students in a particular way (e.g., shared home languages). Once students have completed their dining partner list (see Figure 8.8), you can use that list in a variety of ways. For example, you can have students talk with each of their dining partners one after the other, or you can specify which dining partner they should talk to at a particular time. Another benefit of dining partners is that it can remove some of the anxiety that some students may feel in finding a partner since there are parameters for choosing a partner.

FIGURE 8.8 DINING PARTNERS

DINING PARTNER	PARTNER NAME
Breakfast	
Lunch	
Dinner	

Source: Icons by iStock.com/bounward

 Available for download at **resources.corwin.com/FennerUnlocking2E**

For other examples, of peer learning activities that could be used to support writing, see Chapter 4.

Mentor Sentences (Preparing to Write, During Writing, After Writing)

Mentor sentences are an excellent way to share models of effective writing for MLs and can also be used to incorporate the teaching of language patterns and structures. Anderson and LaRoca (2017) describe a strategy that begins with the teacher selecting a mentor sentence to use as a model and developing a focus phrase that aligns with the language convention or structure that they want to practice. **A mentor sentence is a sentence that provides a strong model of a particular language pattern or structure.** For example, if the class is working on having students make comparisons between two characters, the teacher might share with students a mentor sentence that includes comparative language. Students are then asked to discuss what they notice about the mentor sentence as a way to encourage students to think about the language convention that is being practiced (and to develop those metalinguistic skills that we wrote about in the research section of this chapter). The teacher then introduces a second model sentence which students compare to the first sentence. These discussions around the mentor sentence can be used to create anchor charts that students can refer to as they write their own sentences. After students write their own sentences, they are given very specific feedback to strengthen their sentences. The strategy also includes an opportunity for students to share and celebrate their writing. For more details about the mentor sentence strategy and how to use the strategy with MLs, see Figure 8.9.

FIGURE 8.9   THE MENTOR SENTENCE STRATEGY

	STEPS	EXAMPLE	CONSIDERATIONS FOR MLs
1.	**Select a mentor sentence:** To begin the routine, you should select a mentor sentence that demonstrates an area of focus that you want to work on and is aligned to the standards. For example, you might focus on capitalizing proper nouns, pronoun use, or including text quotation in a text. Anderson and La Roca recommend selecting a piece of writing that "demonstrates the convention's power and purpose" (p. 23).	Example mentor sentence: "Everyone was running—men, children, women carrying babies." —Linda Sue Park, *A Long Walk to Water* (regular and irregular plurals, use of dash)	In selecting sentences, you'll want to be sure to preteach or explain any vocabulary needed for the sentence or select sentences that are comprehensible to all students.
2.	**Develop a focus phrase:** Based on your area of focus, you develop a focus phrase to guide students. This should be written in student-friendly language and clearly define the learning goal.	I use plural nouns to show more than one person, place, or thing.	Depending on the needs of your MLs, you may need to provide additional opportunities for students to practice the skill. For example, with irregular nouns, you might consider providing a resource that they could use for their work or assigning some small-group work to facilitate extra practice with the skill.
3.	**Invite students to notice:** Explain to students that rather than looking at a sentence that needs to be fixed, you'll be focusing on great sentences. Read the sentence aloud two times. Ask students what they notice about the mentor sentence.	• The -y changed to -ies in "babies." • Men and women don't have an -s at the end. • There is a dash before more details are added.	As with all routines, students will need modeling and practice with the process the first couple of times. It is also important to give students wait time. It can be beneficial to have students talk in pairs in order to provide more think time and opportunities for language practice.
4.	**Invite students to compare and contrast:** Develop an imitation sentence and ask students to compare the original sentence with an imitation sentence that you have created. This imitation sentence should closely mirror the mentor sentence but also provide an opportunity to demonstrate how the pattern can be applied to other situations and content.	Everyone was swimming—ducks, fish, and ponies carrying children.	Consider modeling this process through a think aloud. Provide sentence stems and modeling of language used to compare and contrast (e.g., In the first sentence, I see _____, but in the second I don't).
5.	**Give students an opportunity to imitate:** Next, it is the students' turn to create an imitation sentence. This can be done as an interactive or whole-group writing activity, pair writing, and/or independent writing. You might have students first develop an imitation sentence in pairs, and then have them create an imitation sentence independently.	Everyone was flying—fairies, witches, and dragons carrying children.	Be intentional about your pairings in order to provide scaffolded support. For example, you might pair students who share the same home language groups to they can discuss their sentence in their home language. Consider additional scaffolds that students might need to complete this next step, depending on the convention that you're working on (e.g., a list of adjectives, list of irregular plural nouns).

	STEPS	EXAMPLE	CONSIDERATIONS FOR MLs
💬	6. **Share and celebrate:** Anderson and La Rocca specify that during the sharing it is important to celebrate the students' work. We want students to associate positive feelings with their writing. This is a time for students to listen to each other's ideas and also to notice how writing conventions connect across topics.	• Students share sentences with class. • Set up mentor sentence walls with a focus phrase along the top. • Make mentor sentence books. • Share mentor sentences with students in lower grades.	Give an opportunity for students to practice reading their sentences aloud in pairs or to you before they share with the whole class. Consider developing a student-friendly checklist that students can use when writing their sentence (e.g., I capitalized the first letter of the sentence).
✏️	7. **Invitation to edit:** Anderson and La Roca specify that having students edit their own writing is the main skill that it is important for students to master. The invitation to edit can be used to help them hone their "editing eyes" (p. 39). You can ask students what they learned from the mentor sentence. Then, show students the mentor sentence again, followed by two to three other sentences that include errors in the focus area.	Everyone was running—cats, mouses, and dogs carrying childs.	Some MLs could benefit from additional supports with this process. For example, students could work in pairs and be provided a resource such as a list of irregular plural nouns. Also, when introducing this activity it would be good to practice the language that students can use to describe and explain errors.

Source: Adapted from Anderson and La Rocca (2017), Snyder and Staehr Fenner (2021). Icons by iStock.com/Tiyas

One aspect of Anderson and LaRoca's (2017) strategy that we really appreciate is the opportunity to celebrate student writing by students sharing their work. We suggest that all opportunities to share writing be optional and that students be given choice in which pieces of writing that they would like to share. Some ways to celebrate student writing are as follows:

- Have a writing wall to showcase student writing. If you are working on mentor sentences, this wall might include the focus phrase.

- Offer an opportunity for students to share their work in an "author's chair" that is especially designated for students who want the opportunity to read their writing aloud.

- Engage students in a gallery walk of published work in which they can comment on aspects of the writing that they appreciate. They can use stems such as "I like the way that you . . . ," "Your description of . . . reminds me of . . .", etc.

Color-Coded Writing (During Writing)

Color-coded writing is one way to build peer learning into the writing process while still requiring each student to be accountable for the work (Ward Singer,

2018). With color-coded writing, students work in pairs to respond to a prompt. You can ask students to write their response on poster paper, on notebook paper, or in an online document. Each student is required to write a certain amount, and each student should write in a different color. For example, one partner might write in blue, and the other partner might write in green. This allows the teacher to see who contributed what to the writing, and it also helps build individual responsibility for the writing. Students should discuss with each other what they will write, and they can also ask each other for support when it is their turn to write.

Use Student-Friendly Checklists for Self-Assessment and Peer-Assessment of Writing (During and After Writing)

In a move to integrate more peer feedback into the writing process, teachers sometimes ask students to review a peer's writing using a long checklist of items to look for (e.g., spelling, grammar, organization, word choice). These types of checklists can be overwhelming for MLs who may feel that they don't know if there are grammar mistakes or are uncertain about how to add more descriptive language. MLs from collectivist cultures might also feel uncomfortable critiquing a peer's writing, worrying that they might upset a friend. Instead, consider how you can develop short student-friendly checklists that include only the aspects of writing that you have been discussing and practicing in class. The checklists can be used for students to self-assess their own writing or to use during a peer review of writing. You can emphasize that the checklists are designed to support students in becoming stronger writers and are not punitive in any way. These checklists can also be differentiated for students based on their strengths and areas for growth in writing. Figure 8.10 includes two examples of student-friendly checklists. Please note that the elementary example would be used after mini lessons on mechanics and adding details. The secondary example could be used in connection to a unit on persuasive writing.

REFLECTION QUESTIONS

1. How do you support MLs in strengthening their writing, or what ideas do you have to support MLs in reflecting on how to make their writing stronger?

2. How do you celebrate student writing, or what ideas do you have to celebrate student writing?

---

online resources   Available for download at **resources.corwin.com/FennerUnlocking2E**

FIGURE 8.10   STUDENT-FRIENDLY WRITING CHECKLISTS

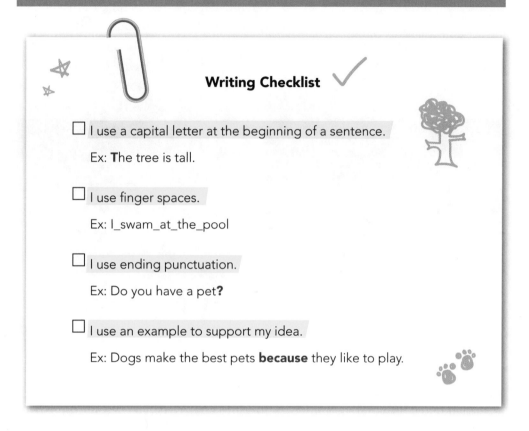

Writing Checklist ✓

☐ I use a capital letter at the beginning of a sentence.

Ex: **T**he tree is tall.

☐ I use finger spaces.

Ex: I_swam_at_the_pool

☐ I use ending punctuation.

Ex: Do you have a pet**?**

☐ I use an example to support my idea.

Ex: Dogs make the best pets **because** they like to play.

Persuasive Writing Checklist

☐ I have a thesis statement that is <u>specific</u> and clearly states my opinion on the topic.

☐ I have included at least <u>two</u> ideas to support my opinion. Each idea includes supporting evidence or examples.

☐ I have included a <u>counterargument</u> to disprove the opposite opinion.

☐ I have a persuasive closing sentence.

☐ I have read my essay aloud to <u>listen for and fix</u> run-on sentences and/or sentence fragments.

Now that we've explored specific strategies to support MLs in reading and writing across content areas, let's take a look at some considerations for ML newcomer students and students with limited or interrupted formal education (SLIFE) and the role of collaboration, equity, advocacy, and leadership when engaging in literacy practices.

ML NEWCOMER STUDENTS AND SLIFE CONSIDERATIONS

What Are Key Considerations for Supporting ML Newcomer Students and SLIFE in Reading and Writing?

Because ML newcomer students and students with limited or interrupted formal education (SLIFE) may have experienced interrupted schooling resulting in gaps in the development of literacy skills, they need targeted supports for developing their reading and writing skills.

Considerations:

- It is essential when MLs who are new to the country enroll in a district that they be assessed for foundational literacy skills (ideally in their home language). **Foundational literacy skills are the skills that students need to develop in order to learn to read such as print concepts, phonological awareness, phonics and word recognition and reading fluency.** Students who have interrupted schooling may need foundational literacy instruction in English and if possible in their home language to support literacy development. In districts where this type of support is not available, teachers should advocate for creative solutions to ensure that this critical literacy instruction is provided. For example, educators might advocate for an after-school tutoring program.

- Some ML newcomer students and SLIFE may come from oral cultures that are rooted in oral transmission of knowledge. It is important to remember that regardless of their foundational literacy skills, these students are competent in many different areas. However, they may not be accustomed to turning to print as a resource for learning and may feel overwhelmed by the role that reading and writing have in classroom learning. In order to orient students toward print and text as a resource, be intentional about the pace and way in which print materials are introduced and used and link these resources to oral language activities (DeCapua et al., 2020; DeCapua, 2023). In addition, use scaffolded oral language activities to tap into prior knowledge, build academic language, and foster writing development.

- DeCapua et al. (2020) highlight the need for administrative support to improve educational outcomes for ML newcomer students and SLIFE. Administrators can establish collaborative learning environments in which teachers of ML newcomer students and SLIFE are given time to share and discuss effective instructional practices. Educators can look for opportunities to connect themes and language skills across content areas. For example, if students are working on elements of persuasive writing in language arts, consider how the tools of persuasion might be used related to the topics being studied in other content areas.

Example: During the intake and enrollment process, it was determined that Joseph, our seventh-grade student from the Democratic Republic of Congo (introduced in Chapter 2), had interrupted schooling and was reading more than two years below grade level. Joseph was fortunate that the district had a foundational literacy program for MLs that prioritized phonics, phonemic awareness, reading comprehension, vocabulary development, and reading fluency within a framework of oral language development. Every week in this foundational literacy course he has an opportunity to engage in activities such as explicit vocabulary practice, collaborative close reading of texts, split dictation in which students work in pairs to dictate sentences to each other, cognate and word study, and informal and formal writing activities. He also has an opportunity to engage in translanguaging practices such as discussions with a peer who also speaks Swahili to support reading comprehension.

What Is the Role of Collaboration in Supporting MLs in Reading and Writing?

Collaboration to build on the strengths of and respond to the needs of MLs as they develop language is more urgent than ever. There has been an increased push for literacy interventions as schools respond to the impact disrupted schooling during the pandemic had on student learning. However, at times these piecemeal interventions can feel disconnected from what students are learning about and discussing in the content areas. For example, if MLs are pulled from their core class to practice letter sound correspondence, they may miss discussions of grade-level content that will impact their ability to engage in other learning activities. As you collaborate with colleagues or as you promote collaboration in an administrative or coaching role to foster MLs' reading and writing, consider questions such as the following:

- What are the language and literacy goals that we have for our MLs?

- How can we embed meaningful opportunities to build these literacy skills across content areas?

- How can we collaborate across content areas to reinforce the language and skills that MLs need to become stronger readers and writers?

- How can we embed opportunities for students to explore new concepts and practice new skills through listening, speaking, reading, and writing?

It's essential that educators have these types of challenging conversations about how to approach meeting the literacy needs of each ML.

What Is the Role of Equity, Advocacy, and Leadership in Engaging MLs in Reading and Writing in All Subjects?

There is an urgent need for advocacy and leadership to support equitable access for MLs when reading and writing. As was emphasized in Chapter 3 and in the research summary at the beginning of this chapter, MLs must have access to grade-level texts as well as the scaffolded supports needed to access these challenging texts. An additional area of consideration when thinking about equity, advocacy, and leadership related to engaging MLs in reading and writing is providing equity of representation in curricular materials and resources and providing opportunities for students to use their cultural and linguistic resources as they engage in literacy practices. Application Activity 8.6 is an opportunity for you to reflect on using students' cultural and linguistic assets as foundations for learning.

APPLICATION ACTIVITY 8.6: LEVERAGING STUDENTS' CULTURAL AND LINGUISTIC ASSETS AS FOUNDATIONS FOR LEARNING

Reflect on a time that you (or an educator that you know) positioned students' linguistic and cultural assets as a foundation for new learning. For example, before beginning a unit on the life cycle of a seed, you might ask students to talk about whether their family has ever grown their own food or plants and how they took care of the plants.

> What happened during the learning? How did you or the educator know how to leverage students' backgrounds as foundations for learning?

In the remainder of this section, we highlight two different activities that offer an opportunity for students to reflect on and use their cultural and linguistic assets: (1) classroom library inventory and (2) identity texts. As you read the description of these two activities, consider how you might adapt them for your context.

Classroom Library Inventory

A student classroom library inventory is an activity in which students evaluate the contents of their classroom library to determine the extent to which the books in the library are mirror books (representing themselves and their experiences) or window books (representing the experiences of others). The concept of mirrors and windows was first described by Emily Style (1988) and then later elaborated on by Rudine Sims Bishop. Bishop (1990) explained the way in which books can also be sliding glass doors that allow the reader to join the world created by the author.

Students need access to both mirror and window books in order to affirm their own identities and experiences and to help them understand and learn about the experiences and backgrounds of others. Students who see themselves and their backgrounds represented in many of the texts they encounter may form an unrealistic picture of the diversity of experiences and world views that exist. They miss an opportunity to learn about the language, culture, and realities of others who are different from them and the opportunity to build empathy for others. Similarly, students who encounter only window books or find characters similar to themselves portrayed in a negative light will miss the opportunity to have their culture, language, backgrounds, and ways of being affirmed by what they read (Bishop, 1990; Style, 1988). A student library inventory is an opportunity for students to think critically about representation and why it matters.

In order to implement a student library inventory, consider the following steps:

1. Introduce students to the idea of mirror and window books as well as the concept of sliding glass doors. Develop student-friendly definitions with students to explain these concepts. It's important for you to have shared language to talk about these ideas. Create an anchor chart with definitions and examples of key terms and home language translations of the key terms as appropriate.

2. Have students think about the different parts of their identity and background that are important to them or experiences that they have had that they would like to see represented in books. Model this by compiling your own list through a think-aloud activity.

3. Over the course of a week, do a series of read-alouds using multicultural resources. For each book, share whether the book is a mirror or a window for you or if it is a sliding glass door. Explain why. Ask students to offer their own responses to the books using the mirror, window, and sliding door terminology. Give sentence stems and frames (if needed) to support them in sharing their responses.

4. Use a template to have students complete the classroom library inventory. As part of this template, they can identify qualities of mirror books that they are looking for and to what extent they see them represented in the books that they review. See Figure 8.11.

5. Ask students to reflect on how they felt completing the library inventory. To what extent are their experiences represented in the books in the library? Are there certain ways that characters who are similar to them are portrayed? Did the characters that looked like them have experiences that they could relate to? What was missing from these stories? Did they find authors who share aspects of their cultural and linguistic backgrounds? You can adapt these questions based on the age of your students.

FIGURE 8.11   CLASSROOM LIBRARY INVENTORY

CHARACTERISTICS BOOKS THAT . . .	YES	NO
Have characters that look similar to me		
Have characters that talk like me and my family		
Remind me of places I have lived or visited		
Have events that remind me of experiences I have had		
Examples of mirror books in my classroom: Examples of window books in my classroom: A book that is a sliding glass door for me is _____ _____ . When I read it, I felt _____ _____ .		

Source: Adapted from Cultural Relevance Rubric (p. 198) in Ebe, A. (2010); Reyes, S. (n.d.); Staehr Fenner & Snyder (2021, p. 221).

There are a variety of ways to incorporate practice in the four language skills (i.e., listening, speaking, reading, and writing) into this activity, make the activity cross-curricular, as well as adapt it for students of different ages. For example, students might draw a table to represent their findings. They could develop a short video to promote a particular book that is a mirror for them. They could write letters to authors or publishers in support of more mirror books. They could research examples of other mirror books that they want included in the school library and make a pitch to the school librarian.

Identity Texts

Identity texts are multilingual, multimodal texts that can be written, spoken, visual, musical, dramatical, or a combination of any of these modalities and provide an opportunity for students to explore one or more aspects of their identity. The term *identity text* was coined by Jim Cummins to represent texts composed by multicultural and multilingual students and that incorporate their varied linguistic repertoires (Cummins et al., 2005; Hamman-Ortiz, 2021). Identity texts can be created individually or in groups.

Identity texts are an opportunity for students to create texts that give value to their own experiences and that can be both mirrors and windows for others in the classrooms and communities. This strategy was also developed with the understanding that increased student engagement and motivation in literacy practices will support literacy growth (Cummins & Early, 2011).

There is no one way to approach opportunities for the creation of identity texts. However, the key principle is that students are given an opportunity to produce multimodal texts that are representative of themselves and their experiences using whatever language they choose. When you introduce an identity text project, give a clear explanation for why you are asking students to take part in the project and explore models of what a finished identity text project could look like. Use strategic grouping during the development of identity texts. Consider grouping students by shared home languages in order to explore the idea of identity texts and discuss examples of identity texts. Following the initial discussion, you could group students heterogeneously to support the creation of multilingual texts and the sharing of varied experiences, or homogeneously to further foster home language integration. The following bullets are some examples of identity text topics.

- Students respond to a prompt about the town or city that they live in (e.g., Philadelphia looks like . . . , feels like . . . , sounds like . . .). Students can respond to the prompt individually but then work collaboratively to create a multimodal, multilingual text that represents their varied experiences (Hamman-Ortiz, 2021).

- Read the book *The Best Part of Me* (2002) by Wendy Ewald or a similar model. Ask students to describe the best part of themselves. Students could take a picture or create a piece of art to accompany their description.

- Students create "I can" books that include images and writing about what they can do as a way to support students in understanding their ability to impact change. This book can be added to with different prompts (e.g., Describe something you can do with your feet or hands. Describe something you can do with your words). "I can" books can also be an opportunity for families to have conversations with their children about all the things that they can do.

For additional examples of identity text projects, see Hamann-Ortiz's (2021) blog post titled "Identity Texts." She highlights different ways students have worked independently and collaboratively to develop identity texts as well as provides background on the development of and rationale for identity texts.

Next Steps

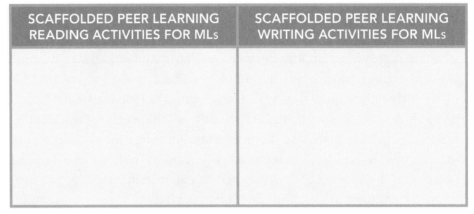

APPLICATION ACTIVITY 8.7: UNIT PLANNING FOR READING AND WRITING

Now that you have had the opportunity to explore some strategies for supporting MLs in reading and writing, it's time to return to the unit planning work that you have been doing with each chapter. Please take a moment to jot down some notes about how you will incorporate scaffolded peer learning opportunities to support MLs' reading and writing related to your unit.

SCAFFOLDED PEER LEARNING READING ACTIVITIES FOR MLs	SCAFFOLDED PEER LEARNING WRITING ACTIVITIES FOR MLs

Next, add your plans to the *Unit Delivery: ML Strategies;* and *Sequence and Activities* sections of the Unlocking MLs' Potential Unit Planning Template (Appendix A). Appendix A can be found on the online companion website. To access the companion website, please visit resources.corwin.com/FennerUnlocking2E.

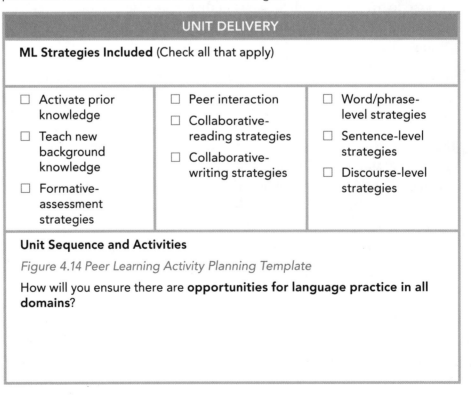

UNIT DELIVERY
ML Strategies Included (Check all that apply)

☐ Activate prior knowledge ☐ Teach new background knowledge ☐ Formative-assessment strategies	☐ Peer interaction ☐ Collaborative-reading strategies ☐ Collaborative-writing strategies	☐ Word/phrase-level strategies ☐ Sentence-level strategies ☐ Discourse-level strategies

Unit Sequence and Activities

Figure 4.14 Peer Learning Activity Planning Template

How will you ensure there are **opportunities for language practice in all domains**?

UNLOCKING RESOURCES

resources.corwin .com/FennerUnlocking2E

UNIT DELIVERY

How will you ensure that **lessons build upon each other to progress toward mastery** of content and language objectives?

For **co-teaching partnerships**, identify the role of the ELD teachers and content teacher.

Outline the unit sequence lesson by lesson. For each lesson, identify the lesson objectives and supporting learning activities.

LESSON OBJECTIVES	LEARNING ACTIVITIES (INCLUDING TEACHER ROLES AS APPLICABLE)

For ready-to-use,
practical tools to support
MLs' reading and writing,
please see SupportEd
.com/unlocking-toolbox.

Conclusion

In this chapter, we have taken a closer look at strategies to support MLs' engagement in reading and writing across content areas. We have discussed research that highlights the benefit for MLs of having reading and writing routines that are differentiated to meet the needs of students at varying language proficiency levels and that incorporate peer learning activities. We have explored specific strategies to provide MLs with scaffolded, collaborative learning opportunities when reading and writing. We also shared activities to leverage MLs' cultural and linguistic assets. Our next chapter, Formative Assessment for MLs, will offer you the opportunity to consider how formative-assessment strategies and tools can help you gauge MLs' understanding of content, acquisition of language, and learning growth and also how you can use that information to adjust your instruction.

CHAPTER 8 REFLECTION QUESTIONS

1. What is one takeaway that you have related to how to strengthen MLs' engagement in reading and writing across content areas?

2. What is a new peer learning strategy that you would like to use to support MLs' engagement with reading or writing?

  Available for download at **resources.corwin.com/FennerUnlocking2E**

FORMATIVE ASSESSMENT FOR MLs

9

Ms. Weber teaches biology in a suburban high school in Washington State, and this is her third year in the classroom. Her class contains a large number of emergent multilingual learners (MLs) at all levels of English proficiency who bring varying amounts of knowledge in biology from their previous education. Although she is working with her school's English language development (ELD) teacher to scaffold her lessons so that her emergent MLs can access the biology content and develop academic language, she is at a loss as to what she should do on her classroom assessments. Her students have to take an end-of-year biology multiple-choice content test in English that is required by the district, and she wants to prepare her students for that assessment measure. However, she recognizes that her students' developing proficiency in English does not always allow them to accurately show what they know and can do in biology without supports. Ms. Weber wants to find a way to create classroom assessments that provide her emergent MLs with a means to demonstrate what they have learned in biology and also give her some insights into where she might need to adapt her instruction.

REFLECTION QUESTIONS

1. What are some challenges you face assessing your MLs' acquisition of language and content?

2. What do you do to address these challenges?

This chapter will highlight the necessity of creating formative assessments that measure MLs' acquisition of academic language and content to support all teachers in sharing the responsibility and joy of teaching MLs. We will first define formative assessment and provide a summary of relevant research on the practice of formative assessment for MLs. We will include opportunities for you to apply the topic, including guidance on creating appropriate classroom assessments for MLs based on MLs' English proficiency levels and how you can use formative assessment results to inform instructional planning for MLs. Finally, we will give you examples and practical recommendations on the use of formative assessment with ML newcomer students and students with limited or interrupted formal education (SLIFE). While there are many ways that assessment can serve MLs, this chapter will focus on formative assessment. The concept of scaffolding formative assessments may be new to you, or you already may be thinking of instructional activities as a type of formative assessment to monitor and measure MLs' progress in language and content. No matter where you are in terms of your expertise on developing and using formative assessment for MLs, this chapter aims to scaffold you up to the next level.

What Is Formative Assessment?

To begin our exploration of formative assessment for MLs, let's first situate formative assessment within a larger context. In her framework of assessment, Gottlieb (2016, 2021a) conceptualizes assessment in three main types: assessment *as* learning, assessment *for* learning, and assessment *of* learning.

- **Assessment *as* learning emphasizes students as active participants in their own learning, with a focus on developing their metacognitive, metacultural, and metalinguistic awareness.** An example of assessment *as* learning is when students create their own language development goals and reflect on their growth.

- **Assessment *for* learning embraces the role of teachers in making instructional decisions from classroom data gathered on an ongoing basis.** An example of assessment *for* learning is when a teacher uses an observation checklist to take notes on students' use of academic language and then adjusts their instruction based on those notes.

- **Assessment *of* learning generates data for summative purposes.** Annual English language proficiency assessments and state content exams used for accountability are examples of assessment *of* learning.

Assessment *as*, *for*, and *of* learning can be thought of as a continuum (see Figure 9.1) as there can be overlap, and they can happen simultaneously.

APPLICATION ACTIVITY 9.1: REFLECTING ON ML ASSESSMENTS IN YOUR CONTEXT

Consider Gottlieb's framework of assessment (as, for, and of learning). Reflect on the different types of assessments you use in your context with MLs. Complete Figure 9.1 by identifying assessments you use with your MLs, whether the assessment is as, for, and/or of learning, and the purpose of the assessment. An example has been completed for you.

FIGURE 9.1   REFLECTING ON ASSESSMENT AS, FOR, AND OF LEARNING

ASSESSMENT	AS, FOR, OR OF LEARNING	PURPOSE
Exit tickets	_for_ learning	I use various types of exit tickets to gather information on ML learning at the end of a lesson and inform my next instructional steps.

(Continued)

(Continued)

REFLECTION QUESTIONS

1. What elements of the FAST SCASS formative assessment definition stand out to you? Why?

2. Which of your ML assessments from Application Activity 9.1 are formative assessments?

3. Where do you see opportunities to embed more formative assessments of MLs into your context?

 online resources Available for download at **resources.corwin.com/FennerUnlocking2E**

APPLICATION ACTIVITY 9.1: REFLECTION QUESTIONS

Review the types and purposes of the assessments you included in Figure 9.1 and respond to the questions below.

1. Which type of assessment (*as*, *for*, or *of* learning), do you see most often in your context with MLs?

_____

_____

2. How do you use the data from the assessments in your context?

_____

_____

 online resources Available for download at **resources.corwin.com/FennerUnlocking2E**

The Council of Chief State School Officers' (CCSSO) Formative Assessment for Students and Teachers (FAST) State Collaborative on Assessment and Student Standards (SCASS) defines **formative assessment as** (2018)

a planned, ongoing process used by all students and teachers during learning and teaching to elicit and use evidence

of student learning to improve student understanding
of intended disciplinary learning outcomes and support
students to become self-directed learners.

Effective use of the formative assessment process requires students
and teachers to integrate and embed the following practices in a
collaborative and respectful classroom environment:

- Clarifying learning goals and success criteria within a broader
  progression of learning;

- Eliciting and analyzing evidence of student thinking;

- Engaging in self-assessment and peer feedback;

- Providing actionable feedback; and

- Using evidence and feedback to move learning forward by adjusting
  learning strategies, goals, or next instructional steps. (pp. 2–3).

This definition of formative assessment embodies aspects of both assessment *as* and assessment *for* learning in that it acknowledges both students
and teachers as part of the formative assessment process. Assessment
as learning empowers students to become more "self-directed learners"
through goal setting, self-assessment, and peer assessment. Assessment *for*
learning honors teachers as decision-makers and leverages their expertise.
Embedded in teaching routines, assessment *for* learning is a direct expression of instruction, inviting student voice and revolving around providing
descriptive, helpful feedback to teachers (Gottlieb, 2016, 2021a; Stiggins,
2005). In this chapter, we examine formative assessment for teachers of
MLs as an example of assessment *as* and *for* learning. Formative assessment
empowers MLs to be active participants in their own learning. Additionally,
it allows for teachers to design, implement, and integrate assessments that
are valid and reliable and, most importantly, provide valuable information
to inform their instruction of MLs.

What Does the Research Say on Assessment for MLs in General?

Our work with MLs and their teachers is based on an advocacy framework in
which the concept of **scaffolded advocacy—or providing just the right
amount of temporary advocacy on the basis of students' strengths
and needs**—is crucial to support their academic achievement (Staehr Fenner,
2014a). The goal of scaffolded advocacy is to support students in being able to
self-advocate. And nowhere do advocacy and equity for MLs play a more important role than in assessment, which can have detrimental consequences for MLs
if not designed with MLs' unique attributes in mind.

To begin, we will explore the issues of assessment in a broad sense for MLs,
focusing on **summative assessments, or assessments that occur at**

the end of a unit of instruction or academic year. These summative-assessment scores are usually compared against a standard or other benchmark. Research has clearly demonstrated that summative assessments designed mainly for native English speakers may not be as reliable and valid for emergent MLs (Abedi, 2006; Abedi & Linquanti, 2012; National Academies of Sciences, Engineering, & Medicine [NASEM], 2017, p. 418). In fact, the average scores for emergent MLs on the 2017 reading and math National Assessment of Educational Progress (NAEP), or "nation's report card," were significantly lower than average scores for native speakers of English, and the gap between emergent MLs and their peers has remained essentially unchanged between 2007 and 2017 (Office of English Language Acquisition, 2018). Data from school year 2018-2019 shows that 46.7 percent of all students who took their statewide mathematics assessment scored proficient or above proficient, whereas 26.4 percent of emergent MLs who took the assessment scored proficient or above proficient, and 51.1 percent of former MLs scored proficient or above proficient. Similarly, data for school year 2018-2019 shows that 50.9 percent of all students who took their statewide reading/language arts assessment scored proficient or above proficient, whereas 23.9 percent emergent MLs who took the assessment scored proficient or above proficient, and 56.6 percent of former MLs scored proficient or above proficient (U.S. Department of Education, 2023). Note that former MLs, those MLs that have been reclassified and exited the ELD program by attaining English proficiency, are outperforming all students, including native English speakers. This fact highlights that while we may not always see immediate, obvious benefits in using the strategies outlined in this book in terms of MLs' scores on assessments, when we look at longitudinal data we can clearly see the value of ML teachers' hard work and the advantages of multilingualism for MLs.

As the data demonstrates, current summative-assessment measures present issues of reliability and validity for MLs. However, if teachers design assessments taking MLs' strengths into consideration, formative assessments hold great promise as a way for MLs to demonstrate what they know and can do in content as well as language. Gottlieb (2021b) writes,

> Classroom assessment can be a powerful linguistic and culturally sustaining process for both MLs and their teachers. Integral to educational parity, classroom assessment can stimulate ML engagement and represent the interplay between content and language as a means of advancing student learning. (p. 1)

What Is the Role of Formative Assessment With MLs?

Assessment of emergent MLs is more complex than assessing non-MLs, as emergent MLs are developing both content knowledge and English language skills simultaneously. Formative assessment allows educators an opportunity to collect evidence on MLs' progress in content knowledge and language development and make immediate instructional decisions based on that evidence. In addition, formative assessment has the benefit of fostering students' engagement with their own learning and acquisition of language.

As educators begin to use formative assessments with MLs in their classrooms, it is important to remember that formative assessments should not take substantial time from classroom instruction and should be seamlessly integrated into instructional routines. Educators can develop checklists, rubrics, and other formative assessment tasks to continuously monitor and respond to MLs' content learning and language development. When creating these formative assessments for MLs, teachers should develop tasks that ask MLs to use multimodalities to show what they know to ensure they are able to accurately measure their understanding (Gottlieb, 2021b; Llosa & Gerzon, 2022). Furthermore, teachers can leverage students' home language and invite MLs to communicate in their preferred language when appropriate. Gottlieb (2021b) shares,

> Students today need to engage in increasingly complex and sophisticated spoken, written, and multimodal texts for different purposes, audiences, and topics. One such communication mode unique to multilingual learners is their interaction in multiple languages. When teachers adopt multiple languages as a multimodal resource for instruction and assessment, multilingual learners benefit immensely, not only academically, but also in helping to shape their identities. (p. 8)

Formative assessment for MLs also has the benefit of increasing student agency. **Student agency means that students are empowered to make decisions about and are actively engaged in their learning.** Using goal setting, self-assessment, and peer assessment as a part of ongoing formative assessment encourages MLs to build metacognitive skills and metalinguistic awareness to progress in their learning. For instance, MLs and teachers can work collaboratively to set individual goals for language development at the beginning of a unit. Then, throughout the unit, MLs can engage in self-assessment and peer assessment to analyze their progress toward those goals and make decisions about how to continue to work toward their goals. To support this process, it is imperative that teachers establish clear success criteria (e.g., student-friendly rubrics, sample responses, checklists) and communicate the criteria to students to ensure that students know they are making progress toward their goal (Brookhart, 2020).

How Do I Structure the Formative-Assessment Process for MLs?

The ultimate benefit of using formative assessment for MLs is that it provides teachers with ongoing insights into students' learning and supports teachers in

UNLOCKING RESOURCES

To see how fourth-grade teacher Taryn Michael uses self-assessment in her classroom, watch the video titled Students Engaging in Self-Assessment (Snyder & Staehr Fenner, 2021).

The video can be found on the online companion website. To access the companion website, please visit resources.corwin.com/FennerUnlocking2E

adjusting their instruction accordingly. Teachers can structure the formative-assessment process in four basic steps, shown in Figure 9.2.

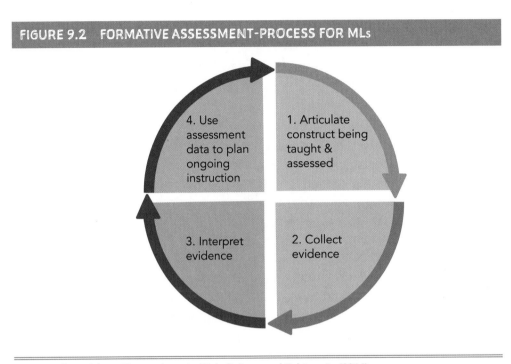

FIGURE 9.2   FORMATIVE ASSESSMENT-PROCESS FOR MLs

Source: Adapted from Alvarez, Ananda, Walqui, Sato, and Rabinowitz (2014).

Figure 9.3 includes more details around each of these steps and describes how each step is unique for teachers of MLs. We apply these steps to one classroom and one student later in the chapter.

FIGURE 9.3   FOUR-STEP PROCESS FOR STRUCTURING FORMATIVE ASSESSMENT FOR MLs

STEP TO STRUCTURE FORMATIVE-ASSESSMENT PROCESS FOR MLs	EXPLANATION FOR TEACHERS OF MLs
Step 1: Articulate the construct being taught and assessed: teacher and/or student articulate learning objectives and success criteria	• Teachers consider what is being taught and assessed, whether content or language are part of the learning objectives or success criteria, and what aspects of content or language are relevant. • Teachers should refer to content and language objectives in this step to ensure assessment alignment. • Teachers and students should have a shared understanding of success criteria, and rubrics or checklists should be aligned to these criteria.
Step 2: Collect evidence about MLs' learning: teacher gathers evidence to	• Depending on the learning objectives from Step 1, teachers can decide how language dependent the formative-assessment task will be. If the focus is content knowledge, teachers may choose to use tasks that are less language dependent (e.g., visual or performance tasks).

STEP TO STRUCTURE FORMATIVE-ASSESSMENT PROCESS FOR MLs	EXPLANATION FOR TEACHERS OF MLs
determine where the student is in relation to learning objective	• Consider using open-ended tasks that allow students at various levels of English proficiency to demonstrate learning (e.g., a prompt that asks students to write and/or draw their response). • Use tasks that have multiple avenues for MLs to demonstrate their learning (e.g., students create a poster with writing and visuals and then explain their ideas orally).
Step 3: Interpret evidence: teacher and/or student look at evidence to provide feedback on the status of student learning	• Language and content are closely linked, but it may be useful to analyze the two separately when looking at student work depending on what you prioritize in Step 1. • Student interpretation can be accomplished through peer assessment or self-assessment using a student-friendly rubric or checklist.
Step 4: Use assessment data to inform ongoing instruction: teacher develops and implements next steps based on data collected in Step 2 and interpreted in Step 3	• Teachers consider the conclusions drawn from Step 3 to inform subsequent teaching and learning activities. • Teachers design learning activities to address content misconceptions, skills needing additional practice, or language development needs. • Students can be involved in next steps by providing them choice in learning activities designed to practice skills or internalize information and setting goals for their learning.

Source: Adapted from Alvarez, Ananda, Walqui, Sato, and Rabinowitz (2014).

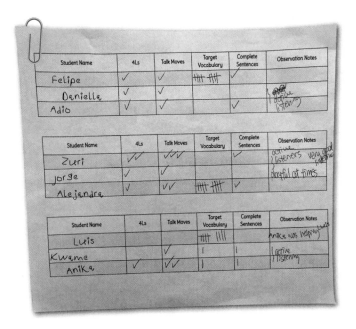

Third-grade teacher Anah Alie and ELD teacher Myunghee Chung use a discussion checklist in math class to collect evidence on students' listening and speaking during small-group discussions. The checklist is organized by group and includes space for the teachers to quickly mark whether or not a student is using the targeted skills along with space for observation notes. After the lesson, the teachers review information from the checklist together to determine next steps. Note that the 4Ls stand for look at your partner's eyes, lean toward your partner, lower your voice, and listen attentively. Student names have been changed.

Source: Anah Alie and Myunghee Chung

How Can I Collect and Interpret Formative-Assessment Evidence to Inform Instruction of MLs?

APPLICATION ACTIVITY 9.2: FORMATIVE-ASSESSMENT BRAINSTORM

There are a variety of formative assessments you may wish to consider for collecting evidence of your MLs' learning. Brainstorm a list of the various types of formative assessments that you already use in your classroom in the box below.

Example: **Exit tickets**

Figure 9.4 includes a sample of different categories of formative assessments and some examples of each. We have built in space for you to indicate which types of formative assessments have been effective for your MLs. You may be surprised at the types of activities that are already part of your practice that you could use for formative assessment.

FIGURE 9.4   CATEGORIES OF FORMATIVE ASSESSMENTS AND EXAMPLES

CATEGORY OF FORMATIVE ASSESSMENT	EXAMPLES	MY NOTES ON THE EFFECTIVENESS FOR MLs
Physical demonstration	• Hands-on tasks • Acting out concepts • Gestures • Other: _____	
Pictorial products	• Drawings • Models • Graphs • Other: _____	
Graphic organizers	• Charts and tables • Venn diagrams • Sorts • Other: _____	

CATEGORY OF FORMATIVE ASSESSMENT	EXAMPLES	MY NOTES ON THE EFFECTIVENESS FOR MLs
Written products	• Captions of images • Reading response or content area logs • Exit tickets • Other: _____	
Oral assessments	• Oral interviews • Reports • Retelling • Role-plays • Audio or video recording • Other: _____	
Student Choice and Self-Assessment Tasks	• Tic-Tac-Toe choice board • Checklist • Rating scale • Other: _____	

APPLICATION ACTIVITY 9.2: REFLECTION QUESTIONS

Review your list of formative assessments and the categories of formative assessment outlined in Figure 9.4.

1. What categories would you divide those assessments into?

   _____

   _____

2. Which types of formative assessment would you like to add to your toolbox?

   _____

   _____

In our work with teachers of MLs, we often find that Steps 3 and 4, interpret evidence and use assessment data to inform ongoing instruction, are the most challenging areas. After teachers collect evidence from a formative assessment, they may be unsure as to how to actually use the evidence to make changes to their instruction of MLs. To provide guidance to teachers on these important steps, we created a tool (Figure 9.5), which details instructional scaffolding and strategies you can use that are tailored to the three levels of academic language (word/phrase, sentence, and discourse) to help emergent MLs move to the next proficiency level. These scaffolds and strategies are suggestions, not mandates, so we encourage you to use this tool as a starting point considering student grade level and English language proficiency level and adapt it for your context.

FIGURE 9.5 INSTRUCTIONAL SCAFFOLDING AND STRATEGIES TO SUPPORT LANGUAGE GROWTH

LEVEL OF ACADEMIC LANGUAGE	STRATEGIES TO SUPPORT LANGUAGE GROWTH
Word/Phrase Level	☐ Bilingual or English glossaries ☐ Dictionaries ☐ Direct vocabulary instruction ☐ Pretaught phrases ☐ Thesauri ☐ Visuals or manipulatives ☐ Word walls and word banks
Sentence Level Language	☐ Academic language practiced with non-academic topics ☐ Mentor sentences ☐ Mini grammar lessons ☐ Sentence frames or stems
Discourse Level	☐ Mentor texts ☐ Paragraph frames ☐ Paraphrasing activities (for fluency and register) ☐ Shared writing ☐ Structured oral language prompts ☐ Text analysis ☐ Text sequencing
All Levels (Word/Phrase, Sentence, and Discourse)	☐ Anchor charts ☐ Cloze activities ☐ Graphic organizers ☐ Repetition ☐ Structured pair and small-group work ☐ Student checklists ☐ Supplementary or home language text or video ☐ Teacher and peer modeling ☐ Teacher-led small groups

What Is Assessment Validity for MLs, and How Can I Ensure My Formative Assessments Are Valid?

Imagine a first-grade teacher assessing all of her students' understanding of word-ending sounds. Ms. Aponte shows her student, Gao-Jer, a Hmong speaker at a beginning level of English language proficiency, the picture seen here.

Ms. Aponte asks Gao-Jer to identify what other word has the same ending sound: *wish, hat, hop,* or *pan.*

Source: iStock.com/DNY59

REFLECTION QUESTIONS

1. What may be standing in the way of this student demonstrating what she knows on this question?

2. What could the teacher do to make this assessment more valid for Gao-Jer?

online resources ⏴ Available for download at **resources.corwin.com/FennerUnlocking2E**

The mop question is an example of validity, which generally refers to how accurately a conclusion, measurement, or concept corresponds to what is being tested. **Validity is defined as the extent to which an assessment accurately measures what it is intended to measure** (American Educational Research Association, American Psychological Association, National Council on Measurement in Education, Joint Committee on Standards for Educational and Psychological Testing, 2014). For example, if you weigh yourself on a scale, the scale should give you an accurate measurement of your weight. If the scale tells you that you weigh 250 pounds, and you actually weigh 200 pounds, then the scale is not valid. If an assessment intends to measure achievement and ability in a particular subject area but then measures concepts that are completely unrelated, the assessment is not valid. In the example of the mop, if Gao-Jer does not know the English word for mop, she will not be able to correctly determine which of the four words has the same ending sound. As a result, it is her knowledge of English vocabulary rather than her knowledge of ending letter sounds that is being assessed. Within the larger umbrella of validity, there are categories of construct validity, content validity, and predictive validity, among others. Figure 9.6 is an overview of different aspects of validity, their definition, and examples that are specific to MLs.

FIGURE 9.6   TYPE OF VALIDITY, DEFINITION, AND EXAMPLE FOR MLs

TYPE OF VALIDITY	DEFINITION	EXAMPLE FOR MLs
Construct validity	The degree to which a test measures what it claims, or purports, to be measuring	A math test in which a teacher has reduced the linguistic load of word problems to ensure it is assessing mathematical knowledge rather than language proficiency
Content validity	The extent to which an assessment represents all facets of tasks within the domain being assessed	A vocabulary quiz that is designed to measure not only MLs' understanding of meaning but also their ability to use the words in context
Predictive validity	The extent to which a score on an assessment predicts future performance	How well an emergent ML's score on the annual state English language proficiency assessment predicts his or her performance on the state English language arts assessment

You don't need to be an assessment expert to work with MLs, but you should have a sense of how the concept of validity can affect MLs differently than non-MLs. In addition, we encourage you to have a plan for addressing different types of validity when you design assessments for MLs to make them more valid. We suggest you also know where to go and with whom to collaborate to better support your MLs in assessment.

APPLICATION ACTIVITY 9.3: WHY IS VALIDITY A CONCERN FOR MLs?

Imagine you are in fourth grade, and your family has moved to Germany for a year for your mother's career. You are enrolling in the German public school system. To determine your mathematics class placement, you are given an assessment to see how much you know in mathematics. In fact, you were in advanced math in the United States and love the topic. You sail through the multiplication problems and the long division until you come to this geometry problem:

Schreibe den richtigen Namen unter die entsprechende Darstellung!

Versuche anschließend zu entscheiden, ob die angeführten Aussagen wahr (w) oder falsch (f) sind. Kreuze Entsprechendes an!

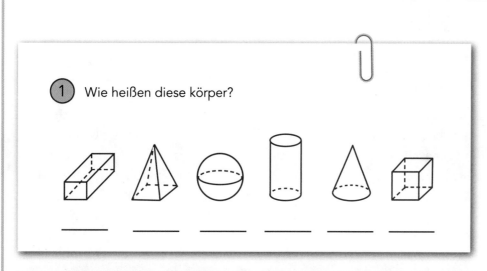

① Wie heißen diese körper?

AUSSAGE	W	F
Der Würfel hat 10 Ecken.		
Die Kugel hat keine Kanten und keine Ecken.		

Source: **Staehr Fenner (2014).**

APPLICATION ACTIVITY 9.3: REFLECTION QUESTIONS

1. Is this a valid assessment for you? Why, or why not?

   _____

   _____

2. Is the main issue at hand construct, content, or predictive validity?

   _____

   _____

3. What kind of support would help you show what you know and can do on these geometry problems?

   _____

   _____

How Can I Ensure That Formative Assessments Are Valid for MLs of Varying Proficiency Levels?

There are several areas that pose validity considerations for MLs. We will next take a deeper look at six areas that may have an impact on validity for your MLs.

Area 1. Assessment instructions. Let's start with the instructions for the assessment. They need to be clear and easy to understand. You may wish to consider communicating the directions orally, as well as in writing, and have a visual cue (e.g., icon to represent direction words) for students to refer to. You can also communicate the directions in the students' home language or have written directions already translated for students (as appropriate).

Area 2. Linguistic accessibility. Look for opportunities to reduce the *linguistic load* in all areas that aren't being directly assessed. For example, you can avoid constructing sentences in the negative and using unnecessarily complex vocabulary and grammatical structures. Teachers should double check their language—both in the assessment and any oral prompting or instructions they give—to avoid the use of idioms (e.g., *under the weather*), which are often confusing for language learners. We also encourage teachers to share a draft of their assessments with another teacher to have a set of "fresh eyes" take a look at it for linguistic accessibility.

Area 3. Format and use of technology. The assessment should be in a familiar format. For example, students should be taught how to engage with a multiple-choice question before using a multiple-choice format for the first time. The technology used, if any, needs to be familiar to MLs as well. Consider the format used and whether the student has had ample time to practice with the technology in class and is familiar with the associated vocabulary, such as *drag and drop* (Staehr Fenner, 2015, 2016). Bear in mind students have various levels of access to technology outside of school.

Area 4. Cultural bias. Cultural biases are often a hidden problem, as teachers may be unaware of these biases themselves. We recommend selecting content for the formative assessment that is something familiar to all students' shared experience, not topics students may not have had access to in their culture, education, or life experience. For example, U.S. American fairy tales, summer camp, and vacations in the mountains or at the beach may not be familiar to all students. Shared experiences, such as class field trips and stories students have read in class, can be used instead as context in assessments.

Area 5. Scoring. Scoring needs to be based on the assessed construct only. Assigning points for spelling and grammar when they aren't the targeted skill or knowledge (on a test on the water cycle, for example) being assessed reduces the validity of the assessment. To determine what construct you're assessing, refer back to your lesson's content and language objectives.[1]

Area 6. Scaffolds. MLs need appropriate supports in assessments, from differentiated assessments to scaffolds, that enable them to demonstrate their knowledge and skills in content while their language is still developing. The assessment does not need to look the same for all students. For emerging MLs at the beginning levels of English language proficiency, nonverbal assessments such as sorts and picture matching, may be used to demonstrate understanding of the concept. For MLs at higher levels of English proficiency, you can use glossaries and sentence stems as supports so that they can demonstrate what they know and can do. Some educators might resist scaffolding assessments for MLs feeling that it is unfair and gives MLs an advantage over native English speakers. However, when used effectively, scaffolds should not change the content being assessed; rather they allow MLs to demonstrate what they know at their current English language proficiency level.

How Do I Scaffold Formative Assessments for MLs?

As we mention in Area 6, providing scaffolds on formative assessments increases their validity for MLs. Scaffolding formative assessments can help prepare MLs to engage with summative year-end state tests that are not likely to be scaffolded. You can gradually reduce the number of scaffolds used on formative assessments to scaffold up to the expectations MLs need to meet on summative assessments. Let's look at an example of one way to scaffold formative assessments for MLs. Suppose that students have had the Chinese folktale "Tikki Tikki Tembo" read aloud several times, have read it themselves, and have discussed it in small groups. Their third-grade teacher, Mr. Leonato, would like students to now demonstrate that they can recount the events of the story and determine the central message. Based on his students' level of proficiency, Mr. Leonato has devised a sketch of what the formative assessment might look like for his MLs who are at three different levels of proficiency, as outlined in Figure 9.7. All three assessment tasks allow his MLs to show they can recount the events of the story and determine the central message, but his students are demonstrating their content knowledge in different ways.

---

[1]See Figure 9.3 for steps to develop formative assessments for MLs.

FIGURE 9.7   STUDENTS' ENGLISH LANGUAGE PROFICIENCY (ELP) LEVEL AND DIFFERENTIATED-ASSESSMENT TASKS

ELP LEVEL	DIFFERENTIATED-ASSESSMENT TASK
Beginning	Place pictures of the story in order. Describe the pictures orally using sentence frames. Answer questions about the central message in writing in the home language or English using sentence frames and a word bank.
Intermediate	Place pictures of the story in order. Describe the pictures orally and in writing using sentence stems. Answer questions about the central message in writing in English using sentence stems or a word bank.
Advanced	Describe the events of the story orally in small groups using sentence stems. Answer questions about the central message in writing in English using sentence stems or pretaught vocabulary.

APPLICATION ACTIVITY 9.4: VALIDITY AND SCAFFOLDING FORMATIVE ASSESSMENTS FOR MLs

As we introduced earlier in the chapter, formative assessments can take many forms: physical demonstrations, pictorial products, graphic organizers, written products, oral assessments, and student choice tasks. Look at the formative assessment examples in Figures 9.8 through 9.11. Answer the following questions for each assessment:

QUESTION	FIGURE 9.8 U.S. GOVERNMENT EXIT TICKET	FIGURE 9.9 DRAWING TO SEQUENCE A STORY	FIGURE 9.10 STUDENT SELF-ASSESSMENT ON TELLING TIME	FIGURE 9.11 PROPERTIES OF MATTER SORTING ACTIVITY
What questions or comments do you have about the formative assessment related to using it with your MLs?				
How can you increase the validity of this assessment for MLs?				
How could you scaffold this assessment for MLs at varying English proficiency levels?				

FIGURE 9.8   U.S. GOVERNMENT EXIT TICKET

Name _____

Directions: Pretend your friend was absent from class today. Write what you would say if you had to explain the difference between a closed primary and an open primary to your friend.

FIGURE 9.9   DRAWING TO SEQUENCE A STORY

Name _____

Directions: Draw pictures to represent the main events from the beginning, middle, and end of the story. Write one sentence to summarize each event. Use the word bank as needed.

Word Bank
First
Next
Then
After that
Last
In the end

Beginning	Middle	End

(Continued)

(Continued)

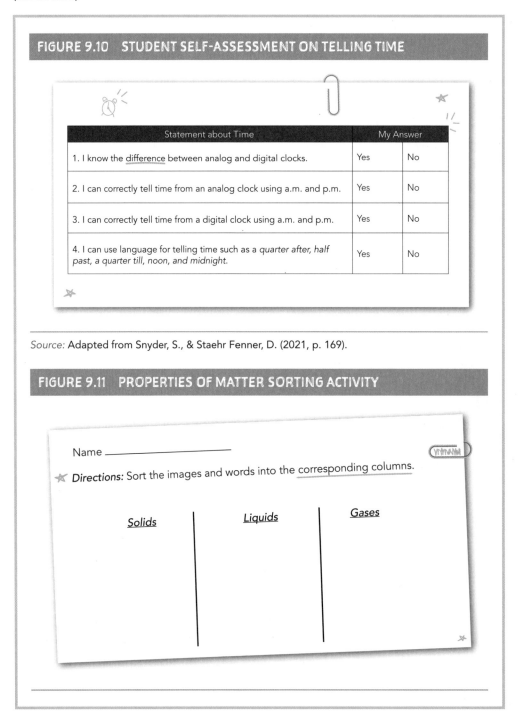

FIGURE 9.10   STUDENT SELF-ASSESSMENT ON TELLING TIME

Statement about Time	My Answer	
1. I know the <u>difference</u> between analog and digital clocks.	Yes	No
2. I can correctly tell time from an analog clock using a.m. and p.m.	Yes	No
3. I can correctly tell time from a digital clock using a.m. and p.m.	Yes	No
4. I can use language for telling time such as a *quarter after, half past, a quarter till, noon, and midnight.*	Yes	No

Source: Adapted from Snyder, S., & Staehr Fenner, D. (2021, p. 169).

FIGURE 9.11   PROPERTIES OF MATTER SORTING ACTIVITY

Name _____

Directions: Sort the images and words into the <u>corresponding columns.</u>

<u>Solids</u>   <u>Liquids</u>   <u>Gases</u>

How Does the Formative-Assessment Process for MLs Unfold in a Classroom?

Now that we've given you some food for thought in terms of formative assessments for MLs, we're going to show you how each of the four steps in Figures 9.2 and 9.3 might look "on the ground" in one fourth-grade classroom that contains MLs. For each step, we'll apply that information to one classroom and one student in particular. As you read through the steps and application, think about how you could adapt this formative-assessment process for your own context.

Step 1: Articulate the construct being taught and assessed.

In this case, the ELD teacher, Ms. Broady, and fourth-grade science teacher, Ms. Cortez, decided to develop a formative-assessment rubric that would capture their MLs' acquisition of academic language at the word/phrase, sentence, and discourse levels while working on complex content. They developed a rubric specific to their emergent MLs' levels of proficiency, which were high beginning, low intermediate, and high intermediate. To develop the rubric, they looked at the WIDA Writing Rubric in Grades 1–12 and made a version just for Grade 4 at their class of emergent MLs' three levels of English language proficiency (ELP). For this assessment, they wanted to focus on how well their emergent MLs were acquiring academic language in writing through an instructional unit on roadrunners. For purposes of this assessment, they were not assessing their emergent MLs' knowledge of roadrunners per se, but rather the focus was on language as a vehicle for their emergent MLs describing their understanding of content. Figure 9.12 displays the rubric that Ms. Broady and Ms. Cortez co-created.

FIGURE 9.12 FORMATIVE-ASSESSMENT RUBRIC FOR ROADRUNNER ASSIGNMENT

ACADEMIC-LANGUAGE LEVEL	LEVEL 2: EMERGING	LEVEL 3: DEVELOPING	LEVEL 4: EXPANDING
Word/Phrase Level	• Writing contains general content words and expressions • Some use of general vocabulary where more specific vocabulary is needed	• Writing contains some specific content words and expressions • Use of vocabulary words attempts to meet the purpose of writing	• Writing contains specific and some technical content words and expressions • Use of vocabulary words generally meets the purpose of writing
Sentence Level	• Repetitive or formulaic sentence structures common in social and instructional situations or some content areas • Variable use of conventions	• Developing range of sentence structures common of the content area • Developing use of conventions	• Range of sentence structures characteristic of the content area • Generally consistent use of conventions
Discourse Level	• Writing is generally comprehensible when text is adapted from a model or source text or when original text is limited to simple text • Writing shows some attempt at organization or an idea or ideas • Some text may be copied or adapted	• Writing is generally comprehensible • Writing shows developing organization of an idea or ideas • Evidence of a developing sense of perspective, register, and genre	• Writing is usually comprehensible at all times • Writing shows an organized expression of ideas • Evidence of some use of appropriate perspective, register, and genre

Source: Adapted from the WIDA Writing Rubric Grades 1–12 (2020b), https://wida.wisc.edu/resources/wida-writing-rubric-grades-1-12.

Step 2: Collect evidence about MLs' learning.

In Step 2, the teachers had Cong, a Mandarin speaker, complete an open-ended task to describe how roadrunners are different from other birds as part of a unit of instruction on roadrunners. To complete the task, Cong was encouraged to look at a word wall in his classroom and to brainstorm a draft of the writing using a mind map. He produced the writing sample shown in Figure 9.13.

FIGURE 9.13   STUDENT WRITING SAMPLE

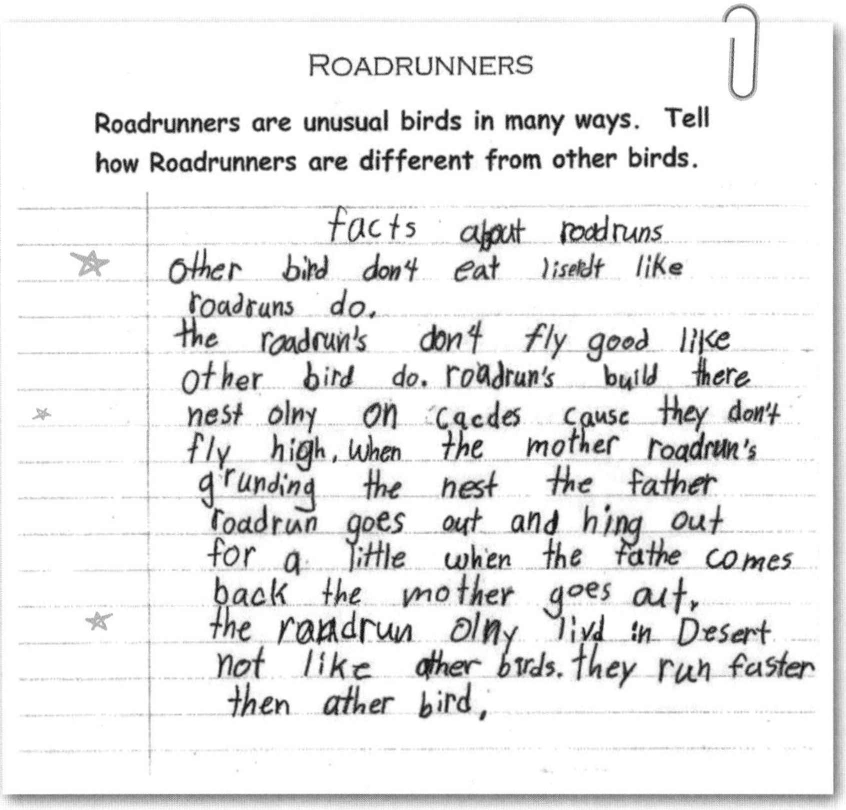

ROADRUNNERS

Roadrunners are unusual birds in many ways. Tell how Roadrunners are different from other birds.

facts about roadruns
Other bird don't eat lisedt like roadruns do.
the roadrun's don't fly good like other bird do. roadrun's build there nest olny on cacdes cause they don't fly high. when the mother roadrun's grunding the nest the father roadrun goes out and hing out for a little when the fathe comes back the mother goes out.
the raadrun olny livd in Desert not like other birds. they run faster then ather bird.

Source: Maureen McCormick, Laurel Ridge Elementary School ELD Teacher, Fairfax, VA.

Step 3: Interpret evidence of student learning.

In this step, Ms. Broady and Ms. Cortez collaboratively analyzed the student's work using the rubric they developed (Figure 9.12). They examined the writing sample's strengths at the word/phrase, sentence, and discourse levels. Figure 9.14 shows their analysis.

The next step is to make a direct connection to the instruction needed for this student to move to the next level of proficiency in each level of academic language and link to future instructional supports for this student. In Application Activity 9.5 we ask you to brainstorm ideas for supporting this student in reaching the next level of proficiency in each area of academic language using the Formative-Assessment Rubric for the Roadrunner Assignment (Figure 9.12) and the Instructional Scaffolding and Strategies to Support Language Growth tool (Figure 9.5).

APPLICATION ACTIVITY 9.5: USING DATA TO INFORM ONGOING INSTRUCTION

Review the teacher's notes on the student's writing and note ideas of how the teachers could support the student in reaching the next level of proficiency in each area of academic language.

FIGURE 9.14   STUDENT SAMPLE ANALYSIS TEMPLATE

LEVEL	NOTES ON STUDENT WRITING (*WHAT CAN THE STUDENT DO* IN EACH OF THESE LEVELS?)	TEACHER SUPPORTS FOR STUDENT TO REACH THE NEXT LEVEL OF PROFICIENCY IN THIS AREA
Word/ Phrase level	The student uses general content vocabulary, such as *build* and *grunding* [guarding]. The student uses specific vocabulary related to the content area, such as *roadruns* [roadrunner], *desert*, and *cacdes* [cactus].	
Sentence level	The student's writing contains simple sentences, such as, "They run faster than other bird." The student also uses a compound sentence, "Roadrun's build there nest olny on cacdes cause they don't fly high." The writing includes an expanded sentence, "When the mother roadrun's grunding the nest the father roadrun goes out and hing out for a little." The writing repeats a comparative structure to contrast roadrunners and other birds— "not like other birds."	

(Continued)

(Continued)

LEVEL	NOTES ON STUDENT WRITING (*WHAT CAN THE STUDENT DO* IN EACH OF THESE LEVELS?)	TEACHER SUPPORTS FOR STUDENT TO REACH THE NEXT LEVEL OF PROFICIENCY IN THIS AREA
Discourse level	The student's writing is generally comprehensible. The writing shows some attempt at organization—all facts are about roadrunners. Errors do not impede the overall meaning.	

APPLICATION ACTIVITY 9.5: REFLECTION QUESTIONS

1. How can you adapt the analysis template for MLs in your context?

   _____

   _____

2. How does framing the writing's strengths allow you to note which supports are needed in instruction?

   _____

   _____

online resources   Available for download at **resources.corwin.com/FennerUnlocking2E**

Step 4: Use assessment data to plan for instruction.

In the final step, Ms. Broady and Ms. Cortez work collaboratively to use the data they gathered about Cong's writing and use of academic language to plan for instructional next steps. Figure 9.15 outlines the supports needed for Cong to move to the next level in each level of academic language, drawing from the support tool provided in Figure 9.5.

FIGURE 9.15   STUDENT SAMPLE ANALYSIS TEMPLATE COMPLETED

LEVEL	NOTES ON STUDENT WRITING (*WHAT CAN THE STUDENT DO* IN EACH OF THESE LEVELS?)	TEACHER SUPPORTS FOR STUDENT TO REACH THE NEXT LEVEL OF PROFICIENCY IN THIS AREA
Word/ Phrase level	The student uses general content vocabulary, such as *build* and *grunding* [guarding]. The student uses specific vocabulary related to the content area, such as *roadruns* [roadrunner], *desert*, and *cacdes* [cactus].	The student uses more specific vocabulary in this writing sample and seems ready for technical words to describe the habitat and life cycle of the roadrunner (e.g., scrub brush, arid, perch, hunt, incubate, predator, and defend). The teacher may support this push to use more technical vocabulary with direct vocabulary instruction, as well as the use of bilingual glossaries, word walls, and word banks (which will also facilitate spelling for this student).
Sentence level	The student's writing contains simple sentences, such as, "They run faster than other bird." The student also uses a compound sentence, "Roadrun's build there nest olny on cacdes cause they don't fly high." The writing includes an expanded sentence, "When the mother roadrun's grunding the nest the father roadrun goes out and hing out for a little." The writing repeats a comparative structure to contrast roadrunners and other birds—"not like other birds."	The student may be ready to use additional sentence structures for comparison. The teacher may introduce a few sentence structures in a grammar mini lesson and create a poster of sentence frames for this student and others to refer to. The student is ready to use more detail and descriptive language. This can be accomplished through grammar mini lessons on how to expand sentences in a teacher-led small group. Reinforcement of this concept can be done through teacher and peer modeling.
Discourse level	The student's writing is generally comprehensible. The writing shows some attempt at organization—all facts are about roadrunners.	The student is ready to begin organizing ideas within a paragraph. The teacher can demonstrate the use of a graphic organizer to group ideas on the same topic together. Another way to practice this skill would through a text sequencing activity in which students cut up the sentences, sort them, and rearrange them. The student is ready to begin writing a topic sentence at the beginning of a paragraph. This could be practiced through a small-group mini lesson and with teacher and then peer support in recognizing the main idea of the paragraph (roadrunners are not like other birds) and turning it into a topic sentence.

Now that you have seen the four-step formative-assessment process in action, you can consider how you might incorporate formative assessment for MLs into your lesson and unit planning. Figure 9.16 is a formative-assessment checklist you can use to self-assess, or a colleague can use to peer-assess, a formative-assessment task you have developed.

FIGURE 9.16   ML FORMATIVE-ASSESSMENT CHECKLIST

	CRITERION	YES	NO	ACTION
	1. Is the assessment **aligned to the standards and objectives** of the lesson?			
	2. Are the assessment directions **easy to understand** for MLs?			
	3. Are students **aware of the teacher's expectations** for the assessment (e.g., a student-friendly rubric), and are assessment results shared with MLs?			
	4. Is the format of the assessment **familiar to MLs**? (For example, if it is an oral presentation, have MLs had practice giving presentations?)			
	5. Are the assessment questions or prompts **linguistically accessible** to MLs? The assessment should not include unfamiliar vocabulary, idioms, or complex sentence structures.			
	6. Are the questions, tasks, or prompts **free from cultural bias**? There should be no references to aspects of culture that may be unfamiliar to MLs from another culture.			
	7. Does the assessment include **appropriate scaffolds** for MLs of varying proficiency levels (e.g., word bank, sentence stems, and pictures)?			
	8. Does the scoring of the assessment **directly correlate to the construct** being assessed (e.g., grammar and spelling are not taken into consideration when evaluating MLs' knowledge of content)?			
	9. If technology is used, have MLs had **sufficient practice** with the technology prior to the assessment?			
	10. Is the assessment used to **inform instruction**? How?			

Source: Adapted from Abedi, J. (2010).

 Available for download at **resources.corwin.com/FennerUnlocking2E**

Let's now explore specific considerations for using formative assessment with ML newcomer students and SLIFE and the role that collaboration, equity, advocacy, and leadership can play in ML formative assessment.

ML NEWCOMER STUDENTS AND SLIFE CONSIDERATIONS

What Considerations Do I Need to Keep in Mind When Using Formative Assessments With ML Newcomer Students and SLIFE?

When developing formative assessment for ML newcomer students and SLIFE there are a number of important considerations to keep in mind.

Considerations:

- Whenever possible, use students' home language on assessments that are not specifically designed to assess English language development (ELD; DeCapua et al., 2020). Using the home language is especially important when ML newcomer students and SLIFE first enter U.S. schools. Providing students with opportunities to demonstrate their knowledge in their home language will paint a more valid and reliable picture of their content knowledge. When making decisions about how to integrate students' home language, be sure to consider their home language literacy skills. Ideally, translations would be developed by trained bilingual staff members in the building. However, we recognize that option is not always available. Online translation tools can be used, but they should be used with caution especially when translating extended text.

- Portfolios are an effective way to assess ML newcomer student and SLIFE's development of language and content over time. Compiling ML newcomer student and SLIFE formative-assessment data into a portfolio will provide educators with a long-term view of growth over time. Additionally, these portfolios can be motivating for students as they are able to see evidence of their progress all in one place and be asked to reflect on their learning (DeCapua et al., 2020).

- It is important that students be assessed using task formats that are familiar to them. ML newcomer students and SLIFE may have had especially limited interaction with the technology used in schools (e.g., typing, dragging, and dropping items on a screen, clicking to select multiple-choice items). Dedicate time to teach ML newcomer students and SLIFE about the format of computer-based assessments. Teach the terms they will need to know to navigate the platform, devote time to practicing test items and navigating the test platform, and make sure they have access to ways to develop their keyboarding skills (Staehr Fenner, 2015, 2016).

Example: Joseph, the seventh-grade student from the Democratic Republic of Congo who was introduced in Chapter 2, is learning about matter and energy within organisms in a unit in his science class. His science teacher, Mr. Yang, and ELD teacher, Ms. Frank, have been collaborating throughout the school year. They worked together to design a series of formative-assessment tasks to be used throughout the unit and compiled into a portfolio. The formative-assessments tasks they designed include opportunities for Joseph to create a visual model of how the systems of the human body function, to act out key concepts related to how matter and energy are processed by organisms, and to complete a graphic organizer on how the body systems work together. Mr. Yang compiles the formative assessment-tasks into a portfolio and together with Ms. Frank analyzes Joseph's content knowledge growth throughout the unit to make instructional decisions. Additionally, Mr. Yang conferences with Joseph periodically using a self-assessment checklist for Joseph to reflect on his own learning and discuss if he needs any additional supports.

What Is the Role of Collaboration in Creating and Using Formative Assessments for MLs?

As we have detailed throughout the chapter, collaboration among content and ELD teachers is crucial in order to integrate formative assessments into your instructional loop. One way in which teachers can collaborate within the framework of formative assessments is to engage in discussions around developing ML formative assessments and reviewing ML formative-assessment results. Teachers and administrators can set up a time to collaboratively plan formative assessments, interpret the results, and determine next steps in terms of instructional supports to help MLs reach the next level of language proficiency and content understanding. Additionally, administrators can demonstrate their commitment to their MLs' equity by setting aside a regular time, place, and collaborative structure for planning to support the analysis of MLs' formative-assessment results. By doing so, they set the tone in their buildings that collaboration is crucial to the success of MLs.

What Is the Role of Equity, Advocacy, and Leadership in Creating and Using Formative Assessments for MLs?

One important step teachers in a school or even a district can take to advocate for more equitable assessments for their MLs is to form a committee that includes the ELD teacher, content area teacher(s), guidance counselor, assessment specialist, administrator, students' parents or caregivers, and even selected students. The committee can meet throughout the year to keep track of how well formative assessments are providing a means by which MLs can demonstrate what they know and can do in language and content. The committee can also discuss any tools, supports, and accommodations to be used on summative content assessments on a case-by-case basis and make sure those supports are also used throughout the academic year, during instruction as well as on formative assessments. In addition, the committee can work together at the building level to conduct a needs analysis of where ML newcomer students and SLIFE could use additional support based on formative-assessment data and offer a time and place for those students to have additional practice with both content and language.

ML FORMATIVE-ASSESSMENT COLLABORATION, EQUITY, ADVOCACY, AND LEADERSHIP IN ACTION

ELD teacher, author, and podcast host Tan Huynh shares how he moved from co-planning individual lessons with content teachers to co-planning formative assessments to be used throughout a unit of study.

Where I once co-planned with content area teachers for the next lesson, I now prioritize co-assessing a long-term project. This shift from co-planning the individual lesson to co-planning the assessments transformed the way I served MLs. When I shifted to planning the assessments, this meant that I magnified my time spent co-planning. Investing time to scaffold formative assessments for a long-term project meant that MLs received support for the duration of that project.

Now that I have been using this approach to engineering assessments (Huynh & Skelton, 2023) during my co-planning for years, my colleagues and I noticed several observations. My colleagues noticed that the scaffolds that are provided to MLs are often the same ones that non-MLs would benefit from as well. Sometimes the scaffolded assessments for MLs become the ones used for all students. That's because all students require explicit instruction to understand and use academic language effectively. As an English language development (ELD) specialist, I can contribute to the team by highlighting the academic-language requirements of the task, something that is less of a focus for my colleagues who teach content.

I also noticed that this approach elevates the ELD teacher from the position of an "aide" to an equal designer of instruction. While my colleagues contribute through their expertise in the content, I share my expertise in scaffolding the academic-language expectations required to be successful in class. I no longer feel that my skill sets are underutilized. On the contrary, I feel that I am able to reach more students in a more effective and meaningful way, especially when many students use the scaffolded tasks designed for MLs.

Additionally, since my support lives in assessment tasks and documents used by students, I feel that my time is multiplied. Every time a student engages with a scaffolded task, I feel like I am there supporting them. When I am not in the room due to scheduling, students are still receiving assistance through the scaffolding and teacher collaboration.

Finally, the most surprising observation I gained from co-planning this way is that it is one of the most effective forms of job-embedded professional learning (Honigsfeld & Dove, 2022). As my colleagues and I work throughout the year, my colleagues develop an understanding of what MLs need, when they need it, and how to provide support. My colleagues frequently share they have taken an assessment or scaffolding strategy I shared during co-planning and applied it to another class or another assignment. This brings me great joy as students in other classes are being supported through our collaboration. In the end, my colleagues are designing instruction with a lens for MLs, which was developed through our teamwork. Though the co-planning is intense and requires time on all parties involved, it is one of the most effective, meaningful, and transformational ways to unlock MLs' fullest potential (personal communication, March 3, 2023).

Next Steps

The following activity will help you synthesize and apply your learning around formative assessment for MLs.

APPLICATION ACTIVITY 9.6: PLANNING FOR ML FORMATIVE ASSESSMENT

To support you in implementing formative assessment with your MLs, we have developed a Formative-Assessment Planning Tool (Figure 9.17). Use the tool to plan for using formative assessment for MLs in the unit you are developing. Parts 1 and 2 should be used to plan for implementation, and Part 3 should be used after the formative assessments have been implemented to analyze the data and develop next steps. Note that The Formative-Assessment Planning Tool can also be used as a standalone tool.

FIGURE 9.17   ML FORMATIVE-ASSESSMENT PLANNING TOOL

Part A. Design a scaffolded formative assessment to use in an upcoming unit or lesson.

Grade level:	ELP level(s) of MLs:

Description of lesson or unit:

Lesson or unit objective(s):

Step 1: Articulate construct being taught and assessed
Describe the construct the assessment will measure. Consider what is being taught. Consider what aspects of language are relevant to the content being assessed (if any).
Describe the criteria you will use to determine how well the construct has been learned.

Describe the steps you will take to ensure that you are collecting valid evidence on the construct being taught and assessed for the MLs in your class.

Write your student-friendly learning objectives and your plan to share these with MLs.

Student-friendly learning objectives:

Plan to share learning objectives with MLs:

Part B. Implement your formative assessment.

Step 2: Collect evidence

Describe the formative-assessment strategy or tool that you will use. At what point will you incorporate the assessment into the lesson or unit?

Describe how you will share your assessment expectations with your MLs.

Describe what opportunities you will provide for self-assessment. Describe what opportunities you will provide for MLs to ask questions about the content and assessment.

Self-assessment opportunities:

Opportunities for questions about content and assessment:

Describe below how you will scaffold your assessment for MLs of varying proficiency levels as needed.

ML Proficiency Level	ML Scaffolds

(Continued)

(Continued)

Step 3: Interpret evidence

Select the tool(s) you will use for collecting and interpreting evidence collected during the formative-assessment process.

- ☐ Checklist
- ☐ Rubric
- ☐ Conferring notes
- ☐ Student rating scales, checklists, or reflection
- ☐ Other _____

Part C. Reflect on your formative-assessment data and plan for next steps.

What do you see?[2] In other words, what data do you have on your MLs?	What do you make of it? In other words, what conclusions can you draw from the data?

Describe your plan for providing feedback to MLs.

Describe the criteria you will focus on in your feedback.

Step 4: Use assessment data to plan instruction

What are you going to do about it?

What conclusions did you draw in Step 3?	What are possible next steps for instruction?

Describe the opportunities that you will provide MLs for revising or re-doing aspects of the lesson or assessment where there were misconceptions.

 Available for download at **resources.corwin.com/FennerUnlocking2E**

[2]Boudett, City, & Murnane, 2013.

Now, add your plans to the *Unit Delivery: Assessment* section of the Unlocking MLs' Potential Unit Planning Template (the portion of Appendix A in Figure 9.18). Appendix A can be found on the online companion website. To access the companion website, please visit resources.corwin.com/FennerUnlocking2E.

FIGURE 9.18 PORTION OF THE UNLOCKING MLs' POTENTIAL UNIT PLANNING TEMPLATE (APPENDIX A)

UNIT DELIVERY

Assessment

Figure 9.17 ML Formative-Assessment Planning Tool

How will you **assess ML student understanding** of unit language and content?

How will you ensure that you are **collecting valid evidence** on the construct being taught and assessed?

What will your **next steps** be based on the evidence collected?

Conclusion

In this chapter, we have presented an often-overlooked aspect of the ML instructional loop, which is formative assessment for MLs. Some topics we explored were assessment *as* and *for* learning, the validity of MLs' formative assessments, and considerations for using formative assessments with ML newcomer students and SLIFE. We shared many examples of creating formative assessments, as well as how to use them to adapt instruction for MLs. Finally, we shared a planning template to support you in planning for ongoing ML formative assessment in your teaching.

CHAPTER 9 REFLECTION QUESTIONS

1. How has your thinking evolved on formative assessment for MLs by reading this chapter?

2. Which ideas would you like to implement from this chapter?

3. What do you think your biggest challenges will be in doing so, and how can you address these challenges so your MLs will benefit?

 Available for download at **resources.corwin.com/FennerUnlocking2E**

Final Thoughts

As we mentioned in the Introduction, since *Unlocking English Learners Potential: Strategies for Making Content Accessible* was originally published in 2017, we have worked extensively with educators of MLs to implement strategies shared in this book. We are excited for the opportunity to share a second edition with you in order to continue to bring you fresh ideas to support you in your work with MLs. The updated strategies, tools, and ideas come directly from our work with educators like you in districts across North America. Our hope is that the updates we have included in this second edition provide you with some tools you need to truly unlock your MLs' vast potential as well as to collaborate with your colleagues in doing so. We are amazed by the MLs you work with each time we're coaching teachers in schools, and we are able to witness firsthand how engaged MLs can be when teachers are intentional about implementing supports in their practice. At the same time, we recognize that your work requires tireless collaboration, advocacy, and leadership in order for your students to succeed. Thank you for all you are doing to leverage the assets and meet the needs of MLs. We wish you continued success and joy.

References

Abedi, J. (2006). Psychometric issues in the ELL assessment and special education eligibility. *Teachers College Record, 108*(11), 2282–2303.

Abedi, J. (2010). *Performance assessments for English language learners.* Stanford University, Stanford Center for Opportunity Policy in Education. https://edpolicy.stanford.edu/sites/default/files/publications/performance-assessments-english-language-learners.pdf

Abedi, J., & Linquanti, R. (2012). *Issues and opportunities in improving the quality of large scale assess ment systems for English language learners* [Paper presentation]. Understanding Language Conference, Stanford, CA.

Adair, J. K., Colegrove, K. S., & McManus, M. E. (2017). How the word gap argument negatively impacts young children of Latinx immigrants' conceptualizations of learning. *Harvard Educational Review, 87*(3), 309–334. https://doi.org/10.17763/1943-5045-87.3.309

Ahmed, Y., Francis, D. J., York, M., Fletcher, J. M., Barnes, M. A., & Kulesz, P. (2016). Validation of the direct and mediation (DIME) model of reading comprehension in grades 7 through 12. *Contemporary Educational Psychology, 44,* 68–82.

Alford, B. J., & Niño, M. C. (2011). *Leading academic achievement for English language learners: A guide for principals.* Corwin.

Alvarez, L., Ananda, S., Walqui, A., Sato, E., & Rabinowitz, S. (2014, February). *Focusing formative assessment on the needs of English language learners.* WestEd. https://www.wested.org/wp-content/uploads/2016/11/1391626953FormativeAssessment_report5-3.pdf

American Educational Research Association, American Psychological Association, National Council on Measurement in Education, Joint Committee on Standards for Educational and Psychological Testing (U.S.). (2014). *Standards for educational and psychological testing.* AERA.

Anderson, J., & La Rocca, W. (2017). *Patterns of power: Inviting young writers into the conventions of language, grades 1-5.* Stenhouse Publishers.

Anne Arundel County Public Schools. (n.d.). *English language development (ELD).* https://www.aacps.org/domain/293

August, D. (2018). Educating English language learners: A review of the latest research. *American Educator, 42*(3), 4.

August, D., Branum-Martin, L., Cardenas-Hagan, E., & Francis, D. J. (2009). The impact of an instructional intervention on the science and language learning of middle grade English language learners. *Journal of Research on Educational Effectiveness, 2*(4), 345–376. https://doi.org/10.1080/19345740903217623

August, D., Golden, L., & Pook, D. (2015). *Secondary curricular units for New York City department of education* (p. 18). Reprinted with permission of American Institutes for Research.

August, D., & Shanahan, T. (Eds.). (2006). *Developing literacy in second-language learners: Report of the national literacy panel on language-minority children and youth.* Lawrence Erlbaum.

August, D., Staehr Fenner, D. S., & Bright, A. (2014). *Scaffolding instruction for English language learners: A resource guide for mathematics.* American Institutes for Research. https://www.engageny.org/resource/scaffolding-instruction-english-language-learners-resource-guides-english-language-arts-and

August, D., Staehr Fenner, D. S., & Snyder, S. (2014). *Scaffolding instruction for English language learners: A resource guide for English language arts.* American Institutes for Research. https://www.engageny.org/resource/

scaffolding-instruction-english-language-learners-re source-guides-english-language-arts-and

Bailey, A. L. (2012). Academic English. In J. Banks (Ed.), *Encyclopedia of diversity in education*. Sage.

Bailey, A. L. (Ed.). (2007). *The language demands of school: Putting academic English to the test*. Yale University Press.

Baker, S., Lesaux, N., Jayanthi, M., Dimino, J., Proctor, C. P., Morris, J., & Newman-Gonchar, R. (2014). *Teaching academic content and literacy to English learners in elementary and middle school* (NCEE 2014-4012). U.S. Department of Education, Institute for Education Sciences, National Center for Education Evaluation and Regional Assistance. https://ies.ed.gov/ncee/wwc/Docs/PracticeGuide/english_learners_pg_040114.pdf#page=20

Banks, J. A., & Banks, C. A. M. (Eds.). (2019). *Multicultural education: Issues and perspectives* (10th ed.). Wiley & Sons.

Banting, E. (2004). *England: The land*. Crabtree Publishing.

Beck, I. L., McKeown, M. G., & Kucan, L. (2002). *Bringing words to life*. Guilford Press.

Bellevue School District. (n.d.). *Our mission and vision*. https://bsd405.org/services/mll/our-mission-vision/

Billings, E., & Walqui, A. (2017). *De-Mystifying complex texts: What are "complex" texts and how can we ensure ELLs/MLLs can access them?* WestEd.

Billings, E., & Walqui, A. (2021). *De-mystifying complex texts: What are "complex" texts and how can we ensure ELLs/MLLs can access them?* Office of Bilingual Education and World Languages.

Bishop, R. S. (1990). Mirrors, windows, and sliding glass doors. *Perspectives, 6*(3), ix–xi.

Blum-Kulka, S., & Snow, C. E. (2004). Introduction: The potential of peer talk. *Discourse Studies, 6*(3), 291–306.

Boudett, K. P., City, E. A., & Murnane, R. J. (2005). *Data wise: A step-by-step guide to using assessment results to improve teaching and learning* (1st ed.). Harvard Education Press

Breiseth, L., Robertson, K., & Lafond, S. (2011). *A guide for engaging ELL families: 20 strategies for school leaders*. Colorín Colorado. http://www.colorincolorado.org/sites/default/files/Engaging_ELL_Families_FINAL.pdf

Brookhart, S. (2020, May). *Five formative assessment strategies to improve distance learning outcomes for students with disabilities* (NCEO Brief #20). National Center on Educational Outcomes. https://nceo.umn.edu/docs/OnlinePubs/NCEOBrief20.pdf

Brooks, K., & Thurston, L. P. (2010). English language learner academic engagement and instructional grouping configurations. *American Secondary Education, 39*(1), 45–60.

Bryan, K., Cooper, A., & Ifarinu, B. (2019). From majority to minority: Advocating for English learners from the African Diaspora. In H. Linville & J. Whiting (Eds.), *Advocacy in English language teaching and learning* (pp. 190–201). Routledge.

Buckley, C. (2023). *Using math manipulatives with cultural connections builds relationships*. Smart Brief.

Bunch, G. C. (2014). The language of ideas and the language of display: Reconceptualizing "Academic Language" in linguistically diverse classrooms. *International Multilingual Research Journal, 8*(1), 70–86. https://doi.org/10.1080/19313152.2014.852431

Bunch, G. C., & Martin, D. (2021). *From "academic language" to the "language of ideas": A disciplinary perspective on using language in K-12 settings*. Routledge Language and Education.

California Department of Education. (2015). *English language arts/English language development framework: Snapshot 7.1: Investigating language, culture, and society: Linguistic autobiographies* (pp. 726–727). http://www.cde.ca.gov/ci/rl/cf/documents/elaeldfwchapter7.pdf

Callahan, R., DeMatthews, D., & Reyes, P. (2019). The impact of *Brown* on EL students: Addressing linguistic and educational rights through school leadership practice and preparation. *Journal of Research on Leadership Education, 14*(4), 281–307.

Carlo, M. S., August, D., McLaughlin, B., Snow, C. E., Dressler, C., Lippman, D. N., & White, C. E. (2004). Closing the gap: Addressing the vocabulary needs for English language learners in bilingual and mainstream classrooms. *Reading Research Quarterly, 39*(2), 188–215. https://doi.org/10.1598/RRQ.39.2.3

Celce-Murcia, M., & Larsen-Freeman, D. (1999). *The grammar book* (2nd ed.). Heinle & Heinle.

Chval, K., Smith, E., Trigos-Carillo, L., & Pinnow, R. (2021). *Teaching math to multilingual students grades K-8: Positioning English learners for success*. Corwin.

Columbo, M., Tigert, J., & Leider, C. M. (2018). Positioning teachers, positioning learners: Why we should stop using the term English learners. *TESOL Journal, 10*(2), 1–5.

Cooper, A. (2021). *Justice for ELs: A leader's guide to creating and sustaining equitable schools.* Corwin.

Core Knowledge Foundation. (2013). *Early world civilizations: Tell it again!™ read-aloud anthology: Listening & learning™ strand: Grade 1: Core knowledge Language Arts® New York Edition* (p. 16). Charlottesville, VA: Author.

Costello, M. (2011, Spring). *The human face of immigration.* Teaching Tolerance. https://www.learningforjustice.org/magazine/spring-2011/the-human-face-of-immigration

Council of Chief State School Officers' (CCSSO) Formative Assessment for Students and Teachers (FAST) State Collaborative on Assessment and Student Standards (SCASS). (2018). *Revising the definition of formative assessment.* Council of Chief State School Officers.

CPO Focus on Life Science. (2007). *Delta education LLC.* https://www.vistacharterms.org/ourpages/download_books/science_books/7th%20Grade%20Science%20Student%20ebook.pdf

Creese, A., & Blackledge, A. (2010). Translanguaging in the bilingual classroom: A pedagogy for learning and teaching? *The Modern Language Journal, 94*(1), 103–115.

Cromley, J. G., & Azevedo, R. (2007). Testing and refining the direct and inferential mediation model of reading comprehension. *Journal of Educational Psychology, 99,* 311–325.

Cummins, J., Bismilla, V., Chow, P., Cohen, S., Giampapa, F., Leoni, L., Sandhu, P., & Sastri, P. (2005). Affirming identity in multilingual classrooms. *Educational Leadership, 63*(1), 38–43.

Cummins, J., & Early, M. (Eds.). (2011). *Identity texts: The collaborative creation of power in multilingual schools.* Trentham Books.

de Oliveira, L., & Westerlund, R. (Eds.). (2023). *Scaffolding for multilingual learners in elementary and secondary schools.* Routledge.

DeCapua, A. (2023). *SLIFE: What every teacher needs to know.* University of Michigan Press.

DeCapua, A., & Marshall, H. (2013). *Making the transition to classroom success: Culturally responsive teaching for struggling language learners.* University of Michigan Press.

DeCapua, A., & Marshall, H. (2023). *Breaking new ground for SLIFE: The mutually adaptive learning paradigm (2nd ed.).* University of Michigan Press.

DeCapua, A., Marshall, H. W., & Tang, L. F. (2020). *Meeting the needs of SLIFE: A guide for educators.* University of Michigan Press.

Delpit, L. (1995). *Other people's children: Cultural conflict in the classroom.* New Press.

Dressler, C., & Kamil, M. L. (2006). First-and second-language literacy. In D. August & T. Shanahan (Eds.), *Developing literacy in second-language learners: Report of the national literacy panel on language minority children and youth* (pp. 197–238). Lawrence Erlbaum.

Dubner, S. (Host). (2021, July 21). The pros and cons of America's extreme individualism (Season 10, Episode 49). In *Freakonomics.* https://freakonomics.com/podcast/season-10-episode-49/

Duggan, J., Staehr Fenner, D. S., & Snyder, S. (2020). *An analysis of state recertification requirements and recommendations for all teachers of English learners.* SupportEd. https://supported.com/wp-content/uploads/State-Recertification-Requirements-and-Recommendations-for-All-Teachers-of-English-Learners-SupportEd.pdf

Ebe, A. (2010). Culturally relevant texts and reading assessments for English language learners. *Reading Horizons, 50*(3), 193–210.

Echevarria, J., Vogt, M., & Short, D. (2004). *Making content comprehensible for English language learners: The SIOP model.* Pearson.

Erickson, F. (2007). Culture in society and educational practices. In J. Banks & C. A. Banks (Eds.), *Multicultural education: Issues and perspectives* (6th ed., pp. 33–61). John Wiley & Sons.

Ewald, W. (2002). *The best part of me: Children talk about their bodies in pictures and words.* Little Brown Books for Young Readers.

Escamilla, K., Olsen, L., & Slavick, J. (2022). *Toward comprehensive effective literacy policy and instruction for English learner/emergent bilingual students.* National Committee for Effective Literacy for Emergent Bilingual Students.

Fabiny, S. (2013). *Who was Frida Kahlo?* Grosset & Dunlap.

Ferguson, C. (2008). *The school–family connection: Looking at the larger picture: A review of current literature.* National Center for Family and Community Connections With Schools.

Ferlazzo, L. (2017, July 6). Author interview: 'Culturally sustaining pedagogies'. *Education Week.* https://www.edweek.org/

teaching-learning/opinion-author-interview-cul turally-sustaining-pedagogies/2017/07

Fillmore, L. W., & Fillmore, C. J. (2012). *What does text complexity mean for English learners and language minority students?* Stanford University, Understanding Language. https://ul.stanford .edu/sites/default/files/resource/2021-12/06-LWF%20CJF%20Text%20Complexity%20 FINAL_0.pdf

Fisher, D., Frey, N., & Lapp, D. (2012). Building and activating students' background knowledge: It's what they already know that counts. *Middle School Journal, 43*(3), 22–31.

Floca, B. (2009). *Moonshot: The flight of Apollo 11.* Atheneum.

Francis, D., Lesaux, N., & August, D. (2006). Language of instruction. In D. August & T. Shanahan (Eds.), *Developing literacy in second-language learners* (pp. 365–414). Lawrence Erlbaum.

Gao, L. (2022). *Messy roots: A graphic memoir of a Wuhanese American.* Balzer + Bray.

García, C. (1992). *Dreaming in Cuban.* Knopf.

García, O., Johnson, S., & Seltzer, K. (2017). *The translanguaging classroom: Leveraging student bilingualism for learning.* Caslon.

Gay, G. (2010). *Culturally responsive reaching: Theory, research, and practice* (2nd ed.). Teachers College Press.

Gee, J. P. (2007). *Good video games and good learning: Collected essays on video games, learning, and literacy.* Peter Lang.

Gibbons, P. (2015). *Scaffolding language, scaffolding learning: Teaching English language learners in the mainstream classroom* (2nd ed.). Heinemann.

Goldenberg, C. (2008, Summer). Teaching English language learners: What the research does—and does not—say. *American Educator.* http://www .aft.org/sites/default/files/periodicals/golden berg.pdf

González, N. (2005). Beyond culture: The hybridity of funds of knowledge. In N. González, L. C. Moll, & C. Amanti (Eds.), *Funds of knowledge* (pp. 29–46). Lawrence Erlbaum.

Gorski, P. C. (2010, April 14). *The challenge of defining "multicultural education."* http://www .edchange.org/multicultural/initial.html

Gorski, P. C. (2015). *Circles of my multicultural self.* http://www.edchange.org/multicultural/activi ties/circlesofself_handout.html

Gottlieb, M. (2016). *Assessing English language learners: Bridges to educational equity.* Corwin.

Gottlieb, M. (2021a). *Classroom assessment in multiple languages: A handbook for teachers.* Corwin.

Gottlieb, M. (2021b). *How can multilingual learners and their teachers make a difference in classroom assessment?* Center for Applied Linguistics.

Grabe, W. (1991). Current developments in second language reading research. *TESOL Quarterly, 25*(3), 375–406.

Graham, S., Kiuhara, S. A., & MacKay, M. (2020). The effects of writing on learning in science, social studies, and mathematics: A meta-analysis. *Review of Educational Research, 90*(2), 179–226. https://doi.org/10.3102/0034654320914744

Grandin, T. (2005). *Animals in translation: Using the mysteries of autism to decode animal behavior.* Scribner.

Grapin, S. E. (2018). Multimodality in the new content standards era: Implications for English learners. *TESOL Quarterly, 53*(1), 30–55.

Hall, E. T. (1976). *Beyond culture.* Doubleday.

Hamman-Ortiz, L. (2021, October). *Identity texts.* Notre Dame Center for Literacy Education.

Hammond, J. (2023). Scaffolding: Implications and equity for diverse learners in mainstream classes. In L. C. de Oliveira & R. Westerlund (Eds.), *Scaffolding for multilingual learners in elementary and secondary schools* (pp. 9–28). Routledge.

Hammond, Z. (2015). *Culturally responsive teaching and the brain.* Corwin.

Heath, S. B. (1983). *Way with words: Language, life, and work in communities and classrooms.* Cambridge University Press.

Heath, S. B. (2012). *Words at work and play: Three decades in family and community life.* Cambridge University Press.

Henderson, A. T., & Mapp, K. L. (2002). *A new wave of evidence: The impact of school, family, and community connections on student achievement.* National Center for Family and Community Connections With Schools.

Hofstede G. (2016). *10 minutes with Geert Hofstede on individualisme versus collectivisme* [Video]. https://www.youtube.com/ watch?v=zQj1VPNPHlI

Hofstede, G., Hofstede, G. J., & Minkov, M. (2010). *Cultures and organizations: Software of the mind.* McGraw-Hill.

Holt McDougal Science Fusion. (2012). *Earth's water and atmosphere.* Houghton Mifflin Harcourt.

Honigsfeld, A., & Dove, M. G. (2018). *Co-teaching for English learners: A guide to collaborative planning, instruction, assessment, and reflection.* Corwin.

Honigsfeld, A., & Dove, M. G. (2019). *Collaborating for English learners: A foundational guide to integrated practices.* Corwin.

Honigsfeld, A., & Dove, M. G. (2022). *Co-planning: Five essential practices to integrate curriculum and instruction for English learners.* Corwin.

Huynh, T. (2016, October 29). *Teaching MLs to deconstruct writing.* https://tankhuynh.com/mentor-texts/

Huynh, T., & Skelton, B. (2023). *Long-term success for experienced multilinguals.* Corwin.

Ingersoll, R. M., Merrill, E., Stuckey, D., & Collins, G. (2018). *Seven trends: The transformation of the teaching force.* CPRE Research Reports.

Jewitt, C. (2014). Multimodality and literacy in school classrooms. *Review of Research in Education, 38*(1), 203–244.

Jorgensen, J. (2019). *Statewide English test finds ELLs performed better than native English speakers.* www.ny1.com/nyc/all-boroughs/news/2019/10/19/statewide-english-test-finds-ells-performed-better-than-native-english-speakers?cid=share_twitter

Kagan, S., & Kagan, M. (2009). *Kagan cooperative learning.* Kagan Cooperative Learning

Kelemanik, G., Lucenta, A., Creighton, S. J., & Lampert, M. (2016). *Routines for reasoning: Fostering the mathematical practices in all students.* Heinemann.

Kester, J., & Daniels, E. (2019). *Making texts accessible for ELs* [webinar]. SupportEd. https://www.youtube.com/watch?v=BHrN_v7_VoU

Khalifa, M. (2018). *Culturally responsive school leadership.* Harvard Education Press.

Kibler, A. (2017). Peer interaction and learning in multilingual settings from a sociocultural perspective: Theoretical insights. *International Multilingual Research Journal, 11*(3), 199–203. https://doi.org/10.1080/19313152.2017.1328970

Kleinfeld, J. (1975). Effective teachers of Eskimo and Indian students. *The School Review, 83*(2), 301–344.

Ladson-Billings, G. (1994). *The dreamkeepers: Successful teaching for African-American students.* Jossey-Bass.

Ladson-Billings, G. (2004). New directions in multicultural education: Complexities, boundaries, and critical race theory. In J. A. Banks & C. A. M. Banks (Eds.), *Handbook of research on multicultural education* (pp. 349–378). Jossey-Bass.

Lai, T. (2013). *Inside out & back again.* Harper.

Liang, L. A., Peterson, C. A., & Graves, M. F. (2005). Investigating two approaches to fostering children's comprehension of literature. *Reading Psychology, 26*(4–5), 387–400.

Lindholm-Leary, K. J. (2015). *Sobrato family foundation early academic and literacy project after five full years of implementation: Final research report.* Sobrato Family Foundation.

Llosa, L., & Gerzon, N. (2022, October 18). *Leading voices: The role of formative assessment—enhancing educational opportunities for multilingual learners.* WestEd. https://www.wested.org/resources/role-of-formative-assessment-enhancing-educational-opportunities-for-multilingual-learners/

MacDonald, R., Boals, T., Castro, M., Cook, G. H., Lundberg, T., & White, P. A. (2015). *A four-step process: Formative language assessment for English learners.* Heinemann.

Mackey, A., & Gass, S. (2006). Introduction to special issue on new methods of studying L2 acquisition in interaction. *Studies in Second Language Acquisition, 28*(2), 169–178.

Marquardt, M. (2016). *The radius of us.* St. Martin's Griffin.

Marzano, R. J. (2004). *Building background knowledge for academic achievement: Research on what works in schools.* ASCD.

Matthiesen, N. C. L. (2017). Working together in a deficit logic: Home-school partnerships with Somali diaspora parents. *Race, Ethnicity and Education, 20*(4), 495–507. http://dx.doi.org.ezproxy.bethel.edu/10.1080/13613324.2015.1134469

Maxwell, L. (2013, October 28). ESL and classroom teachers team up to teach Common Core. *Education Week.* https://www.edweek.org/policy-politics/esl-and-classroom-teachers-team-up-to-teach-common-core/2013/10 McLaughlin, B. (1987). *Theories of second language learning.* Edward Arnold.

McNamara, D., & Kintsch, W. (1996). Learning from texts: Effects of prior knowledge and text coherence. *Discourse Processes, 22*(3), 247–288.

Merriam-Webster. (2023). *Culture.* https://www.merriam-webster.com/dictionary/culture

Michaels, S., & O'Connor, C. (2015). Conceptualizing talk moves as tools: Professional development approaches for academically productive discussions. In L. B. Resnick, C. Asterhan, & S. Clarke (Eds.), *Socializing intelligence through academic talk and dialogue.* American Educational Research Association.

Moll, L., Amanti, C., Neff, D., & Gonzalez, N. (1992). Funds of knowledge for teaching: Using a qualitative approach to connect homes and classrooms. *Theory Into Practice, 2,* 132–141.

Molle, D., de Oliveira, L. C., MacDonald, R., & Bhasin, A. (2021). Leveraging incidental and intentional vocabulary learning to support multilingual students' participation in disciplinary practices and discourses. *TESOL Journal, 12*(4), e616. https://doi.org/10.1002/tesj.616

Murphy, J. (1995). *The great fire.* Scholastic.

Murphy, J. (2006). *The great fire.* Scholastic.

Najarro, E. (2023, February 21). *The English learner population is growing. Is teacher training keeping pace?* https://www.edweek.org/teaching-learning/the-english-learner-population-is-growing-is-teacher-training-keeping-pace/2023/02

Nation, P. (2021). Is it worth teaching vocabulary? *TESOL Journal, 12*(4), e564. https://doi.org/10.1002/tesj.564

National Academies of Sciences, Engineering, & Medicine (NASEM). (2017). *Promoting the educational success of children and youth learning English: Promising futures.* The National Academies Press. https://doi.org/10.17226/24677

National Academies of Sciences, Engineering, and Medicine (NASEM). (2018). *English learners in STEM subjects: Transforming classrooms, schools, and lives.* The National Academies Press. https://doi.org/10.17226/25182

National Center for Culturally Responsive Educational Systems (NCCREST). (2008). *Module 6: Culturally responsive response to intervention.* Mary Lou Fulton College of Education. http://www.niusileadscape.org/docs/pl/culturally_responsive_response_to_intervention/activity1/RTI%20Academy%201%20FacMan%20over%201.1%20FINAL%20kak.pdf

National Center for Education Statistics. (2021). *English learner (EL) students enrolled in public elementary and secondary schools, by state: Selected years, fall 2000 through fall 2019.* U.S. Department of Education, Institute of Education Sciences. https://nces.ed.gov/programs/digest/d21/tables/dt21_204.20.asp

National Center for Education Statistics. (2022). *Characteristics of public school principals. Condition of education.* U.S. Department of Education, Institute of Education Sciences. https://nces.ed.gov/programs/coe/indicator/cls

National Governors Association for Best Practices, Council of Chief State School Officers. (2010). *Common Core state standards for English language arts and literacy in history/social studies, science, and technical subjects. Appendix A: Research supporting key elements of the standards. Glossary of key terms.* https://achievethecore.org/content/upload/corestandards_appendix_a_text_complexity_ela.pdf

National Reading Panel. (2000). *Report of the national reading panel: Teaching children to read: An evidence-based assessment of the scientific research literature on reading and its implications for reading instruction.* National Institute of Child Health and Human Development.

New York State Testing Program. (2016). *2016 Common Core mathematics test.* http://edinformatics.com/testing/2016-released-items-math-grade7.pdf

Nieto, S. (2016). *Culturally-responsive pedagogy: Some key features.* https://www.sabes.org/sites/default/files/resources/Culturally-Responsive-Pedagogy.pdf Northouse, G. (2007). *Leadership theory and practice* (4th ed.). Sage.

Office of English Language Acquisition (OELA). (2018). *English learner (EL) trends from the nation's report card* (OELA Fast Facts). https://ncela.ed.gov/sites/default/files/legacy/files/fast_facts/ELs-NAEP_Card.pdf

Office of English Language Acquisition (OELA). (2021a). *English learners absenteeism, suspension, and retention.* National Clearing House for English Language Acquisition. https://ncela.ed.gov/resources/fact-sheet-english-learner-absenteeism-suspension-and-retention-september-2021

Office of English Language Acquisition (OELA) (2021b). *English learners in advanced placement and international baccalaureate programs.* National Clearing House for English Language Acquisition. https://ncela.ed.gov/resources/fact-sheet-english-learners-in-advanced-placement-and-international-baccalaureate-courses

Office of English Language Acquisition (OELA). (2021c). *English learners in gifted and talented programs.* National Clearing House for English Language Acquisition. https://ncela.ed.gov/resources/fact-sheet-english-learners-in-gifted-and-talented-programs-february-2021

Office of English Language Acquisition (OELA). (2021d). *Profile of English learners in the United States.* National Clearing House for English Language Acquisition. https://ncela.ed.gov/sites/default/files/legacy/fast_facts/DEL4.4_ELProfile_508_1.4.2021_OELA.pdf

Office of English Language Acquisition (OELA). (2022). *English learners in college credit-bearing courses.* National Clearing House for English Language Acquisition. https://ncela.ed.gov/sites/default/files/2022-09/OELACollegeCreditBearing_09012922_508.pdf

Ogbu, J. U. (2003). *Black American students in an affluent suburb: A study of academic disengagement.* Lawrence Erlbaum.

O'Reilly, T., Wang, Z., & Sabatini, J. (2019). How much knowledge is too little? When knowledge becomes a barrier to comprehension. *Psychological Science, 30*(9), 1344–1351. https://journals.sagepub.com/doi/10.1177/0956797619862276

Paradisi, P., Raglianti, M., & Sebastiani, L. (2021). Online communication and body language. *Frontiers in behavioral neuroscience, 15,* 709365. https://doi.org/10.3389/fnbeh.2021.709365

Paris, D., & Alim, H. S. (2017). *Culturally sustaining pedagogies: Teaching and learning for justice in a changing world.* Teachers College Press.

Pearson, P. D., Palincsar, A. S., Biancarosa, G., & Berman, A. I. (Eds.). (2020). *Reaping the rewards of the reading for understanding initiative.* National Academy of Education. https://eric.ed.gov/?id=ED608448

Pierce, L. J., Chen, J., Delcenserie, A., Genesee, F., & Klein, D. (2015). Past experience shapes ongoing neural patterns for language. *Nature Communications, 6,* 1–11.

Restrepo, M. A., Castilla, A. P., Schwanenflugel, P. J., Neuharth-Pritchett, S., Hamilton, C. E., & Arboleda, A. (2010). Effects of a supplemental Spanish oral language program on sentence length, complexity, and grammaticality in Spanish-speaking children attending English-only preschools. *Language, Speech, and Hearing Services in Schools, 41*(1), 3–13.

Reyes, S. (n.d.). *Diversity in your classroom library mirrors and windows project.* Teachers Pay Teachers. https://www.teacherspayteachers.com/Product/Diversity-in-your-Classroom-Library-Mirrors-and-Windows-Project-4320636

Riggio, R. E., & Tan, S. J. (Eds.). (2014). *Leader interpersonal and influence skills: The soft skills of leadership.* Routledge/Psychology Press.

Sackman, D. (2018). *Guest post: The writing recipe – How "essay framing for ELL' creates confidence writers in all of us!* https://larryferlazzo.edublogs.org/2018/12/01/guest-post-the-writing-recipe-how-essay-framing-for-ell-creates-confidence-writers-in-all-of-us/

Safir, S., & Dugan, J. (2021). *Street data: A next generation model for equity, pedgagogy, and school transformation.* Corwin.

Sahakyan, N., & Cook, H. G. (2021). *Examining English learner testing, proficiency, and growth: Before and throughout the COVID-19 pandemic.* Wisconsin Center for Education Research, University of Wisconsin–Madison.

San Francisco Unified School District, Mathematics Department. *San Francisco Unified School District Mathematics Department: The 3-Read Protocol.* https://www.sfusdmath.org/3-read-protocol.html

Sanchez, J. T. (2021). *We are not from here.* Viking Books for Young Readers.

Sandler, M. W. (2004). *Island of hope: The story of Ellis Island and the journey to America.* Scholastic.

Sayre, A. (2007). *Vulture view.* McGraw Hill.

Schaeffer, K. (2021). *America's public school teachers are far less racially and ethnically diverse than their students.* Pew Research Center.

Senzai, N. H. (2011). *Shooting Kabul.* Simon & Schuster.

Shanahan, T. (2013). Letting the text take center stage: How the Common Core State Standards will transform English language arts instruction. *American Educator, 37*(3), 4–11.

Shanahan, T. (2020). *How can we take advantage of reading-writing relationships.* https://www.shanahanonliteracy.com/blog/how-can-we-take-advantage-of-reading-writing-relationships

Singer, T. W. (2018). *El excellence every day: The flip-to guide for differentiating academic literacy.* Corwin.

Snyder, S., & Staehr Fenner, D. (2021). *Culturally responsive teaching for multilingual learners: Tools for equity.* Corwin.

Snyder, S., Staehr Fenner, D., Smith, S., & Singh, J. (2023, March). *Terminology to describe* multilingual learners: Labels and their implications. SupportEd.

Soto, I. (2021). *Shadowing multilingual learners* (2nd ed.). Corwin.

Staehr Fenner, D. (2013a). *Background knowledge: A key to close reading for ELLs* [Web log post]. http://www.colorincolorado.org/blog/background-knowledge-key-close-reading-ells

Staehr Fenner, D. (2013b). *Determining how much background knowledge to provide for ELLs* [Web log post]. http://www.colorincolorado.org/blog/determining-how-much-background-knowledge-provide-ells

Staehr Fenner, D. (2014a). *Advocating for English learners: A guide for educators.* Corwin.

Staehr Fenner, D. (2014b). *What's your "elevator speech" about your expertise with the Common Core for ELLs?* [Web log post]. http://www.colorincolorado.org/blog/whats-your-elevator-speech-about-your-expertise-common-core-ells

Staehr Fenner, D. (2015). *Computer-based Common Core testing: Considerations and supports for ELLs* [Web log post]. Colorín Colorado. http://www.colorincolorado.org/blog/computer-based-common-core-testing-considerations-and-supports-ells

Staehr Fenner, D. (2016). *Fair and square assessment for ELLs.* ASCD.

Staehr Fenner, D., Kozik, P., & Cooper, A. (2015). *Evaluating ALL teachers of English learners and students with disabilities.* Corwin.

Staehr Fenner, D., & Snyder, S. (2015a). *Socratic circles and the Common Core: An introduction* [blog post]. http://www.colorincolorado.org/blog/socratic-circles-and-common-core-introduction-part-i

Staehr Fenner, D., & Snyder, S. (2015b). Using pair and group work to develop MLs' oral language skills [blog post]. Retrieved from http://www.colorincolorado.org/blog/using-pair-and-group-workdevelop-ells%E2%80%99-oral language-skills.

Staehr Fenner, D., & Snyder, S. (2017). *Unlocking multilingual learners' potential: Strategies for making content accessible, first edition.* Corwin.

Staehr Fenner, D., & Teich, M. (in press). *Social emotional learning for multilingual learners: Essential Actions for Success.* Corwin.

Stanford Center to Support Excellence in Teaching: Understanding Language (n.d.). Supporting ELLs in mathematics: Language of mathematics task templates. https://ul.stanford.edu/resource/supporting-ells-mathematics

Stiggins, R. J. (2005). *Student-involved assessment FOR learning* (4th ed.). Pearson.

Stogdill, R. M. (1950). Leadership, membership and organization. *Psychological Bulletin, 47*(1), 1–14. https://doi.org/10.1037/h0053857

Stroink, M., & Lalonde, R. (2009). Bicultural identity conflict in second-generation Asian Canadians. *Journal of Social Psychology, 149*(1), 44–65.

Student Achievement Partners. (2022). *Juicy sentence guidance.* https://achievethecore.org/page/3160/juicy-sentence-guidance

Style, E. (1988). Curriculum as window and mirror. *Listening for all voices.* Oak Knoll School Monograph. https://nationalseedproject.org/Key-SEED-Texts/curriculum-as-window-and-mirror

Summit Hill School District 161. (n.d.). *ELL vision statement.* http://www.summithill.org/Documents/Ctrl_Hyperlink/ELL_uid10282014241332.pdf

survive. (2016). http://www.merriam-webster.com/dictionary/survive

Teaching Channel. (n.d.). *Scaffolding text structure for ELLs* [video]. https://learn.teachingchannel.com/video/scaffolding-text-structure

Teaching Channel. (2014). *Series Engaging ELLs in academic conversations: Participation protocol for academic discussion.* https://www.teachingchannel.com/k12-hub/blog/ells-academic-conversations/

Thomson, S. L. (2010). *Where do polar bears live?* HarperCollins.

U.S. Census Bureau. (2019a). *Characteristics of people by language spoken at home, 2019 American community survey 1-year estimates subject tables.* The Census Bureau. https://data.census.gov/table?q=S1603:+CHARACTERISTICS+OF+PEOPLE+BY+LANGUAGE+SPOKEN+AT+HOME&tid=ACSST1Y2019.S1603

U.S. Census Bureau. (2019b). *Language spoken at home, 2019 American community survey 1-year estimates subject tables.* The Census Bureau. https://data.census.gov/table?q=S1601:+LANGUAGE+SPOKEN+AT+HOME&tid=ACSST1Y2019.S1601

U.S. Department of Education. (n.d.). *Academic performance outcomes for English learners.* https://www2.ed.gov/datastory/el-outcomes/index.html#introText

U.S. Department of Education National Center for Educational Statistics. (n.d.). *Race and ethnicity of public school teachers and their students.* U.S. Department of Education, Institute of Education Sciences. https://nces.ed.gov/pubs2020/2020103/index.asp

U.S. Department of Education, Office for Civil Rights. (2021). *Education in a pandemic: The disparate impact of COVID-19 on America's Students.* Author.

U.S. Department of Education, Office of Career, Technical and Adult Education. (2016). *Adult English language proficiency standards for adult education.* Author.

U.S. Department of Education, Office of English Language Acquisition. (2023). *The biennial report to congress on the implementation of title III state formula grant program: School years 2018-2020.* Author.

Valdés, G., Kibler, A., & Walqui, A. (2014). *Changes in the expertise of ESL professionals: Knowledge and action in an era of new standards.* TESOL International Association.

Valencia, R. R. (1997). Conceptualizing the notion of deficit thinking. In R. R. Valencia (Ed.), *The evolution of deficit thinking: Educational thought and practice* (pp. 1–12). Palmer Press.

Valenzuela, A. (1999). *Subtractive schooling: U.S.-Mexican youth and the politics of caring.* State University of New York Press.

van de Pol, J., Volman, M., & Beishuizen, J. (2010). *Scaffolding in teacher-student interaction: A decade of research. Educational Psychology Review, 22*(3), 271–296.

Villegas, L., & Garcia, A. (2022). *Educating English learners during the pandemic: Insights from experts, advocates, and practitioners.* New America.

Villegas, L., & Ibarra, M. (2022). Former English learners outperform English-only peers on Texas' state assessments [blog]. *New America.* https://www.newamerica.org/education-policy/edcentral/former-english-learners-outperform-english-only-peers-on-texas-state-assessments/

Walqui, A., & Heritage, M. (2018a). *Meaningful classroom talk: Supporting English learners' oral language development.* American Federation of Teachers. https://www.aft.org/ae/fall2018/walqui_heritage

Walqui, A., & Schmida, M. (2023). Recoceptualizing scaffolding for English learners. In L. C. de Oliveira

& R. Westerlund (Eds.), *Scaffolding for multilingual learners in elementary and secondary schools* (pp. 29–46). Routledge.

Webb, S. (2019). Chapter 15 incidental vocabulary learning. In S. Webb (Ed.), *The Routledge handbook of vocabulary studies* (pp. 225–239). Routledge.

WIDA. (2013). *WIDA focus on group work for content learning.* http://stem4els.wceruw.org/resources/WIDA-Focus-on-group-work.pdf

WIDA. (2020a). *English language development standards framework, 2020 edition: Kindergarten–grade 12.* https://wida.wisc.edu/sites/default/files/resource/WIDA-ELD-Standards-Framework-2020.pdf

WIDA. (2020b). *WIDA writing rubric grades 1–12.* https://wida.wisc.edu/resources/wida-writing-rubric-grades-1-12

WIDA. (2022). *Scaffolding learning for multilingual students in math.* https://wida.wisc.edu/resources/scaffolding-learning-multilingual-students-math

Zaboi, I. (2017). *American street.* Balzer + Bray.

Zacarian, D., & Staehr Fenner, D. (2020). From deficit-based to assets-based. In *Breaking down the wall* (pp. 1–20). Corwin.

Zwiers, J. (2008). *Building academic language: Essential practices for content classrooms.* Jossey-Bass.

Zwiers, J. (2010). *Building reading comprehension habits in grades 6–12: A toolkit of activities* (2nd ed.). International Reading Association.

Zwiers, J. (2014). *Key strategies for developing oral language* [blog post]. https://www.teachingchannel.org/blog/2014/10/29/strategies-for-developing-oral-language-ousd

Zwiers, J. (2019). *Next steps with academic conversations: New ideas for improving learning through classroom talk.* Stenhouse.

Zwiers, J., & Crawford, M. (2011). *Academic conversations: Classroom talk that fosters critical thinking and content understandings.* Stenhouse.

Zwiers, J., & Soto, I. (2016). *Academic language mastery: Conversational discourse in context.* Corwin.

Index

Adjectives, 141–42, 178, 184, 250
Advanced Placement (AP), 10
Alim, H. S., 41, 52
American Sign Language, 130
Anchor charts, 67, 70–72, 78, 85, 116, 121,
    222, 235, 241, 249, 257
  color-coded, 189
  of strategies, 78
Anderson, J., 249–51
Anticipation guides, 129, 144, 203
Antonyms, 148–50, 154, 157
AP (Advanced Placement), 10
Apollo 11, 179
Assets, 1, 11, 26, 58–59, 61, 82–83, 296
  cultural, 15, 256
Assignments, 48, 56, 90, 229–30, 233, 291
Audio resources, 70, 72, 85, 273
August, D., 98, 123, 140, 232
Autism, 212–13
Awareness, metalinguistic, 232, 264, 269

Baker, S., 78, 140–42, 146, 149–50, 154, 233
Banks, C. A. M., 11, 35, 38, 40
Banks, J. A., 11, 35, 38, 40
Banting, E., 213–14
Barriers, 13, 19, 31, 34, 40, 58–59, 175
Biases, 18, 41, 278
  cultural, 278, 288
Billings. E., 71, 201, 231–32, 237, 239
Bingo, Conversation 112
Bishop, R. S., 257
Bunch, G. C., 132–33

Callahan, R., 18
Cards, 119, 153–54, 190
  bingo, 154
  index, 83, 119–20, 151, 153
Carousel
  activity, 122, 216–17
  brainstorming, 207, 218

CCSSO (Council of Chief State School Officers'),
  66, 266
Charts, 166, 179, 207, 272
  juicy sentence, 182
  language charts, 116
Checklists, 91, 96, 114, 157, 163, 176–77, 180, 247,
  251–53, 269–71, 273, 294
  classroom, 23
  formative assessment, 287–88
  for Academic-Language Development, 194
  for Increasing Academic-Language Awareness,
    163, 176, 194
  student, 229, 274
Chunking text, 71, 181, 238
  chunks, 181–82, 237
Chval, K., 219
Clauses, 136, 167–69, 172, 177
  dependent, 168–70
  independent, 167–69
Cognates, 72–73, 152, 156–58, 177, 255
  false, 154, 156–57
  understanding, 154, 156, 162
Cohesion, 136, 171, 173, 187
Comparisons, 65, 70, 84, 90, 249, 287
Conferences, 33–34
Conjunctions, 74–75, 77, 168–70, 235
Continuums, 198–99, 264
Conversations
  academic, 77, 96, 99, 105–6, 122–23, 126
  Bingo, 112
  meaningful, 14–15, 22, 29
Core beliefs, 8, 14–15, 17, 19, 22, 24, 29–32
  five, 2, 4, 7, 13–14, 29, 32
Coteachers, 7, 22, 107, 115
Council of Chief State School Officers' (CCSSO),
  66, 266
Cultures
  collectivist, 36, 60, 90, 121, 252
  differences, cultural, 36, 40
  home, 40, 43, 53, 96

knowledge, cultural, 41
    misunderstandings, 38
    understanding, 34
    unfamiliar, 47
Curricula, 25, 41, 201, 222, 229, 235
    curricular units, 41, 146

Daniels, E., 240
DeCapua, A., 60, 89–90, 158, 191, 221–22, 254, 289
Definitions, 257
    embedded, 71, 170, 237–38
    student-created, 76
Delpit, I., 40
Department of Education, 10, 71, 142, 149, 268
Development, professional, 4, 11, 13, 18, 26, 62
Devices
    cohesive, 136, 178, 187, 189
    literary, 75
Dialogue, 18, 117, 185
Discomfort, 45, 61
Dove, M. G., 7, 24–25, 159, 291

Elevator speeches, 8, 30–31
Emotional charge, 37–38
Emotional load, low, 36–37
Empathy, 23, 27–28, 34, 47, 257
Energy, 56, 110–11, 289
errors, 102, 137, 251, 286
Escamilla, K., 74, 96, 98, 140, 231–33
ESSA (Every Student Succeeds Act), 57
Essays, 188, 190, 253
Every Student Succeeds Act (ESSA), 57
Expectations, 23, 40, 43, 50, 60, 84, 96–97, 100,
        107, 192, 235
    cultural, 99, 106–7, 123
    high, 49
    for students, 40
    of teachers, 40, 106
Explicit instruction, 73, 105, 129, 136–37, 156, 159,
        202, 291
    of vocabulary, 130, 148

Fabiny, S., 238–39
Familiarity, 82, 84, 146, 203
Feedback, 22, 102, 105, 117, 137, 229, 249,
        266–67, 271, 294
    providing, 28, 101–2, 137, 294
Fences, 213, 216–18
    low, 213–18
Folktales, 115–16
Food, 36–37, 145, 181, 183, 204, 222, 242, 256, 282

Frayer Models, 130, 148
Fun, 130, 238–39

Galleries, 240, 246, 251
Games, 112, 150–51, 153–54, 169, 219
Gaps, 10–11, 15, 18, 59, 202, 254, 268
Gay, G., 11, 41
Genres, 136, 172, 185, 187, 283
González, N., 43
Gottlieb, M., 264, 267–69
Grammar, 134, 167, 177, 182–83, 252, 279, 288
    mini lessons, 287
Grandin, T., 212

Hamman-Ortiz, L., 259
Hammond, Z., 36–37, 49, 67
Histories, 49, 52, 90, 214
Hofstede, G., 36
Honigsfeld, A., 7, 24–25, 159, 291

Identities, 44, 50, 134, 148, 257–58, 269
    linguistic, 30
    texts, 256, 258–59
Immigration, 53–54
Indigenous Americans, 74, 99–100
Information gaps, 151, 162
Informed demander, 49
Ingersoll, R. M., 11
Interactive Word Walls, 77, 151
Interpreters, 19, 34, 58–59

Journals, 206, 229
Juicy sentences, 181–82

Kagan Cooperative Learning Strategy, 248
Kahlo, F., 238–39
Kester, J., 240

La Rocca, W., 251
Libraries, 241, 257–58
    multicultural, 61
    school librarians, 56, 61, 258
    student library inventory, 257
Linguistic loads, 80, 276, 278
    reduced, 70, 80, 85
Look-fors, 24, 42, 46, 49, 58–59

Martin, D., 132–33
Manipulatives, 70, 76, 85–86, 109, 121, 220, 274
McNally, 65
Mentor texts, 185, 187, 274

Mini lessons, 20–21, 80, 82, 113, 155, 176–78, 180, 182, 192, 221, 252
    language-focused, 22, 80
    small-group, 287
Modalities
    multiple, 79–80, 87, 160
    and translanguaging, 80, 87
Molle, D., 132–33, 139–40, 150, 154
Money, 146–47, 222, 237, 244
Multiple meanings, 138–39, 141, 143, 157, 170, 177, 219

NAEP (National Assessment of Educational Progress), 268
National Assessment of Educational Progress (NAEP), 268
National Center for Educational Statistics (NCES), 11
NCEE, 142, 149
NCES (National Center for Educational Statistics), 11
Neurodivergent students, 107
New York State Testing Program, 175
Nieto, S., 41
Non-academic topics, 70, 80, 85, 274
Nonexamples, 130, 146, 148–50, 157
Nontechnical words, 137
Nonverbal communication, 106–7, 114, 124
Nouns, 136, 141–42, 173, 184, 250
    noun groups, 136, 173
    plural, irregular, 250–51

OELA, 10–11, 13

Paintings, 117, 134, 238–39
Parents, 8–9, 33–35, 43, 47, 59, 290
    parent-teacher association (PTA), 47, 59
Paris, D., 41, 52
Participle phrases, 180
Pearson, P. D., 201–2, 231, 233
Perspectives, 16, 47–48, 53, 58–59, 61, 183, 237, 283
    assets-based, 16, 43, 46–47, 62, 201
    deficit, 43, 47, 62, 193
    diverse, 15–16, 41, 54, 123
    strengths-based, 27
Photographs, 73, 209, 241–42
Pictures, 66, 69, 72–73, 76, 144, 146–49, 153, 180–82, 184, 211, 218, 220, 239–40, 244–45, 280–81
    students match, 146, 173
Plants, 86, 103, 216–17, 256
PLC (professional learning community), 3
Posters, 88, 119–20, 151–52, 181, 216, 240, 252, 271, 287

Precision, 134, 136–37, 172
Predictions, 138, 156, 240, 246
Prefixes, 141, 143, 152, 156
Preteaching, 180, 204, 209, 250
Professional learning community (PLC), 3
Protocols, 101, 121, 235, 240, 243–46
PTA (parent-teacher association), 47, 59

Reading levels, 49, 54, 141, 193, 213, 223
Refugee students, 15
Routines, 23, 165, 235, 250, 262
Rubrics, 22, 269–71, 283–84, 288, 294

Sackman, D., 190
SCASS (State Collaborative on Assessment and Student Standards), 266
Schaeffer, K., 11
Sequencing, 67, 187–89, 196
Shanahan, T., 98, 123, 140, 193, 206, 232–34
Snyder, S., 8, 15–16, 42–45, 57–58, 73, 85, 87, 90, 113–14, 121, 155, 201, 208, 209, 211, 246, 251, 282
Sociocultural contexts, 40, 134–35, 178, 180
Socratic circles, 117–18
Spaces, safe, 13, 23, 60, 122
Spanish, 48, 55, 156, 165, 179, 182
Staehr Fenner, D., 8, 13, 15–16, 18, 22, 24, 26, 40, 42–45, 47, 49, 57–58, 62–63, 87, 90, 96, 106–7, 114, 121, 201, 205, 208, 209, 211, 215, 277–78
Standards, 91, 133, 179, 250, 275, 288
    -based content tasks, complete, 140
    frameworks, 133
State Collaborative on Assessment and Student Standards (SCASS), 266
Sticky notes, 80, 106, 152, 207, 240
    categorized, 207–8
Success criteria, 266, 270
Suffixes, 141, 143, 152, 156
Swahili, 60–61, 122, 159, 255
Synonyms, 148–50, 157, 178, 181–82, 238

Technology, 45, 278, 288–89
Teich, M., 13, 15, 22, 40, 96, 106–7
Tiers, 137–38
Toppel, K., 183–84
Translanguaging, 54–56, 70, 79–81, 85, 87, 255
    translation and opportunities for, 55
Translation, 54–56, 72–73, 130, 146, 159, 212–13, 289
Transportation, 19, 34, 47, 58–59

Valencia, R. R., 43

Valenzuela, A., 43

Validity, 268, 275–76, 278–80, 295

Verbs, 141–42, 168, 170, 184, 186

Virtual learning, 1, 10

Vision statements, 30

Walqui, A., 71, 101, 137, 201, 231–32, 237, 239, 271

Webb, S., 139

WIDA, 8, 19–20, 66, 79–81, 132–37, 167, 171–72

    ELD Standards, 20, 79, 134–36, 167, 171, 173, 178

Zwiers, J., 22–23, 96, 98, 101–4, 106, 170, 191

A Sage Company

Helping educators make the greatest impact

CORWIN HAS ONE MISSION: to enhance education through intentional professional learning.

We build long-term relationships with our authors, educators, clients, and associations who partner with us to develop and continuously improve the best evidence-based practices that establish and support lifelong learning.